Omerta – a code of silence by a powerful group to protect their own interests…

…enter the closed shop world of l~   …
a world of cover-up with im~

You will meet simp
whose honour and in.

This true story gives an   _.ing insight into the real workings of our legal sys.cm… are judges as clever and honest as they would claim, and you would hope….
it questions the blind faith we are asked to hold in our trustees of justice…
…will that faith survive without proper public accountability?

Simon Kaberry

Published by:
Chipmunkapublishing Ltd
PO Box 6872
Brentwood
Essex
CM13 1ZT
United Kingdom

Chipmunkapublishing is dedicated to raising awareness of all mental health issues and facts

Second Edition 'B'

To

Holly and Louise

and to

All those who put their faith
in lawyers and judges

Simon Kaberry

INTRODUCTION

They say life is what you make of it.   Or is your destiny determined by events over which you have no control.

If you are wronged, you seek redress in accordance with the law. You look for 'justice' - be it simple truth, compensation, retribution, or understanding. We entrust enormous power to our legislature and executive; they account to us - a vital protection from corruption. The third part of democratic life is the Judiciary- our trustees of justice. By accident of history, we have no sanction on our Judges; they know that - one of the few 'jobs for life' - appointed from within their own, and covered by a powerful omerta - a silent code of 'their greater good' which they arrogantly call 'the importance of independence.' Some judges even deny they are public servants. By rules of human nature, any public system whereby those who control it and are also unaccountable, is open to abuse, corruption and cover-up at the public's expense. It can ruin anyone's life and we are powerless.

This true story gives you an insight into the real workings of our civil and criminal legal systems from all courts, to the vital importance of our jury system - we can't trust lawyers with justice.

You or I will be punished for our criminal wrongs or breaches of duties owed to one another. High duties of care are imposed on doctors and surgeons; breach that, and they will be ordered to compensate you and even be sent to prison if reckless. If a police officer breaches or abuses the trust placed in him – he is sent to prison to maintain confidence. But if a Judge delivers a judgment which dishonestly robs a man of justice by abuse of his trusted position, he causes greater loss than that caused by the criminal or negligent doctor, but as a law officer, he knows there is no sanction for his wrong; quite the reverse - there is an omerta to protect him. This true story explains what happens when you try to expose dishonesty within legal and judicial ranks.

' They' say it is right that there should be 'double standards' when judging them; but they would, wouldn't they. Now read this...

Simon Kaberry

CHAPTER ONE

Could this be your worst nightmare?

He spoke with the calm assurance of a senior barrister, advising with his wide experience. Quietly but sternly he addressed his client, as part of the defence team seated in the Consulting room outside Court, with trial about to start. The four defence lawyers present each wore a grim solemn face.

In firm slow monotone, the QC continued - "Now look, it's time to come to your senses." He paused for effect…
"I don't know this Judge - he's new here in Newcastle, but I have made inquiries. He can be very fair to those who admit their wrongs. Nevertheless, believe me, he can be very harsh on those who will not admit their crimes - their wrong. As I have told you, you are looking at many years if you continue as you intend, but maybe, *just maybe*, with your mitigation - you could get away with five, possibly six years if you admit your guilt. But fight it... deny it, and you could well be facing a severe sentence as I have told you - ten… maybe twelve years".

Then, with frustration again threatening, for he knew he had a stubborn client, the QC snapped -
"Damn it man, can you not see that you have not one chance in a hundred of securing just one acquittal on these fourteen counts. Just look at the evidence against you !"
-'*allegations - yes, but what evidence*' mused the silent man.
The accused sat opposite his lawyers. Leading counsel, junior counsel, fully gowned for court combat, solicitor, and his assistant; they liked to be called 'the defence team.' The forty-seven year old client said not a word, smartly dressed in clerical grey suit from Bond Street, fine white Jermyn Street shirt and quietly patterned tie, all remnants from bygone days, for now he was very poor. He listened politely, matching their expressionless faces calmly.

Aidan Marron QC continued.
" So look…I'm going to leave you now to think. And 'think carefully' - consider your position. With this professor, you have excellent mitigation - just don't blow it all. I will come back soon - in about ten minutes but I just want you to think…. just think."

The barrister raised another plea to this determined client:
"Look, it makes no difference to me; I'll be driving home to Ripon whatever happens, and you'll be going elsewhere."

Argument was pointless, as it had been for the past fifteen months - plead and go down. The defence team moved with the importance of lawyers from the small room. Aidan Marron QC, in his early fifties, just over six foot tall led the exit, followed by the junior Nicholas Paul, in his early forties, up from London, and his friend, solicitor Michael Thurston, approaching fifty, who had been entrusted to investigate and defend the charges. The younger girl clerk, Kate Moyler, was in her early twenties.

The accused took a deep breath. Time to think - something he had done every day for the last three years, and thirteen days since arrested, and kept on bail ever since, in the hands of this system. This lawyer, now defendant, who had called in the police for forgery at his bank, and thefts from his account, was on trial as the thief. Judge, jury and media would never know that.

The team had never stopped to think, never asked the question - "what *really* had happened? Where is this million pounds? Or is it two millions? A solicitor of twenty years had allegedly helped himself to more than a million pounds of client's money in just one year. The Law Society's Court had already published he had stolen it to gamble - "in the worst case of unbefitting conduct possible." Duly vilified by media, he was immediately charged. Then a slow helter-skelter to court, where he must plead and go to prison with the truth brushed aside. The 'Legal Establishment' had already taken his home and career, adjudged him bankrupt for another man's debts and destroyed his reputation and family - "in the public interest." He had been in solitary for three years awaiting these moments. This defence team would now ensure the Establishment got the final order - prison.

Not one witness had been seen, no accountant instructed, and he had no formal proof of evidence. His detailed answers to charges were unread by the team. Fear was set aside for a steely determination to beat them. Panic and he will lose for sure. Outside, the media were waiting, ready to slaughter him again.

He had a small card - it was 8th April. As the weather warms, everyone feels happier. Arriving at Crown Court at 8.30 am, he had beaten the cameras; trial had been moved to Newcastle to avoid just that prejudice a hundred miles away in Leeds, where he was already guilty -"Shame and Disgrace - Solicitor struck off for gambling away over two million of client funds" screamed the banners. He had vowed revenge – but any such double grave digging must wait. The immediate issue was trial; would the team ask the right questions?

Louise had told him one of his biggest problems was that he didn't look as though he had suffered a jot: "can't you just try... I mean... you still look like a pompous lawyer... what'll they make of you?" But rules are we must always present ourselves at our best. Quietly he kept telling himself - "*don't insult 'the team'* - *stay calm... drag the evidence out - somehow.*" Thank god also that for this defendant that this was no lost day, with spinning head, screwed up eyes and tight chest. – "*keep your cool - it's up to you now... be polite*" - he kept talking to himself.

Ten minutes or so, and the team returned. Long serious judicious faces sat as before opposite.

"Well - what's it to be?" started Aidan Marron.

Calmly and without expression came the quiet reply:

"OK then - I'll plead."

It was all over and he could be locked up that day. Marron QC began to note the Instruction...

"Provided...." the client hesitated... "I can go in the box"

"Well you can't."

But this accused was a lawyer - they had forgotten.

With an inquisitive tone, junior counsel Nick Paul joined in: "er...maybe he can - sometimes it's allowed."

"So, what's it you want to say?"

"Simple really. I have never been dishonest in my life - and I've never stolen anything nor intended to deceive anyone; I've helped everyone I've ever met. It defies common sense to dope a man up, rob him blind and then convict him as a crook, for things over which he has no control, or has no knowledge, whilst those who robbed him retain their funds and his money... even now".

Aidan Marron's cheeks flushed. An air of self-righteousness permeated the room. He was right; no, the other was right. One was wrong - it was stand-off time.   Swiftly he put the pen away and arose to leave.

"Very well then, it's you're decision. Let's get on with this."

They strode out, leaving the defendant alone with the ever re-assuring solicitor Michael Thurston. Just older than the defendant, his build was similar - at six foot, but with a full crop of hair unlike the defendant's bald pate, and of similar social background. Mike of the brilliant bedside manner - who actually never does anything save come out with lines like -"well, I think that was a jolly good meeting" and "well, we're all up to speed now" - after more costs racked up as papers were shuffled. Now the client needed him, but where was the evidence? He hadn't done it.

"Well, I did warn you it'd get tough... but - it's your decision," offered Michael, resigned to this stupidity.

Responses would be pointless; it was too late.

A quick visit to the gents was appropriate. Walking in he heard Detective Sergeant Jock Clark, the investigating officer from Leeds Fraud Squad, making polite conversation with a colleague from another force, whilst attending to nature's call. Temptation took over; he stood behind him and murmured:

"Don't say a word about me... it's bad enough being shat on in life."

Startled, the policeman half-turned to look.... "Oh...Hello" is all he could manage. But whilst the accused was the one on trial, the policeman was surely the one in need of the loo.

The defendant entered the near empty Court Five and made for the dock at the back. First sighting was of the Judge's Clerk or Court Associate, seated below the Judge's empty bench; and quite a sight, in her mid-thirties, he guessed, gowned and wigged with a peaches and cream complexion, with tufts of blond hair aside. 'What *a lovely vision to wake up to*' thought the accused, followed quickly by '*stop that; this is serious, just because its a sexy blond dressed in a black gown, no time to go weighing up the talent in court; anyway, she's probably got thunder thighs.*' A Securicor man took him to the back cell to frisk him for weapons. Then the Defendant saw him arrive at the front of court.   He took furtive side-glances at him: "*I've seen him before - it's that poncy git with the bow-tie I used to see from my office window in Leeds... him - now a QC - good god!*"   This was David Hatton QC, now his prosecutor - '*what does Hatton really know of the case*'. That quiet inner confidence - "*I can beat this man....*" Then - "*eyes are on you.... no expression at all*". It's all part of the game.

Court was filling with the few concerned in the trial. From the back, the defendant faced the Judge's empty seat. In front, to his right, facing the judge was first his learned QC, with junior Nick Paul behind. Behind them sat Michael and Kate to hold the papers. Four people to do one man's job. Below the Judge's seat, facing the lawyers sat the luscious Court Associate. To the defendant's left, backs to him, sat the prosecution team; they were full of it - they were going to win. Everyone had that air of importance, carrying bundles of duplicated papers. Front row the dapper Hatton QC. Behind him his junior counsel little Robin Frieze, who had prepared the prosecution case - the defendant had stolen all this money for three reasons - to gamble, invest in businesses and pay debts. What a nasty man he must be. But then Frieze concluded at the end he 'hadn't lived well' - on two million pounds in just over a year. Must be a fool as well.

Behind Frieze and just to the front of the dock sat 'the team' who had put it all together at CPS and pull the strings of a prosecutor. Pamela Hudson, the solicitor in her thirties, in charge, and her caseworker Hazel Kitson. CPS had chosen this defendant and briefed the two barristers. Whenever one reads, "the Crown is considering its position," it means faceless and nameless civil servants such as these two - unaccountable to the public they are meant to serve. If their conduct or decisions are questioned, anonymous people say decisions were made "within the Code of Practice" - and the public can't argue with that for they don't know who made the decision nor on what facts. They have the power.

To his left, the defendant espied four press from the corner of his eye. They were certainly not friends. Split Ends of YTV, with two women and a man. Didn't know any of them. Must be Yorkshire Post, Evening Post and The Times.
 -"*How can I get my predicament to them?*" He reasoned. - "*don't bother - they're here to damn you not save you.*"

Soon it was action time. The usher announced "All 'rise", and the Judge duly robed for the occasion entered the minefield. Leading counsel introduced themselves and the junior counsel, sitting behind them with nothing to do, to His Honour Judge David Hodson, the Recorder of Newcastle, entitled to be addressed as if a High Court Judge. The usher left from the back to collect a jury. This would be alien to them - being judges. Thirteen bodies of varying sizes, ages and sexes came in from a door to the right.

It's part of our centuries old system of justice - the right to be tried by your peers. One by one, the Associate called each forward by name to take a seat in the jury bench, opposite the witness box. There being no challenge, the final one wasn't needed and left. Each juror stood to read out the oath publicly that he or she would try this case honestly according to the evidence. The defendant observed without turning his head towards them. It was a comforting moment. These are real people not pompous self-opinionated lawyers.

-"*Don't look at them... look straight ahead - they'll be nervous enough as it is.*"

Aidan Marron QC asked that the Counts be all put again. Was he giving one final chance to plead so he could never be blamed, or allowing the jury to hear the defendant's voice - 'there's a human being involved here.'

He stood to answer as the Associate put the Counts one by one.
"Count one. Theft. Simon Edmund John Kaberry. You are charged that between February 1992 and January 1994 you stole £85,000 from Northern Rock Building Society (details set out)…... How say you. Are you guilty or not guilty?"
"Not Guilty"
"Count two. Theft. You are charged that between March 1992 and January 1994 you stole £68,000 from Abbey National Building Society…(details followed)…."
"Not guilty"
"Count three. False Accounting. You are charged that between November 1992 and January 1994, with a view to gain, you dishonestly falsified a document, namely a client ledger card, required for an Accounting purpose…."
"Not Guilty"
"Count four. Theft. That you stole £60,000 from Northern Rock Building Society between September 1992 and March 1994"
"Not Guilty"

It was all three, four or five years earlier. A few minutes passed as she concluded fourteen Counts, being ten of theft of Building Society funds, one of theft of £20,000 cash from a client, one of deception to make gain and two of 'false accounting' in the lawyer's practice in Leeds over a sixteen months period ending February/March 1994. Over £600,000 – not a bad little spending spree, but that was just the petty cash. Soon they would hear the real figure was more like 2 million.

To each charge, he quietly but firmly replied "Not Guilty." So, the jury knew his voice. The Associate turned to the Judge:
"M'lord - the Defendant pleads Not Guilty to all fourteen Counts"

"Thank you." The judge then invited the Crown barrister David Hatton QC to set the case for the jury. They brought unpolluted minds to court. That was why the trial was in Newcastle - in Leeds, where these offences had allegedly occurred, the newspapers, gossip and Law Society had already told everyone he was very guilty. This would be a long labour of mudslinging - *'fling n' hope some sticks'*.

To 'take silk' or be a 'Queens Counsel' is historical, like so much of the system we have. To take silk a barrister has to be accepted by his contemporaries, and the Lord Chancellor's office, as having 'an enhanced professional reputation', usually in court, gained over years. He would then earn much more for doing the same work as before. Most High Court Judges were previously QC's. Some silks then make fortunes, whilst others price themselves out of the market. Like a footballer, they're still only as good as their form; lose it and no one wants you, although some has-beens linger on. The idea is that this archaic practice should be ended, but it's a self-serving system - part of the self-appointing circle within the legal establishment. Next stop is judge; and they like a system which created them. And best of all no one can do anything about it for these boys are, in reality, unaccountable save to those who run the system; there is no true protection of the public or an individual within our legal system (not that they will admit it – quite the reverse). Try to complain about a judge and drive through treacle; likewise a senior counsel. Read chapters 15-19 if you think you can effectively do anything about these people. It's a living, operating closed shop - created over centuries, which they call "vital independence." We call it a serious flaw. Present reforms don't begin to address it - they make it worse.

Hatton QC was being paid a lot of state money by CPS to ensure this defendant was convicted. A QC is meant to have 'outstanding ability', 'sound knowledge of the law' and "independence of mind and moral courage." Just how independent they can be when they rely on doing as told by their paymaster is another matter. Are they exempt from the usual rules of human nature?

David Hatton QC turned towards the jury. It's called the Opening. As he started, so solicitor Mike Thurston nodded farewell and slipped out: he was off 200 miles down the A1 to his Nottingham office, never to return. Next time he saw his client, he would be in prison. The Establishment was starting to roll.

Each juror had a large lever-arch of papers prepared by the CPS girls, to set much of the 'evidence.' Hatton QC would take them through the pages of documents slowly. They started with three separate documents containing pages of handwritten confessions by the defendant. In those he admitted he had simply stolen to meet the desires to gamble and gamble – "I took that money to the Grand National" and "all I did was lose, lose, lose". Three separate but slightly different confessions; why three - was one not enough? CPS chose what goes in - and much was missing. The bundle had copies of incoming cheques to his company client accounts and bank statements, which confirmed receipt of the client funds - each properly banked. But…. something of incredible importance was missing. Had none of these lawyers noticed?

> "All of us must trust solicitors", Hatton QC told the jury, "to safeguard our money when moving house or re-mortgaging our homes. Solicitors hold that money on trust for one specific purpose in accordance with that transaction. Mr. Kaberry was such a solicitor with offices in Leeds city centre and undertaking financial work for the public, who had trusted him. But this man was not to be trusted. Instead of undertaking the work, he would help himself to their money and conceal what he had done by paying interest on it to banks and building societies, pretending all was well. That way, no one knew what he had done."

This way, he had stolen over £600,000 from his clients as charged in the fourteen Counts, and covered his tracks. Why had he done it?

> "Ladies and gentlemen – there were three reasons for these thefts - to pay debts, to cover shortfalls in his own accounts... and to gamble."

But then he added,

> "...and for other reasons" which interchanged with "but it doesn't matter where it went... the point is that it didn't go where it should have gone..."

- '*oh yes it does matter*' mused the accused again - '*it's vital.*'

The Frieze Case Summary identified Murgatroyds - a large Fast Food Fish & Chip Business as one of the Defendant's failed businesses funded by the stolen money, but Hatton now made no reference to it.

> "How had he been able to do it ladies and gentlemen?

> "There are two principal ways in which he went about these thefts. Sometimes people change the mortgage on their home for one reason or another or any number of reasons", - he explained...

> "That required work by a solicitor who would act for the lay client and for the old mortgage company and the new one. The solicitor would receive money from the new building society, intended to repay the old one, and account to the client with difference between the two, less his fees and costs, with a detailed 'Completion Statement' of what had happened. Simple enough and that is what should happen, as set out in the Completion Statement. But what Mr. Kaberry – the defendant – did, was to pay the client his small share - the difference between the old and new mortgages - BUT - rather than pay off the old mortgage company, as he should have done, he would steal that money, but pay interest as the client used to do. That way, no one would know what he had done."

Sounds a simple and practical fraud operated by him. That was dishonest and was theft as charged, said the Crown. But did he really commit a crime he had no chance of getting away with? The defendant sat in the box expressionless, just listening.

"On other occasions, he would act for a client in the sale of a house which had a mortgage on it. After the sale, he would send the client a Completion Statement, showing the proceeds of sale on one side. On the other – to balance it, he would show the old mortgage amount – allegedly paid over to the building society, together with the costs of sale, and the balance being the amount due to the client, for which amount he sent them a cheque. But ladies and gentlemen, what Mr. Kaberry did was to help himself to the sum shown as due to the old Building Society and pay the interest due to them so - again - no one would know what he had done. That is how – the Crown says – he concealed his dishonesty, but eventually he had been caught out."

But again Hatton QC didn't mention the obvious – on a re-mortgage the new lender will want the deeds quite soon and on a house sale, the buyer will want a deed of release from the old Bank within two weeks - so one must be even dumber to try that one. This must be one very foolish lawyer - trying to commit offences that have no chance of success.

"And ladies and gentlemen - what had he done with this money? And how does the 'Crown' know this?...(pause) We know it - because it is in Simon Kaberry's own words - we have his own words and his own handwriting that this is what he did with money entrusted to him. Ladies and gentlemen I ask you to read documents 1, 2 and 3 in the bundle before you, each being in his own handwriting, and typed copies following to assist you. He has taken it to gamble on races like the Grand National, the Derby and 2000 guineas."

So he read extracts… "*I took it to the Grand National*" and later "*if I wasn't out by now, I soon would be……all I did was lose lose lose.*" And "*I was greedy.*" Moreover, later he referred to '*robbing Peter to pay Paul*'.

"But ladies and gentlemen, that wasn't true because he was actually robbing <u>both</u> Peter <u>and</u> Paul!"
- was the prosecutor's joke.

This was just as Law Society had published earlier when vilifying him to media and taking his career. Hatton QC then took them to bank statements and copy cheques all showing the receipt of the money. Gradually, the balance held reduced - too low over time - the money had 'gone' - "so obviously he has stolen it - it certainly has not gone where it should have gone, although exactly where it has gone *'doesn't matter'*".

Sitting expressionless the guilty defendant mused...

- *"oh yes it does.... where this money went certainly matters."*

> "But one Count is different - that of theft of cash of £20,000 from a client. Mr. Kang was buying a house ladies and gentlemen. He took £20,000 in cash to Mr. Kaberry for that purpose. You will see in the bundle that Mr. Kaberry wrote to the client - the letter is dated November - acknowledging receipt of that cash to buy a house. What did Simon Kaberry do with this man's money? We have it in his own words - *"you can guess where that went."* Well, ladies and gentlemen of the jury - you can indeed guess where it went - and it certainly did not go where it was intended."

The Defendant listened - unmoved; it didn't sound good, but was this the truth? What house? What price? Why £20,000?

Hatton's opening address continued for the rest of the day as he went over and over the fourteen different Counts. He explained how money is requested and released to the solicitor from a lender - how it is banked in a special client account. How, for each client, there is a separate client ledger. The totals of all ledgers must equal the total sum held in the bank. Whenever he could, Mr. Hatton took the jury back to the confessions. Then he told the jury that he had even stolen his own brother's money, albeit not a charge in this list, due on a house re-mortgage - over £120,000 - "that is how low this man had sunk." It was in the 'admissions' - so he showed them that admission; this was a mudslinging exercise. The media boys and girls were writing avidly – great copy. A greedy, dishonest lawyer – gambling client accounts away. A lamb to be slaughtered. But was it true? Something was missing.

- *'Take it all on the chin SK - my day will come'.*

Finally he finished, media left and the jury filed out. The Judge extended bail to the following day and left. Tomorrow it would really start. The defendant mumbled to his Securicor guard:

"What's it sound like?"
"Not very good for you."
-'*Well - ask a stupid question...*'

The accused joined his QC and junior counsel Nick Paul in the small Consulting Room.
"Well... I warned you," said his QC - "and it'll get worse."
Yet this defendant was happy. Trial was going as well as he could hope - just had to take it on the chin a while longer; it was the only way out. Then hit them with the sucker punch. But would his counsel deliver it? That was the problem.
- '*oh yes... my day will come* '".
He set off to walk around Newcastle, called in at the bookies in the Bigg Market to see the day's results and read the Racing Post (got to keep up to date) then the Metro to his hotel in Jesmond.

On arrival at the hotel, he espied the two CPS girls – Pam Hudson and Hazel Kitchen were staying in the same small hotel.
"*This should be fun*" – thought he. "*I'll wave to them each breakfast over their scrambled eggs.*" Reality struck in – "*no way - these are the enemy; two very unaccountable girls - and with enormous power - never forget that - this isn't funny - they are out to destroy me*'; but oh - that look of shock-horror on their faces! They fled and checked out.

Eventually it was time to check in back in Leeds, ringing Louise at 6.30. She should have watched the early evening local TV news.
"Well, dare I ask?"
"Oh don't. It's awful. As you said Split Ends at Yorkshire Television has done a hatchet job on you"
"Yes. I saw her leaving early and expected it... she's had her card marked by someone...probably police. What's she saying?"
"They've done homework...she was filmed outside Newcastle Court but back in Leeds, they were all prepared. You were the lead story – solicitor stealing over £600,000 to gamble. Pictures of your home, your office.... your bank - Yorkshire Bank in Infirmary Street - how did they now that in advance? Of course and a photo of your father - Lord Kaberry and MP for Leeds for thirty years, who died after the IRA bombing of the Carlton Club - you're being slaughtered - she says you've admitted it"
"It's simple; people feed them in advance. It could be barristers, CPS, or police. It goes on all the time... go on..."

"Well you've stolen hundreds of thousands to gamble and she had a shot of a Ladbrokes betting shop – presumably where you took the money and lost it..."

"Ladbrokes!" He exclaimed with incredulity "but they banned me long ago, and it wasn't for losing too much!"

"Yes I know that, but they don't. She said you live in a tip and were robbing Peter to pay Paul to cover you tracks – you even stole from your brother. And one poor client gave you £20,000 to buy a house in cash and you stole it... it's not good".

He paused...

"I know - I know...but this is the prosecution case. What about Murgatroyds - did she say by chance I have a large Fish & Chip Restaurant, as well as taking fortunes to racetracks all over England? That was missing from Hatton's address which makes me think he knows the truth; he didn't dare play that one."

"No, she didn't say anything about that or Calibre"

There was a moment's silence.

"Look - there's a jury here. Seven women and five men. Not bad eh? They look decent people and *they* are my judges – not the judge, not Hatton, not the Marrow, not Split Ends, nor the Editor of the Yorkshire Evening Post - oh damn it - you've got that to come tomorrow; whether it's true is an irrelevance to them. They have agendas of their own to justify their positions. *They* are not my friends – I know that. I offered YEP the full inside story and they don't want to know. Expect nothing but grief from the boys at Yorkshire Post papers and Yorkshire TV. That's life."

"How are you getting on with - what is it - 'your team'?"

"They won't talk to me. Mike's done a runner - gone back to Nottingham, leaving me with this young girl. Gets up my nose - keeps calling herself my solicitor. Walks about with files of papers... a sort of duplicate of Mike"

"I don't know... I really hope you know what you're doing. Really it's just getting worse all the time...

"Look - it's as you said... the jury - they either believe me or they don't. Right now they think I'm a right little bastard who's stolen fortunes to gamble. What will they think of Hatton when the truth comes out - who'll be the little shit then? The Marrow doesn't want to know - won't talk to me... so getting the truth out won't be easy."

"I wish I was as relaxed as you sound," she said. But of course, he was not relaxed; terrified, and in denial that he was on a hiding to nothing. One hears and reads of injustices but they only happen to others. This was real and happening and no one could do anything to stop it.

"OK I'll speak tomorrow - but I warn you it'll get worse before it gets better - we've tomorrows papers to come yet and I saw someone from The Times. The rags are no problem - there's no sex in any of this."

The phrase is shit scared, but he was smiling. Well - what else does one do when surrounded by adversity.

Across Leeds Graham Carter answered his phone:

"It's me, give us a minute" said Tony Heatherington in his blunt Yorkshire accent

"I dorn't know that I wanna talk to you"

"Naw - dorn't gor... 'ang on, this is different... - did you see it. I 'aven't laft so much in a long time - still got tears rolling down me cheeks - I can't believe it. They've gone for everything *again*... Simon's on trial now".

"Yeah - I know… I saw it.... okay I can't see 'ow they can touch anyone else now. I've already spoken to my solicitor... ee' told me - nor *wey* can the' stand all this on it's 'ed now; and say it weren't 'im and were us – they'll look fools...

"Yup - spot on... by then ee'll be locked away… they can't say it were us all along can they?"

"An' ee's alone – they let Harpo go as well…."

"Swines – is there no justice in this world" he laughed

"But... how long will Simon get".

"Ah he won't get long. Any'ow 'ee can tek it - just like public school fer 'is sort. But that letta we 'ad im writin' in Yarmouth... now its main evidence – but there seem to be more!"

"Yeah - amazin'. But look I dorn't wanna talk to you - just keep away…"

"Look - I'll explain one day. You was arrested wasn't you – I heard. Whatcha tellum about the moni?"

"As agreed - said it was to pay Simon's gambling debts - they had to accept that, as Law Society said so. But I'm still on bail - 'ave they bin fer you?"

"Well - they came, an' I just sat there - said not a word. Without Simon, they can't touch us...... 'an Law Society - dorn't laff - they repaid all lenders fer us!!'"
"Yeah - you owe me big time... But I dorn't wanna see yu again... not after what happened.... so you keep away
"Look - ferget about all that other stuff... I didn't do owt; it were them others. I had some problems going back a bit... you went away, so dorn't knor what 'appened.. I'll tell ya one day".
"Look – I'm off'

And there was no prospect of getting any of it into trial. Lawyers needed this defendant to lose, to justify a Law Society Establishment Sting. Little wonder he put his faith in ordinary people.

Over in North Yorkshire, old Harpo rested uneasily against his golf club bar.
"Hello Peter... I see that pal of yours is getting his come uppance. Absolutely *disgraceful* if you ask me. Hope he gets a long stretch. Never liked him anyway," offered a passing member. "I knew his parents – they must be turning in their graves. Thank god they don't have to put up with this."
"It's what he did to me, and my family, that bothers me. I never saw it. He just took us to the cleaners. Cost me my business and nearly my home"
"Yes, I heard" offered the interested party, who knew only the gossip proffered by the Yorkshire Evening Post and idle digs of uninformed lawyers - "but he should get at least ten years for that lot, and you're OK now aren't you. Keep your pecker up old chap – don't let types like him get you down"

"Thanks - I'm OK - Law Society paid me £270,00 compensation for what he did to me, but that's only scratching the surface..."
"Good - excellent" And off he went to join his group. Smugly Peter chuckled to himself - *'I stuffed them with over £500,000 I'd already got from him. Prats all of them'*

Ever since the Law Society's Court had published Kaberry was guilty of these allegations, they were accepted as true. No one thinks to question such people and there is no procedure to – at all. It's a closed shop with judicial protection. If the public knew the real truth, what confidence would it have in the Law Society? The Legal Establishment had discredited this defendant and now needed him convicted.

Down in Leamington Spa and across in Cardiff, Robin Penson, a clerk in charge at Law Society, and solicitor Geoffrey Williams, respectively enjoyed their suppers, in complete indifference to the destruction they had caused to this man's life and the judicial system. Likewise in London solicitor Anthony Isaacs who had sat in the Law Society Kangaroo Court which had published these false stories as true, of a man who couldn't talk; they destroyed him. This defendant had avowed that one day he would have them, and he had sat in silence since. For his part he made this plain; no way would they keep him from that witness box. But he was not ready for press-gags.

This is no story of fiction. It is my personal story of how the system works - lawyers at work. I relied on the cleverness of ordinary folk to see that hole. These allegations were not true and the facts were grossly misrepresented.

'Let's see what tomorrow and the next days will bring - if only I can sleep.' - trial was marked to last three weeks, but would I be allowed a fair trial? Would my counsel expose lawyers?

CHAPTER TWO

A Medico -Legal Scandal – and still it continues

"One day we will look back and wonder how our society can have been so barbaric... to our citizens."

"They re-routed my mind... everyone was running rings round me...."

"They stole my life..."

At this point, I must digress. This is my personal story of the blind faith we are expected to keep in life-changing systems over which we have no control - the legal and medical systems. This story also illustrates why we must always keep faith with ordinary people, and the inherent dangers of unaccountable power. It could so readily have been you in that court, with that advice. Lawyers won't accept this true story - it whistleblows.

You probably know nothing of the true story of the lawyers who spent 35 million pounds of taxpayers' money, paying themselves, in a civil claim for many thousands who claimed to have been injured by a generic group of prescribed drugs. Effectively their own lawyers blocked the claim, leaving thousands with lives in tatters - ruined careers, families destroyed and ongoing ill-health for life. No evidence was ever heard. It is a scandal.

Pose this question - why are you as you are, and what right do you have to remain, the person you are? Silly question - the right to your own working mind is always there. No one can rob you of your mind - you take that for granted. We live in a society with inflated ideas of 'rights,' but the right to your own mind and to be yourself must surely be unquestioned.

Remember the words of one of the world's best-known philosophers Renee Descartes - "*I think, so I am*" ('*cogito, ergo sum*'). A few years ago, a Neurosurgeon Prof. Antonio Damasio published a book "Descartes Error" - '*you may have a brain all right, but you're certainly not all there!*' And I'm sure we have all jested whether some people, even ourselves, have any brain at all sometimes.

Damasio reviewed a few old cases starting with the tragic story of Phineas Gage. He was a nineteenth century navvy working on railway construction when gunpowder blew a bolt through the front of his head. Miraculously he survived, but had lost a large section of his forehead. He still was human; his physical injuries were visible and obvious. The injury also robbed him of the ability to think and reason. He lived on, becoming a circus freak, robotically exhibited alongside the bearded woman. 'C' was a commercial lawyer in his thirties in New York State. He developed a brain tumour the size of an orange. Surgical skills saved, cured, and injured him all in one operation. All appeared well at first. But during the operation, it seems the surgeon cut a tiny part of his frontal lobes, possibly within the limbic system, which deals with emotion and impulse. Even now, neuro-surgeons, psycho-pharmacologists, and psychiatrists don't fully understand all the causes of damaged minds, or the consequences. 'C' was left a man incapable of emotion - devoid of feelings for himself or anyone. But that was not all; he lost all ability to make any decision. He could give options, but make no decision, whilst responding to instruction, hold detailed conversations about life and politics, but make no decision. From a clever and successful lawyer, he was now a man with no feeling for anyone. Unable to rationalise, he was unemployable, ending up living in a relative's attic bedroom. The professor nearly cries for the patient who had no feeling for what had befallen him in life.

Their destinies were controlled by what happened to them. We can readily understand a body can't work properly until a broken bone or physical injury is repaired – when the computer hardware is damaged. But, what happens if the 'way we think' and the ability to hold emotion is damaged internally? - when the software is damaged. We don't readily or really understand that.

Over the last century, a multi-national, international global industry of pharmacy and pharmacology has grown, far more powerful than here-today-gone-tomorrow governments, unaccountable and with very considerable wealth, which brings power and influence. These are the truly wealthy - colossal, with access to and control of global experts, and power over our daily lives in so many respects. One successful drug can earn them billions. Yet, just one error can break a company, so they don't admit it, and we can't prove it because it is rarely an exact science.

Some say it's the most corrupt business possible - too powerful. Remember thalidomide? They denied responsibility until eventually one would have to lack common sense to deny the connection between the drug given to pregnant women to calm them, and the injuries sustained by the newborn child. That said, the lawyers advised settling at 40% of potential liability, as they feared being unable to persuade a Judge that the supplier of the drugs, which caused such devastation, breached the duties of care. What happens to men once tied up in gaiters with horsehair atop?

Prescribed psychoactive drugs - by simple definition 'mind altering' drugs - are controlled by a regulation system. On a simple level that is why it's a criminal offence to drive a car when under the influence of the drug alcohol, that slows the brain and can make the driver reckless, negligent, and downright stupid. When it comes to the prescribing and usage of drugs, our doctors have to rely upon guidance from the data sheets and from lectures they attend – usually put on by the Industry which supplies the drugs - i.e. they rely on the very people who have a vested interest to make money from the product, for its efficacy.

The generic Benzodiazepines scandal

This story does not concern recreational drugs and abused drugs or amphetamines and steroids, nor the anti-depressants about which you receive so much misleading information in the media. 'Anti-depressants' in today's terminology and pharmacy are generally the SSRI's (selective serotonin re-uptake inhibiters) – they target serotonin levels. Things like Prozac.

The scandal concerns tranquillisers, known generically as Benzodiazepines.

Some of the more common benzodiazepines set overpage

Benzos are both common tranquilliser and sleeping pills. Many media writers confuse anti-depressants and tranquillisers, calling them all 'happy pills.' Happiness is a consequence of fulfillment or an anticipation of good times, and you don't get either when sedated.

All benzodiazepines have these **five** pharmacological actions

Generic Name	Brand Name	Manufacturer	Introduced	half-life	UK Usage
chlordiazepam	Librium	Roche	1960	5-30 hours	anxiety
Diazepam	Valium	Roche	1963	20-100 hrs	Anxiety /insomnia
Nitrazepam	Mogodon	Roche	1965	15-38 hrs	insomnia
Oxazepam	Serenid	Wyeth	1969	4-15 hrs	anxiety
Medazepam	Nobrium	Roche	1971	36-200 hrs	anxiety
Lorazepam	Ativan	Wyeth	1972	10-20 hrs	anxiety/ insomnia
Clorazepam	Tranxene	Boehringer	1973	[36-200 active]	anxiety
Flurazepam	Dalmane	Roche	1974	[40-250 active]	insomnia
Temazepam	Normison	Wyeth	1977	8-22 hrs	insomnia
Triazolam	Halcion	Upjohn	1979	2 hrs	insomnia
Clobazolam	Frisium	Hocchst	1979	12-60 hrs	anxiety
Fluni-trazepa	Rohypnol	Roche	1982	18-26 hrs	insomnia
Bromazepam	Lexotan	Roche	1982	10-20 hrs	anxiety
Prazepam	Centrax	Warner	1982	[36-200 active]	anxiety
Alprazolam	Xanax	Upjohn	1983	6-12 hrs	anxiety
Ketazolam	Anxon	Beecham	1980	2 hrs	anxiety

(i) Anti-anxiety; - (ii) anti-convulsant - (iii) muscle relaxant - (iv) sedative/hypnotic, and (v) amnesic (enabling the user to forget what's troubling them - *and other things too!)*

This generic benzo group was foisted on us in the late 1960's; the doctors were told they were safe, as opposed to the highly toxic barbiturate sedatives, which they replaced. Remember the tragic blonde, overdosed and died from sleeping pills; those were the barbiturates. It's much more difficult to top yourself on Benzos.

'Benzos' are central nervous system depressants, which means they slow the activities of a variety of nerve cells in the brain. Apparently, they increase activity of a natural chemical in the brain called gamma-amino acid (GABA), which then suppresses nerve cell activity. Put another way, Benzos block some of the brain receptors thus preventing the transfer of information - including warnings that danger is afoot, which would otherwise enable you to take evasive action; the user's brain is 'sedated' - unable to work things out as before. By 1970's they were referred to by one distinguished psychiatrist as 'the opium of the masses' –

'here's a patient complaining of something - here try one of these; Valium - it'll make you feel better.' Some GPs prescribed willy-nilly. But, they were only intended for short-term use (2-3 weeks).

Ignorance remains widespread. A good friend of mine suffered a bad back for years; in the mid 1980's, he was prescribed Ativan, as a muscle relaxant, to ease the pain. So he ingested a drug for anxiety, convulsion and to cause amnesia and sedate his working brain for over a year - for a bad back! His feisty wife relates that divorce was on the cards - 'I can't begin to tell you how impossible he became,' said she - but in the nick of time, information came to hand, the prescribing stopped and they were saved. The mother of another friend is charming but has a reputation of being eccentric and difficult, even aggressive and readily drunk. It transpires, she cannot live without mogodon – which she still thinks is 'just a sleeping pill'. Thousands of lives have been ruined - and the users thought they were the problem.

Following initial use, the user feels better or sleeps better as they work well; so they become dependent. The user has 'a belief' he needs them - addicted. And the longer you have been taking them, then, generally, the longer it takes for your mind and body to recover, or kick the habit. What you need is a good doctor to explain and control usage to 7-10 days. However, at any one moment there are about 8,000 drugs reps plying their bosses' wares to GP's with vast hospitality on offer.

None of them saw or sees themselves as drug addicts. They were taking harmless pills as prescribed - and stopping is horrible.

However, the real truth, masked by these disbeliefs and misplaced faith, was that horrendous damage was being done to thousands who kept 'taking the tablets', beyond two or three weeks – their intended term. Patients were 'so ready to accept that the pill was doing them good.' Common sense tells us now that a brain which is physically sedated, cannot work as well as one that is not. Insidiously, they had been robbed of their own working mind and the right to be themself - *the computer software damaged.*

Let me explain the effects. Imagine you're a reasonable chess player. Sedated, you still know and understand the mechanics of the game, but you can't plan a game, or see what your opponent has in store for you. You're there to be had in a Fool's Mate. Transfer that to daily professional, social and commercial life; the consequence will be utter chaos, and gullibility. And your normal family life – without emotion? Worse still, anyone taking any benzo must abstain from all alcohol. The two synergize' doubling at least the effect of each drugs. Hence the 'date-rape' with rohypnol (flunitrazepam) but you'll get a similar result with many benzos.

The consequences will and do vary from one person to the next. Some of the effects *include* (and I take all this from pharmachologists reports):

- Poor concentration: an inability to sit down - find a solution to a problem; or do something non-routine. Daytime confusion: mild or severe. Daytime drowsiness: Lightheadedness; muscular problems (including diarrhea or constipation.). Impaired short-term memory (the chemicals are intended to cause amnesia e.g. the date-rape experiences.). Emotional anesthesia (you no longer feel for people *or yourself.*). Depression: suicidal desires; and agoraphobia (you avoid mixing by 'fear of the market place.'). Obsessive conduct: Aggressive and bizarre behaviour, including lack of inhibition (a sort of 'couldn't care less' attitude.); and violent outbursts: Slurred speech and drunkenness, especially if alcohol is taken before the chemical has been excreted, which could be days after ingested. There is more; the list is near endless. You live divorced from the real world, unable to see things as you normally would.
- All this and more from apparently 'harmless' pills.

It doesn't end there. Many thousands are left **permanently injured** from long-term exposure to the drugs, but here the evidence has to be anecdotal. To do otherwise would require taking an individual, exposing him to the drugs for years, then waiting to see how much harm had been done: 'utterly unethical.' Nevertheless, that anecdotal evidence is whopping.

There are *thousands* of horror stories from real people living with those problems in England and all over the world. Look at website www.benzo.org.uk. under '*stories*' or '*media*' and read comments of the site of '*petition*'.

It took the Committee for the Safety of Medicines (CSM – now NICE) to January 1988 before it formally warned prescribers to limit the prescribing of all Benzos, to those who really needed them for daytime sedation or help with disabling sleeplessness. They warned of the consequences of *over-prescribing* including addiction, confusion, amnesia and suicide, and that in any event, all prescribing should be for short-term only. Moreover, in 1990 Roche issued a similar warning to prescribers – 'these drugs are for short-term usage only.' But it did little good.

Sleeping Pills

Sleeping pills are probably more dangerous than 'tranquillisers' because the user thinks he/she has just taken something to help him sleep. When up, showered and about he assumes the effect is over. Try to come off them after a while and you can't sleep; if you cannot sleep, you can't function properly, and feel dreadful and worse – although that is also withdrawal. So, you 'keep taking the tablets.' Many people, even today, don't know a sleeping pill is virtually the same as a daytime tranquilliser.

By the early 1980's the experts knew these drugs were causing problems. Well-known types such as actor Burt Reynolds and the infamous case of Richard and Karen Carpenter's addiction to dalmane. So the pharmaceutical industry pushed shorter acting pills, excreted from the body more quickly - Temazepam, Flunitrazepam (rohypnol) and Triazolam (halcion). But there are terrible horror stories about Halcion - "*Sweet Dreams or Nightmares*" is one of the newspaper headlines. Things reached a climax in late 1980s with the Grundberg case; after taking Halcion for over a year she became paranoid and killed her mother. She sued Upjohn - that they had marketed a drug responsible for her bizarre conduct. On the eve of trial, the towel was thrown in and although secret, it is thought they paid her $6 million to settle. They were not going to admit fault readily, and they have the power and money. There was no judgment against them and they said – 'you've got to rely on science, anecdotal evidence doesn't cut.' That means common sense plays little part.

The Legal Benzo Scandal – *lawyers*

In the mid-late 1980's, people started to consult solicitors about the effects of Benzos generally. One lawyer tried to sue the regulator CSM for acting too little and too late (in 1988), but you can't win against such power – unless perhaps you can find a judge who has been affected personally or within his family. Unaccountable Judges like to protect the Establishment of which they feel a central part.

Legal Aid funded a 'Group Claim.' Thousands came forward and a central committee was set up with Nottingham lawyers Freethcartright, headed by a young man called Paul Balen. The clients wanted compensation for ruined lives, families destroyed, careers and businesses lost, and ongoing ill health. They had been robbed of the right to be themselves, and often with terrible consequences.

Lawyers were getting stories of differing effects of different drugs from a variety within the generic group. Ativan seems to have been severely criticised. Sometimes it can't have been easy to distinguish what was causing the problems – something in them, or the treatment and duration of it. Against that, many never needed any mind-changing drugs, so with them at least it was fairly simple - if the lawyers could grasp that. And of course many who could have come forward knew nothing about the claims and litigation, and were still taking the drugs, oblivious to the cause of their problems – or that they even had a problem; that only comes clear when they try to stop. Some are still taking them – oblivious to the truth, and with GPs ignoring their trust and duties.

The solicitors passed the facts and supporting medical evidence to barristers to advise how best to proceed. That's the way our messy system has evolved; you get two men to do one man's job, and 'falling between two stools' is not a meaningless saying. Lawyers and judges defend this system by saying you get a specialist second opinion; but they would, wouldn't they? Judges are endemically trained to protect their system. Solicitors charge as if they are experts - then say 'now you need an expert' - buck-passing. These were big claims of real loss and serious injury. *But - against whom?* - the prescriber or manufacturer? If you were in their powerful shoes of Wyeth, Upjohn and Roche – what would be the easiest way to block the litigation? Think on that as you read to the very end of this story, then reflect – how sinister?

This was a huge claim worth many millions of pounds. How do you value a life? What is it like to be confused for years, and left permanently unwell? What about the housewives who weren't working anyway? Barristers included one Oliver Thorold, who advised and drafted one of the claims, filed at court – i.e. he 'pleaded' the claim, which set out the allegations of breach of duty of care, injury caused, and losses arising. They issued two 'Group' Claims – one against each BOTH the prescribers, and manufacturers. Of the GP's they claimed they had wrongly prescribed addictive drugs constantly. That was largely the claim drafted by the barristers - that they had failed to 'wean' the addicted patient from the drug – nothing of poor diagnosis or treatment, nor the terrible effects on a working mind, and nothing about the long-term injuries for those who never recovered. The real consequences of addiction and drugs effects were never pleaded - the turmoil that will cause to daily life, or what it is like to live with a sedated mind, that can't work things out any more, devoid of real feelings ('tranquillised'). It was never 'pleaded.'

I suggest the lawyers got it hopelessly wrong; the investigations and pleadings were poor, possibly incompetent. Another problem would be that their own experts agree there is a place in medicine for the generic drugs – generically they are not dangerous. The problem is in overuse. First, to apply to strike out the 'pleaded claim' before any evidence was heard were the doctors' insurers. In the claim against the manufacturers, the barristers pleaded the doctors hadn't been told the drugs were addictive - so, what was there for them to answer? They had prescribed what the Regulator licensed, and they were still prescribing them. They had nothing to defend on the claim the lawyers had pleaded. It was struck-out by the High Court.

The lawyers were surrounded by problems largely of their making for failing to investigate the facts, issues, and effects thoroughly, and gather the evidence from the experts – *and* defendants' own records and research, and plead a powerful case. The problem was the length of time many patients had been prescribed them – and some should never have been prescribed mind-changing drugs at all. The real case wasn't pleaded.

Not then actively engaged in litigation, I knew none of this, but reading the events later, it seems to me it was inevitable that the pleaded Group Manufacturer claim would also be struck out. The lawyers must have known that as inevitable. Yet, *millions* of pounds of public money had already been paid over to these lawyers - on their advice to the Legal Aid Board to fund what they had done. How would you react as advising barrister in such situation? Hold your hands up and say 'I got it wrong' – and go unpaid. Or is it more sinister than that? As I say, 'keep an open mind'…. I hold one of the 'Reviews' for the Legal Aid Board Audit purposes of barrister Thorold on the merits of proceeding with more money on his pleaded case. He said people talked of their 'Lost Years' when 'life was barren.' Little is said of the ongoing injuries and the hell they still lived whilst trying to rebuild their shattered lives, or how long this would continue (some never recovered). But the ongoing defendants – the pharmaceutical industry - hadn't 'diagnosed and treated' any claimant; doctors had done that. Thorold then proceeded to put a monetary value on a 'Lost Year', and compared it to living in a damp house – a figure of about £1,500 for each year. You get that for a cricked neck in a good whiplash case. That Opinion and other Advice was submitted by the lawyers in Nottingham to the Legal Aid Board with the *inevitable* consequence – the LAB decided that the group claim was 'not financially viable,' when you set that level of compensation against the millions lawyers had already taken for their fees, and would yet take.

Accordingly LAB withdrew funding. Media got hold of the story in early 1994 – "**Sad Story of the Happy Pills**" – '*six years on and the legal system cannot cope with a group compensation claim for tranquilliser addiction… after 30 **million pounds** had been paid over to the lawyers.*' (Others say 35 million.)

The very lawyers who held themselves as champions of the claimants had effectively advised the LAB to pull the plug. That media report recorded that '*lawyers are bitter.*' Paul Balen said the decision 'called into question the entire English system.' But he had filed the Opinions, which made that decision inevitable. The solicitors and barristers 'withdrew' leaving the claimants without lawyers. One man wrote directly to the judge setting out his losses at a million pounds - and he wasn't alone. Many of the group claimants never recovered and never returned to work – some were put on Incapacity and Disability Benefit for life; others just accepted their lot in life – we are powerless. One of their number ** later remarked to me - 'yes, you can live, but it's a different life, and go to work – the problem is what happens when you get there' (you can't work or understand reality). Thousands will agree with him. They were all denied access to justice – on their own lawyer's advice (but they didn't know that).

> ** - he removed himself completely from the 'Group Claim', and continued alone in Scottish (no strike-out) courts. He had been prescribed the sleeping pill mogodon, when a successful businessman. His world and business fell apart with his mind. He claimed millions from the manufacturers for not telling his GP what the pills really were and did (*a different Pleading*) and was due finally to come to trial in 2007. But those years in litigation took an enormous toll, and, at the court door, he settled - 'a secret deal struck' - no trial or admission.'

Frighteningly, lawyers Balen and Thorold continue to hold themselves out as experts on the effects of Benzodiazepines. Imagine a heart surgeon, and all his patients died, still held out as an expert. Lawyers would skin such a doctor alive! But there is no similar control over lawyers. Quite the reverse - judges to the very top in the House of Lords will protect them, as this account relates. It's the Legal Omerta.

A group continued the claim without lawyers. Their appeal against strike-out without trial came before Lords Justices Stewart-Smith, Brooke and Aldous. Sir William Aldous is prominent later in this account, protecting the lawyers. The three judges said the lawyer's advice to LAB left them 'dead in the water,' and saying it was 'flawed ab initio.'

Thousands have had their lives ruined - forever; it's about responsibilities; nothing to do with a compensation culture; this was no accident. Well, if Boots gave you the wrong prescription with disastrous consequences – you'd sue for the losses so caused.

Modern Medicine – the position post 1994
- *The problem continues*

Most doctors have heard the horror stories, but not all of them by any means, and the problem continues. It's terribly sad and a waste of life. There are some non-benzo sleeping pills but NICE have confirmed they work on the brain just the same way as Benzos.

Doctors who ignore the Benzo warnings and expose their patients to these drugs long-term <u>should be sued and disciplined</u>. That would end the scandal – *simple as that.* <u>But it hasn't happened</u>. The trouble arises from the group action – lawyers generally have wrongly been told the Claim was 'lost.' But that isn't true.

The knock-on effect of the wasted 35 million runs much deeper. Recently, in USA victims of an arthritis drug were awarded $2*billion* for their injuries. In UK funding isn't allowed for such group claims so they got - nothing for their injuries.

I offer just a tiny few of the *thousands* of comments found on the website of individual's remarks:
- "It was as if my mind had been re-routed, as sure as if the points had been changed; *everyone was running rings round me...*
- "Taking these drugs *ruined my life....*
- "*I went through mental hell....*
- "These drugs are deadly – they should be banned...
- "**Someday I can only hope that the truth will be told** of what these benzodiazepine drugs have done. We will look back and wonder how our society could have been *so barbaric to have prescribed these to millions of unsuspecting citizens.*
- "We all need to come together and find a solution and inform people... this must stop
- "**I have suffered years in recovery – please do something now.**
- "**5 years on Benzos ruined my life, and so far it's been 5 years in recovery...**
- "**They stole my life....**
- "These unnecessary and irresponsibly prescribed drugs have devastated **not only my life,** *but of those around me who had to face this with me*

I could continue another five pages and more....
- *Can they all be so wrong?*

Save this is fact; not everyone was adversely affected, as we each respond differently to psychoactive drugs. Some recovered and some did not – rather like gulf-war syndrome.

Many still try petitioning Parliament to stop this scandal. But Parliament doesn't 'diagnose and treat' patients. The issues are medico-legal - and the courts….. men like Lords Bingham, Phillips, Scott and Brown, who will allow no evidence. Read on

This Story
You will have guessed: I was prescribed the sleeping pill Dalmane for four years. Dalmane (flurazepam) 'puts and keeps' the working mind to sleep - far longer acting than its brother flunitrazepam (rohypnol, used also to sedate before sexual attack). The prescribing was 'top-end' negligence by my GP. I led a full life as a lawyer with my own practice. Over those years, my social, domestic, professional, and economic life gradually fell apart along with my mental faculties. I had no idea I was ingesting a psychoactive daytime sedative drug, and no need for one. As I lost the ability to think-straight and concentrate, I sat on work I could no longer do, and my practice fell apart. Simultaneously Law Society failed to regulate me, as I filed and kept no accounts, and fraudsters took advantage of my impaired condition; I was cleaned out - my signature was forged to cheques. Eventually rendered suicidal, in despair for what seemed to have happened when I was in charge, I took personal blame for all 'missing money,' and, as directed, wrote admissions, which could not be true when set against the facts. You've just heard them in chapter 1. I was arrested, and as police investigated (one man arrested told police in Interview I became an 'Easy Touch' for money), I discovered the cause of my woes, and was referred to Balen and Thorold, who were immediately granted legal aid to sue the negligent prescriber.

Aware of all this, Law Society published in a ten-minute sitting of it's Kangaroo Court (Tribunal), that I had stolen millions from clients to gamble. They knew it wasn't true, but they are well protected by our Judges. With police investigations ruined, and in chaos - for I could be no witness after that, I was charged and you have just read the start of my trial. How would you cope?

In the first part of this account, I explain what it is like to be doped up, defrauded and deceived, then set up by Establishment - and put on trial. The second part is more worrying - our unaccountable legal system, and two questions - how sinister is all this? - and what can we do with unaccountable and bent judges who breach their oath to do justice without fear or favour, protecting their own first (chaps 16-18). It's pretty sordid. We have no sanction (chap 19) on them at all – in our democracy.

Supported as I was by the facts, a jury ruling in a press-gagged trial, and all medical experts, my own lawyers then blocked the best prescriber claim, which would have made up for the wasted 35 million. Why and how? Read on… I ask you to keep an open mind throughout, then judge the lawyers and judges. I explain how readily they do it, and name the names.

The Legal Omerta – the judicial cover-up

With essential funding to sue the negligent doctor lost on my lawyer's bad advice, and in an impossible position in law, I had to sue the negligent lawyers, funded by taxpayers money. Here I was confronted by the Omerta of legal protectionism. That 'Silent Code of the Closed Shop' that you look after your own first. The Hearing of any claim would expose serious wrongdoing, criminality, and deceptions by Law Society staff, on the public; our judges wouldn't allow that, for it kicks their closed shop.

The jury had met me and wished me well getting back to work and re-building a very shattered life. Events which follow make one want to re-write those old school essays - *'Power Corrupts, Absolute Power Corrupts Absolutely?'* - for judicial power is absolute and unaccountable, entrusted to unelected jobs-for-life types. Any claim by me, and publication of the truth, would reveal how Law Society, by its top lawyers had committed criminal offences for which others are sent to prison – our judges wouldn't allow the dangers of their closed shop exposed.

Lords Bingham (then LCJ) and Phillips (then MR) led the line of cover-up, that no evidence be allowed of what Law Society had done, so no career or life could be restored, and I live out my days condemned a dishonest thief. That would blight anyone, and no compensation claim heard – so the scandal continues. My pension was taken by law, offering poverty for life, and both Bingham and Phillips ruled no evidence could be given of how Law Society had set me up to media, and left three crooks laughing like extras from a smash advert with millions from their frauds. I give you the detail of these men of honour and chivalry. Two High Court and five Appeal Court judges (two blatantly dishonest) followed their lead, striking out all civil cases from proceeding. Three highly duplicitous law lords (chap 18) followed suit – *"we find there is nothing for us to consider"* – to hell with justice without fear or favour. Sadly, they are too unaccountable for me (or you) - Lords Bingham, Phillips, Nicholls, Scott and Brown all ruled - no evidence in any trial involving me. Sordid or corrupt? Serious public interest and legal issues were blocked by these men. You read the evidence and consider if I'm right.

I petitioned Lord Bingham (as senior law lord) ten times to review this, as he had started it (see Epilogue). He viewed all thru Nelson's eye, saw nought, then travelled to Windsor to accept the highest honour of chivalry (a courageous defender of the weak). This is the Legal Omerta. He knows, as they all do, that there is absolutely no accountability to the public they serve.

A lady was wrongly prescribed dalmane at the same time as me. She suffered similarly. She used 'non-expert' lawyers to sue the prescriber and was awarded a six figure sum to 'settle.' So it can be done with half-competent lawyers.

They had made us subject to European Courts to protect 'human rights'. But I'm not a homo-sexual, crook, prisoner, or asylum-seeker; did the Convention have anything for a native anglo-saxon seeking an ounce of justice? Was it not my 'human right' to have a trial before losing my career, home, family, capital, reputation and pension? It's ruling (chap 18) would surely make a radical Muslim extremist chuckle like a mellow Christian.

One person who read this book in draft said – *"you keep reading, believing... surely... this couldn't happen in England... then you vote... and fifteen minutes later you're smiling."*

At the end (chapter 19) I set out the system we have to bring dishonesty in legal circles to account. There isn't anything effective and the recent reforms (like the OJC) make a bad situation worse – it reports to the very man who participated in it all. And I set how events affected all those in this true story. You judge...

Simon Kaberry

CHAPTER THREE

Could this have been you?

As this is a personal story, I have to tell you who I am. How would you cope if put on trial? I ask you also to make allowance for, and understand any prejudices I may have, however none PC.

Like you, I will be a consequence of 60-40% genetic inheritance and 60-40% life experience to explain the way I am. I was born in Horsforth near Leeds, the last of three boys for my parents. My early memories are that all was safe and well; we didn't know our families had just been in a five year world war. My father was a solicitor, businessman, and politician from fairly humble beginnings. The War saw him go in as a volunteer and leave a Lieutenant Colonel. In 1950, he was elected as conservative MP for Leeds North-West, where he would stay until 1983 - part of the new middle class taking over the Conservative Party. Placed in the Whip's office, he can be seen on early 1950's newsreels on platforms seated behind or adjacent to The Great Man (then PM again). At six foot six and with a rotund girth, he had a commanding presence. But he was no toff-type public schoolboy Tory, yet he would have been on the periphery of the Magic Circle. They made him Deputy Chairman 1955-9; as such, in 1956 he interviewed a lady candidate, and reported she would be 'an asset to the party - find her a good seat.' She later became Prime Minister. He was paid off by Macmillan with one of the last (hereditary) baronetcies – 'thank you very much, but no further on the Front Bench'. It was the way of the time. His motto chosen was 'Laboro Fide - and I would also always 'strive with faith.'

We didn't need words for honour, integrity, duty and respect; the qualities we were taught, and always to do what is right - don't compromise standards. Mother was surely one of the most cheerful 'ever happy' people one could hope to meet. She accepted her lot - her husband was effectively away all her life. It was an era of - 'if you can't find something good to say, then don't say anything.' That said, mother was one of those who had to say something whether it fitted or not, but spoken with a glint of comedy. "Well, I may as well be slain for a sheep as a lamb" - that sort of remark.

My eldest brother was typical of such - bossy and outgoing, whilst the middle one was so shy, he would disappear if anyone visited, later found in the loo, and at school he couldn't be a prefect. It was pre-written that he'd later be picked up by, and marry the first passing hairdresser, with me as Best Man. But he's a nice chap.

In 1957 we moved to a large house in several acres in Adel, another suburb of Leeds, with housekeeper, cook, and gardener and his wife in the cottage. Old values lingered on. Understatement and polite manners were expected. One must do nothing ostentatious and talking or flaunting money or success was vulgar; still should be and is to many of us. If one did something wrong, one admitted it and accepted punishment - as a matter of course. It was disgrace to do wrong - hang your head in shame; but worse, it was dishonour not to admit wrong when caught.

Age six, I was sent off to boarding school; best lessons were in manners. For sex education matron Jones gave practical training; so, at an early age I knew what an old wanker was – she'd get 5-6 years nowadays. Next school was Repton. It's not a very top-notch public school but far more than very adequate. An early incident explains how I react. I was sixteen and watching cricket on the Square - mid Saturday afternoon. I've backed horses since I was eight. Hepworth was going to the village bookie - "do you want a bet Kaberry?" - "Okay I'll have two shillings on this double." At about 6.30, I was called to see the headmaster. Hepworth had been caught, and claimed to be my runner; bad enough being caught, but then to blame me! "Was that true Kaberry?" - "Yes sir." That is honour - always admit your involvement. My punishment was to be hit six times. As we do, I said 'thank you sir' – but not 'how kind.' The event was soon forgotten, save I didn't speak to Hepworth again. A year on the housemaster made me 'Head of House' and the headmaster appointed me a school prefect. The responsibility gives you a confidence to present yourself; an excellent experience for life generally. My Final Housemaster's Report referred to my *'ability to get others to tow the line and accept his authority 'in his own quiet wa*y.'' That is how I have always been. A big weakness.

I left with the mandatory three 'A' levels. Career was pre-written - I would be a lawyer and work in father's office in Leeds. University was a no-no. I sat alone for hours learning by rote, sometimes went to court to listen, and sometimes a little commercial law went in. After being Secretary of the Law Students, I knew I could get nowhere in that firm; I moved to London. First week, I stayed at father's Club, so I encountered him with his London chums. I joined him for drinks and was introduced to Peter Do-Da, 'your Foreign Secretary' and Peter So-and-So, 'your Attorney General'; fine men, very different to the grass roots politics I had become a part of. Ten years later Peter Do-Da, was back as FS, and resigned after his office had failed to note the build-up of troops around the Falklands - acceptance of responsibility. Ministers don't do that now, as without Office, they are nothings and nobodys, without proper jobs or careers.

Next day father asked me to join him in the Court of Appeal to listen to a case; I noticed him nod to the old codger on the right. On my way out I stupidly said – 'and which judge is in your pocket' - receiving a very stern rebuke - "Don't you *ever* dare say or think any such thing. These boys are completely independent, and will do what is right in accordance with the law. They owe no favour and have no fear. They will only do as is right in accordance with the law." That lesson would cost me dear. That aside biggest lesson I learned in London was never to trust clerks.

For Finals I shared digs in Guildford with Yorkshireman John Patchett. I spent more time in Heathorns (the local bookies) and the lovely redhead in my amour. Normal youthful irresponsibility. At Easter I saw the feared Dr.Bedford - often tired, was I suffering relapse glandular fever, as warned? He prescribed *'something to buck you up.'* John and I called them my 'little poppers' because suddenly I was full of energy - mentally flying. I had no idea what Ritalin was, save that I could read an article, case-law, book, paper, Act of Parliament, précis an answer after just one swift read. Only twenty-five years on, was I to discover what Ritalin is. They don't 'sedate disruptive children' (ADHD). They speed up the dopamine in the brain, so the brain is more able to process information. Thus, with a turbo-charged Ritalin-inflamed brain, I breezed my finals and was admitted a qualified solicitor in 1974.

Life was not the silver-plated spoon other's may have thought. And having one's father as a politician can be very awkward - imagine my embarrassment when reading father signed off a report as Chairman of the Select Committee on Trade and Industry – "We find that Concorde will never be a viable financial proposition." How out-dated he was, for everyone knew supersonic flights were the future and this was just the start. Ten years after he died, Concorde was taken out of service - not an economic proposition.

I started my first job as an assistant solicitor in dowdy offices in Wakefield; they only worked on conveying houses. Most days, I was finished before 10.00 am. I wanted more than that and, bored, saw Dr.Bedford again - could I have some of those marvellous Ritalin things again? He gave me some, but if I was tired (my excuse), then he said I needed sleeping pills, so he gave me some as well - just on, the market - called Dalmane. In other words, he gave me uppers (amphetamines) and downers (sedatives) in one swoop; I didn't know that. Soon I was hooked.

It didn't take long for things to go wrong - *first time round.* That summer we had two weeks sharing a house in the Spanish sunshine. But I'd lost all drive and was drifting. My nightly Dalmane had taken a hold - not that anyone knew; mid-twenties, I was actually sedated by Valium. It was not a good holiday; I had lost my way in life for no apparent reason.

I returned to be confronted by my employers - over the coals for work I wasn't allowed to do, but had been doing. Worst, the day prior to holiday, I'd seen a client over lunch; the cashier was out. I wrote on the file that he gave me £30 for a Registration fee and gave him a receipt. But I knew nothing of the event at all. Where was the £30? The buck stops with me - personal responsibility. I said it could only be me - I was out there and then.

I found the cash in the top front pocket of the suit I must have been wearing that day, but not on my return; no one would believe that, and anyway, the real reason I was out was there was no work. I got a better job in Bradford as a common law lawyer. Doped up maybe, but you can work and live in that condition - just not as well as you could. I was carried, with my fees not matching my overhead to them. Not surprisingly, mon amour dropped me. I wasn't the person she had met two years earlier. I had retreated to a little world. Doped up, life was passing me by.

Father sold Adel Willows - to be divided into five houses and gardens, but retaining the adjoining 6 acres of field and paddock. One day that would be worth a considerable sum; we all knew that. Without motivation, I had nowhere to go. So he sold me the front main part – and I paid market value. A 100% mortgage was arranged, so I came to own a lovely home with three big bedrooms and two bathrooms and super garden down a tree-lined drive.

My employers didn't seem to mind my arriving for work at 9.40 or later; but there was no pay rise. Actually, often I got very confused - eg basic spelling. Mr.Mistry and 'mystery' baffled me. On many Fridays after work, I went to the well-known Regent in Chapeltown. Two pints and I was drunk as a skunk - behaving as a fool. One Friday night some pushy blonde seemed to take a shine to me - so I came to engage in a fling by default.

Elaine told me to 'get out of that dead end job' and she moved on. Truth was I was the dead loss. In November 1979 I moved to a small firm, in Leeds city centre. Drugged up, I soon felt oppressed; I couldn't hack it in the real world. Then my memory problems repeated. The man who breezed his finals was now a zombie.

In early February 1980, I did what too many others, subjected to these generic drugs, have done. It was midweek; I took all that I had of the Dalmane, and for good measure a good swig of scotch. My mind and outlook on life had been destroyed. It's the reverse of human nature – certainly not me.

Next morning at 11, the phone shrilled by my bed - why was I not in court? Everything was spinning and groggy, as I dragged myself under the shower, tried to shave, drank some tea and in a very dishevelled state drove into town. My employer told me to go home. The following day he suggested: "things aren't working out." We agreed I would leave in six weeks - end of March. Could this have happened to you?... of course it could.

Simon Kaberry

CHAPTER FOUR.

The Seeds of Destruction

Six-weeks drug free (not that I knew I had taken any 'drug') and I was returning to myself. We excrete drugs and recover the younger we are. So in April 1980 I opened my own legal practice. My broad training would stand me well, and I present quite well, albeit a little pompous to those who don't understand my reserve and love of trickery. I could do most legal things.

My confidence returned; but always my upbringing of modesty and moderation prevailed. Having marked my Notes not to give me Dalmane, the GP re-started a supply, but I only used them occasional weekends. Make no doubt - Dalmane is a very effective sleeping pill.

Gamblers are frowned on by some, so I kept my horsey hobby quiet. Until I wrote this, no one bar a couple of managers knew of my successes; the proximity of Tote meant I used it often. Years later, manager Malcolm signed a statement for my lawyers, that I was 'not good business', and twice they barred me, although my 'stakes' have never been big but my love was doubles, trebles etc - so any returns would be good. My lawyer Thorold advised – he's a racing loser! You'll meet many clever lawyers in this story.

More than anything, I was an ante-post punter, looking for the big win at long odds – an ante-post punter always has something to look forward to; the perpetual optimist. And a losing punter always looks forward to tomorrow, when it will be so different. The love of a gamble, and there's nowt wrong with it. I am sorry for you boring types who frown on life's optimists, albeit readily confused with life's tossers, who historically go to the pub with the wage packet, then the bookies and blow it all, then go home and knock ten bells out of the wife for complaining there's no money.

Life was for living again – a joie de vivre you don't get when on drugs. I had a narrow escape when failing to avoid one of life's neurotics, who drove me bananas - no pills needed. Lovely, not gorgeous, but I didn't know some women are born liars. One morning, mother phoned - "Simon - I have some news - do you know your father has been honoured?" That's how we spoke in our family - in the objective. "You are now the Honourable Simon Kaberry!"- *'I don't think so!'* My father had been rewarded for a lifetime's public work by elevation to the House of Lords. I took morning tea upstairs - "Your tea - delivered by the honorable butler." Don't we all know the girls love even a little knob? Mother had some 'calling cards' printed with my address etc 'the Hon Simon Kaberry' - *joke*; these twists of life.

She left, and I started a new life, only for her to return months later. These women, you know, they can do that to us when under the skin. She left again; I returned home a couple of weeks later to find she'd been back and removed any trace that she had ever been any part of my life. Then, the inevitable call - "Simon, I'm getting married." A mountain had been lifted from my shoulders, for she couldn't return to plague me again. Really good times would follow. Always look for good in bad times and you'll find them - I realised all my women were good-lookers; so I'd got something - just had to leave the neurotic ones to better men.

The lost love seemed to spur me to lose track of my own values. At 34, I behaved like a rampant 21-year-old, and had 'flings' without too much thought. But always quietly, so no one knew. I don't like bedroom talk, but 48 year-old mother, and twenty-five year old daughter, at the same time, and neither knew - nor did I know they were, till too late. Yet I sourced that well-known saying - and it's true. How the washing machine worked overtime to ensure all traces of distinctive perfume were removed. Golly... imagine being caught - torn limb from limb. I speedily downed tools on both. The point I make is that I am utterly normal, and capable of being naughty, but I'm pretty discreet.

My lifetime's hobby evolved; I was generally winning on horses - 1981 onwards. But it's only a hobby. In March 1985 I collected about £4,000 from my small ante post Cheltenham doubles etc, and decided to put half of it back on to supplement my wagers for the guineas in May. I tried a £1,000 double at 8/1 and 10/1. Hills knocked me to a lesser stake (i.e. Hills wouldn't stand a £99,000 to a £1,000 bet on a double in 1985). I got more on later In May they both scraped home - at evens. My pal PD watched as my lucky mascot, but I don't talk. I was short of the £99,000 + that should have been, and as ever I took it all in cash; people in banks talk.

The following year 1986 was Dancing Brave year – backed each week at 14/1 from October to March and won at 15/8. With extra income like that, I didn't need to earn much from the practice; I often charged next to nothing to clients, or nothing at all. My practice was growing.

There were some short and long flings as I sought what none of us quite know what - save we know it when we have it. In 1986, I met Petrina, thirteen years my junior. Her happily vibrant personality contrasted with my reserved and outwardly quiet ways, and well balding head. I persuaded her to move in with me in; I could readily provide for both of us. Not perfect, pretty, but no neurotic fantasist, and by then I was well adjusted, confidant, financially sound and relaxed - ready to settle down. I gave her as much rope as possible; if she was unhappy, she could leave. It works - people stay together because they want to, not when pressured. If they want to go: let them – you can't ever force a relationship to work well. You have my views.

I rebuilt (after a failed partnership with Richard Jackson) a very busy small general legal practice. Gambling wise, 1987 was not good. In early April, I decided Maori Venture would either win the National or fall. The 50/1 was too tempting to my mind. I took £1,000 from my depleted kitty and tried to get the whole lot on spread among the bookies – 'win only' at 50/1 in the week before, just failing to get it all on. The following Saturday, he stood up and sped up past them up the run-in; 28/1 returned. My lady and I had an indulgent five star Easter weekend in London and the peace of Woodstock the week following. But I got the Guineas and Derby hopelessly wrong that year. You can't win 'em all.

September 1987 and we indulged ourselves in our child substitute - my best friend for the next thirteen years - a super Rhodesian Ridgeback to whom we gave the rather uninspiring name of Holly, rather than Africa or 'killer.' I remember sitting down with this tiny bouncing puppy, and promised her a good secure and happy life. It was not to be.

1988 was a 'special' year in my gambling life. Everything won. I needn't go into detail, but in 1987 I backed the favourite for the guineas (Warning) at 33/1, then set about using potential winnings from it (£4,000++), to back against it. On Cheltenham, the

National and Guineas I won in excess of £400,000 - a lot of money then (well over one and a half million in house price money today). [ironically the best horse was Warning - but he was poorly, so I was lucky] Then the Derby/Oaks - another £80,000. The night before the Oaks I invited brother Andrew and his wife to a celebration dinner out; I couldn't lose the next day. Let's be clear, this was just a good hobby; visits to races were 3 or 4 times a year at York in spring and summer - that's all.

I took it all in cash save £150,000 which I thought I should admit to a non-business bank account; didn't want anyone to know. I remember collecting the smallest of the wins from Corals; amazing how £70,000 can be placed in cash about one's jacket and trousers without showing. The sun shone brightly as I strode with a rather superior air in my step, across town. For Ladbrokes I took a briefcase to their bank - 'some advice on investments sir?'
- 'Well, thank you, but I like my own advice at the moment.' Surely one can be excused being a little smug; just the once.

All the while, 1985-6-7-8 I was rebuilding my practice. I did work; many work harder, but it was more than enough. The intent was to find a partner, or merge.

By then, Petrina had started to wear my ring on her left hand. I was happy and content enough to say - do you want to stay forever? After my successes of spring and summer 1988 we went for some sunshine in May then for a month in October that year – a Five Star 'Grand Tour' of the Far East - the Hong Kong, Singapore, Bangkok, and Bali one. The bookies banned me for two years from taking any price about any horse, and Tote banned me completely.

I thought a few sleeping pills would soon sort any jet-lag problem. We landed in Hong Kong in late afternoon after no sleep in many hours, so I took Dalmane and went to bed. I never quite adjusted.

We returned from the Far East trip with my renewed belief I needed dalmane to sleep; I knew they were harmless. Gradually into 1989 I became hooked again, unable to sleep and then feeling very rough if I hadn't (slept), although I avoided them at weekends so as not to being dependent. That's what I thought.

Aged forty I had cash all over my house – the attic, cellar, wardrobe, and wherever. But life was about to implode again; people on Benzodiazepines can't plan or carry out plans. They don't see reality. I'd planned to rekindle my early twenties involvement in politics, but my zest for life began to wane as 1989 passed - nothing seemed to matter much. I had no emotional feelings - not just for Petrina but anyone, even myself. I went to the office but later and later, came home and went over the motions of life. I couldn't even understand some clients; often I didn't even know who they were! By 1989/90/1, I had started to sit on work – putting it aside until tomorrow, when I would probably feel like doing it. Doped up, tomorrow could never come. I went to the bookies most days as I had for the last ten years, but now cared not a toss, win or lose; I found it all funny. If I won, I just wanted to put it all back on. Life was slipping into autopilot.

In 1988-9 I bought three houses for about £30,000 each - now each worth about £250,000 plus. All I will say is this - how can anyone 'lose' a house. I know I bought three, but I could only find two later. Who got my house?

I had known Graham Carter since 1986-7 when he worked for mortgage advisors in the downstairs office. A little man with a baldhead, he reminded me of Tin-Tin. He came from 'Bradfud' – that's how they say it there. He introduced house purchase and re-mortgage work. In 1989, Graham left Leeds to set up on his own in Bradford. He needed a loan and I needed work to continue to flow in. So I loaned him £20,000. Why not? - when established he would repay me, and in the interim would introduce work. I'm sure it happens often.

I had known Peter Harper since the early 1980's. He was my junior by about eight years, excellent on a one-to-one basis; both a man's man and a woman's man - chalk and cheese from Graham. One small without pretense of style – the other robust and a lover to all things stylish and grand. Having inherited his father's plastics business, he was set for life. But what I could never quite fathom, was how all Peter's businesses went bust, whilst he progressed in life to better and better homes and standards of living. He had learned it was simpler to go into Receivership, for that way no one properly investigates – you don't often face irate creditors. About seven of his business went west in five years.

Being an only child, he always thought anything by him – was his. It would not be unfair to observe that, with him, you don't get what you see, nor see what you get.

1990 onwards, the idiosyncratic and insidious effect of the Benzos was changing me. I didn't want any holiday; I no longer wanted to mix socially. I got up and staggered to the shower later and later, getting to work as late as 9.45 (a 15 minute drive away). Horse racing? - I couldn't give a toss, win or lose. And bookies had started to let me bet again – *uggh!* At work, the foundations of negligence claims were laid, as I sat on work I could no longer think through. Trying to write a new Lease I would get as far as the first line… "This lease is made the…." and stop - I couldn't plan it; it then sat on the back table. Lacking confidence, I felt an underdog to many people, and, as such people do, I remember once trying to be bold, writing to a good client not darken my door again. I fear there were a few similar incidents. Transfer these incidents to daily life and multiply them over 1991-2-3 - all becomes chaos.

Without emotion, I came to see Petrina as 'just someone living in my house'. And she would tell the jury I became 'impossible to live with' - I would come home, ignore her, eat, watch TV and go to bed with Horlicks and sleeping pills. At work, I never saw my accountant so my accounts weren't checked or filed as required by the Law Society 1989/90.

Summer 1990: Law Society wrote an Accountant was coming to inspect my books. I finally motivated myself after work to start to go over the records - every kind of error possible so far as I could see. At about 9.45 (this was largely pre-mobile days) the office phone rang:
"Oh there you are" said Petrina "I've been looking everywhere…. now, there's been a bomb in London at the Carlton Club - IRA they think - and your father's been injured, and taken to hospital. You've got to ring Kit (eldest brother down south) and he'll explain." I listened and said nothing. Although retired, father still went to London each Monday, as he had the last forty years, sat in the Lords, and stayed at the club in St.James'.
"And look, you'd better come home, your supper's in the oven, and Holly knows where it is and is guarding it - she wants it".

Holly, as I say, is the daughter we didn't have. She'd grown into a real character and a very good-looking Ridgeback.

The Law Society Inspector stayed three days, found nothing was wrong, save confirming my Accounts were a mess. The book-keeper must be sacked and all re-written. Then I went to visit father in Westminster hospital. Andrew's wife went on TV to say he was fine; you must never talk about things until you know the facts - fact.

My father had never been ill – no one in our family had anything but A1 health. He was a big strong proud man. But people of 82, however robust, can't take Semtex blasts from nasty people who don't give a damn for the devastation they needlessly bring for no possible gain. He had tubes from all angles of his body, and was a mess. Outwardly, he was as stoic as ever, and I couldn't grasp he had suffered a stroke, impairing his speech, which for such a man was an insult. His possessions were still being recovered, covered in thick soot, for it seems he had been carried out in darkness, as a fire blazed. He knew a man who had been burned alive in such a terrorist blast and mentioned his name; that's all. Once he broke for a moment; we pretended it hadn't happened - that's the way we are - stiff chins. But we are all so vulnerable.

To illustrate his natural strengths, my old man forced himself from what was his deathbed from that event to stand as President of the Dunkirk Veterans - 50 years celebration - the month following with the Queen. It all had taken a big toll and for the next nine months, he was to and from hospital. Occasionally he was sent home to Harrogate, and then returned to Leeds General Infirmary. The blast had caused severe renal failure.

Even by then, my life was becoming a troop, punctuated by wonderful times when I believed all was so well; I had no idea I was taking *any* drugs. I still backed horses most days, but without any care or plan. There was no plan or thought to anything. I had been accustomed to business lunches, but found that just one glass of wine and I was on my way to orbit.

It became too much for Petrina. One evening in July I ignored her as ever and went to bed at 10. About twenty minutes later, she came in and physically beat me up as I lay there, shrieking at me, hysterical at my indifference. She moved to the front room and wanted out. I was responsible, for I had asked her to move to Leeds and I had to help her find security. Holly felt it, but our best friends don't complain.

At work, I started to windmill anything I couldn't do. Use of that phrase 'windmilling' would get me into awful trouble later with my expert lawyers. What I did was windmill problems... put them all up in the air, hoping to solve them 'tomorrow'.

I transferred one of the houses I had bought to Petrina to do up. She took Holly, but would return her to my office each Friday and collect her from my home on a Sunday evening - just as you share joint custody of a child.

In January 1991 I attended the Solicitors Disciplinary Tribunal in London. The girl prosecuting me for Law Society told me:
"Well, you've not been stealing.... you haven't been robbing Peter to pay Paul.... your books were just a mess." The Tribunal's Order 'would follow later'. I was sent away more baffled than before. Self-regulation - there was no ruling!

Father died in March; he'd never recovered [verdict - homicide]. I was incapable of any feeling. He'd had a very rich and full life since 1907, a man of complete integrity - but the last nine months, back and to from hospital must have been demeaning hell for him. I reacted as trained - the British way - "The King is dead, long live the King - *Hurrah.*" Life moves on. The retribution part of us says that the man who mindlessly did this to him should also have his retirement cut short and spend his last nine months of life in and out of hospital. Why not? His mother had lived to 96 so he still should have had a few years left. Four days later, just before the funeral, I received another call from eldest brother Kit:
"What the hell's going on?... you could have told us..."
"Umm... what do you mean?"
"Your mother's just had the Yorkshire Post wanting her views, or rather father's views from some numbskull reporter, on Law Society's fine just imposed on you."
"I don't understand - there was no Order or fine."

Law Society had chosen now to publish to media (not to me) their judgment, and fined me £2,500 for failing to file accounts. It was front page of the Yorkshire Post. Next day I attended father's funeral - the humiliation of it all. In church there were cameras up our noses. I think a detailed ruling came by post later, but I never read it. I was in the benzo mire.

1991 passed into 1992: the books were at the Accountants and I had no bookkeeper - so no accounts, save those I tried to write up at home after dinner. Peter Harper needed to refinance his house to raise money. He would borrow £150,000 from Bradford and Bingley to pay off £90,000 to Nationwide and £40,000 to his bank, as he had guaranteed his last failed business. So he would have £20,000 for his latest business – it went something like that. A week or so later I had a call:

"Simon - what the hell are you doing! I've got the bailiffs coming tomorrow to evict us for the bank. Haven't you done it yet... I mean - for god's sake.... transfer £55,000 (not £40,000) to the Bank *now*.... or we'll have nowhere to live..... Don't you understand... pull your bloody finger out man."

The £150,000 was there, and I transferred £55,000 immediately to pay off the bank. Then the settlement figure came - he was in arrears and it was £105,000 (not £90,000)

"Peter – there's a problem. I'm over ten grand short to pay off Nationwide."

"That's your problem. Lend it to me, you've loads of money – transfer it from your client account"

"Don't be silly, I can't do that"

Putting it simply, I'd been done; but I saw it as yet another of my errors. I would hold over for a month, which I could get away with, and he would pay me the £10,000 from a new facility being put in place by his latest bank. I think it went like that - so it was forgotten. And I held £95,000 in client account, which he knew. In no time:

"Right you've got that £95,000 of mine in your account. The bank won't yet let me draw on uncleared effects.... so get me some cash from your bank and I'll give you a cheque to cover it."

Anything for peace - as ever, I did as told. Joanne or Alison would go to my bank and get him the thousands in cash from client account, and he gave me his new cheque to cover it. This is strictly a breach of rules - but I think you'll find most solicitors have drawn on uncleared effects; I was just helping him through tough times. He wouldn't do me, would he? Two months passed and he came to see me:

"You're getting interest on that £95,000 (I'd told him that)... you've got this problem now....." and he showed me an arrears letter on his old mortgage I couldn't redeem.

"You should've paid them off by now"

"But Peter... I haven't got £105,000 in that account - now it's more"

"That's your problem. You're getting the interest on it.... so you've got to pay this interest."

For years I had paid interest to clients or given them discount if I'd sat on their money, or paid their mortgage company. That was the right thing to do, and is now a rule. So I paid off his arrears, telling the old mortgagee there was 'a delay' in completing the transaction. His new business was doing well, but had no bank facility yet, and he kept swapping cheques for cash. But I was living with amnesia and other payments were being made - I would know nothing about for years.

Each Friday at about five o'clock Petrina would bring Holly to my office. Big dog would come bounding in, very pleased to see her daddy. On the following Sunday Petrina would collect her, and usually tidy up a bit; my standards were going and the house really was a tip. There would be about six bottles of fine claret, with just one glass taken from each; I couldn't drink, but tried to live as before (PD later remarked that was about the most criminal thing I ever did!). I would visit mother at her Harrogate home overlooking the famous Stray. For some while she had complained of 'problems down there.' In May 1992, just 14 month after father died, she went into the Harrogate Nuffield for exploration. I visited on the last day of the spring bank holiday. Petrina had called earlier. Kit had been up from the south and even brother Andrew had called. I left at about seven at the end of one of those lovely sunny May days; the sun was streaming through the windows. I turned left out of her room, instead of right, reached a dead-end, did an about turn, and as I passed her room, I heard her non-stop cheerful voice, irrepressible as ever, saying to the nurse:

"Aren't I lucky...three sons and they've each been to see me today"

- '*typical; non-stop, always something to say*'
Next morning at work, Kit phoned:
"Are you alone?"
"Yes thank you"
"Well, I'm sorry to say mother died this morning"
I didn't understand she had been struck down with bowel cancer just like that. I sat at my desk looking straight ahead – incapable of feelings. Later Petrina explained - 'but didn't you see?' - 'see what?' - 'she'd undone all her tubes and drips - she knew.' I never saw it - my mind wasn't assembling the information before it. Mother's funeral was embarrassing - I had a drink.

Weeks passed into months; summer 1992 sped by. Law Society sent another Accountant to check me - nothing was wrong or missing. I continued to back horses without care, and had a new fascination - even obsession - backing dogs; traps 1-2-3 the finish 1-2-3 the sort of things you see tossers doing in bookies. I thought it was funny - £100 per race. I was a dumbo. It was funded by my supplies of cash at home in various hiding places, but depleting, as I was earning nothing.

Graham was becoming a complainer - why should he give me all this work when he had clients complaining about my not doing it. My actual income, as I wasn't really working, was minimal, but with big overheads, and I had come to realize that it paid to sit on work as I had hundreds of thousands in client account earning interest. I kept paying the interest of Peter's mortgage – no sign of any money from him. That way the problem was 'windmilled.' But a new problem arose; his cheques for cash from my client account were bouncing or marked 'payment countermanded.' Chaos everywhere. Some stories are amusing. For one of Graham's clients, I did all the work, paid off his mortgage, didn't bill him, then paid the interest on the new one! "Great lawyer!"

Graham had a new mate called Tony Heatherington, over ten years our senior in his mid fifties - dare I politely say 'something of a rough diamond.' Later it became apparent that Tony had just served time for fraud; I never asked why and what.

Life drifted by... I never had another holiday and had no urges to involve myself with people or females. Well, I tried, but not very well - you may recall from chapter two that even Oliver Thorold admits benzo users talk later of 'lost and barren years.'

August Bank holiday is relevant for one incident. The Tote had allowed me to start backing again, but I wasn't allowed to take a price about any horse – S.P. only. For no special reason I picked four horses to watch on TV that Saturday. In what's called a £2 'Lucky 15,' with an extra £40 win accumulator - total stake £70. I won just short of £100,000 when all won. The same month Kit sent me about £43,000 being my share of the net proceeds of mother's apartment in Harrogate (in today's money, the flat would have fetched about £750,000 – then £170,000). But the allegation from Hatton to the media and jury (chapter 1) was that I started to steal client money then - because I was short! By then I wasn't even going to any racecourses to enjoy my 'hobby.'

I only worked for people who made me jump, and if it was routine. Work I couldn't do sat on the back table or went to staff. If they couldn't do it, it wasn't done. Being polite, one could say my desk was 'cluttered.' For Glen M. I was instructed to do a re-mortgage; but I hadn't finished his work from the previous year. He pressed me to 'get it bloody done'. So I drew the money he needed, paid him what he said he was due, then stopped. Peace. But then there was a new problem; his unfinished work. Simple solution - same as with Harpo, just pay the interest, then no one would know I couldn't do it anymore – the money just sat in the account.

Without detail, there were six similar instances; they each were charges you have read about in chapter 1. My own mortgages were not dissimilar. In the chaos, I ended up with two mortgages as I argued about settlement figures. The money sat in client account earning interest. Whenever I didn't know where to put an entry - I charged it to me, if I charged it anywhere. I did similar for brother Andrew. I drew funds down and received funds from him to complete in late 1992. But I couldn't work it all out so did nothing. Then each month a woman rang from his old mortgage company asking for interest which I sent. So that problem was windmilled as well throughout the year.

Without putting the first problem right, Peter needed yet another re-mortgage as his latest venture failed as well. I did as told, drew down more money from another lender he arranged, and paid his bank off. Now I was effectively sitting on £200,000 due to his mortgagees. I didn't know what to do, with insufficient money – so did nothing. Chaos everywhere and unregulated. My Accounts were a mess; even I didn't follow what was what. But I had to pay everyone and Peter!

By that year, Graham was 'in business' with Tony. It was a crucial year - over a million pounds allegedly 'disappeared', but of course it didn't disappear. True I lost at horses, but that was my money. I later told my lawyers I was living (in hindsight) *'on habit, impulse and direction of others'*; none of them understood. Graham always appeared with his shadow Tony Heatherington; they talked of 'million pound deals' to buy and develop land for conversion to housing. Other mortgage work continued, but rather than John Smith and Fred Brown, strange new foreign names appeared on my desk, all arranged by Graham with Tony. I did as asked and saw no problem. I trusted everyone.

Peter Harper, with Martin Pickard, found a site at Yeadon by the airport for a large fast food fish and chip business - initially to be called 'Mr.Big Fish Emporium' intended for the children's market. Peter told me he would soon put things right with me – and at the best of times I'm a trusting so-and-so. Simultaneously, Graham and Tony had found a mill in Dewsbury, ripe for development into flats. Their company Calibre would buy it for about £200,000, convert it into thirty flats and sell each for £38,000 (in those days).

By then, I had no bookkeeper and tried doing the books at night after dinner. Baffled, I would look at the stubs in the cheque-book and many would be blank. To find what was what, I would take out the next bank statement and enter the value of the cheque as presented and cleared by my bank. Then came the real problem - to which file did it relate and who was the payee? I either guessed, left it blank, or put it down to my name, as there was loads of cash in that ledger - mine and my brothers. You have heard that called 'false accounting with intent to deceive.' Truth was I couldn't hack it any more.

"Right then" said a smiling Graham, flushed with a bravado he had never had before – "we bought us an 'orse from Richard."
These two, skint as they come, had bought a racehorse from a local trainer. The two year old filly, was either £5,000 or £10,000 and

somehow they got me to take out my personal Lloyds chequebook from my right hand drawer, and write out a cheque. To whom I don't know, but it seems that I paid for their horse. Late Friday following, they were in my office when Petrina arrived with Holly, for my access weekend.   And so came Petrina Bay, owned by Graham and Tony - paid for by me. Why would anyone do that?

Holding a Business Plan, which showed turnover at 2 million, Peter told me Martin was now 'out' and I was his partner:
"Let me give you a secret" he told me earnestly, "this idea is going to be big.... really big. As soon as it opens, I'll be able to sell it for a million." I couldn't grasp it, was a solicitor, not a fish and chip man.   I was made a director of his company - Northernfolks Limited. But he had the shares; I was falling into place as stooge and fall-guy, my name on everything.

Peter took me all over the north of England inspecting other fish and chip emporiums. The best was Trenchers in Whitby. A joint favourite eating place in Leeds since 1970s has been the Pizza in Street lane. So a large fish and chip Emporium – called Murgatroyds, was constructed from an old AFG garage site in Yeadon, a cross between Whitby and the Pizza. And my name would guarantee everything; he said we were 'partners', with everything in his name. He hadn't had income for ages, so he said 'I was paying him' to work for me – thus justifying all the money he was getting from me. From August storefitters arrived and I was to pay for everything.   View it today, and you see what I mean. Doped up - I was being cleaned out. Everything asked, and I supplied. No way, in my normal mind, would anything like this happen - I'd have said 'get lost!' Just how all this was funded? – I don't quite know, but it wasn't right. [*Police interviews follow.*] Sedate someone and you can rape them (and they join in) or, in my case, deceive them and then call them a crook. Life's twists.

Peter would visit my office and 'take over' whilst I would move to the outer open plan general office. Once or twice Jennie lost her cool… as I jumped to each command:
-"*Why......why......why do you do it.......allow it.   You let them all walk all over you*" she said thru gritted teeth. She could see I'd lost the plot, but too polite to say more.

Tony and Graham demanded - was I 'in or out' with them, on their property deals. I said 'out' but would be their solicitor on the purchase and sales; that's all. Later I discovered they also used my name and made me a director of their company – although I had nothing to do with it at all. Two men who had no money were buying the Mill for £200,000 to renovate and sell on. Where did that money come from? My accounts? I don't know to this day. The closed shop world of cover-up by lawyers and judges you meet soon, would ensure no one ever knew the truth.

Then August/September to February their company 'Calibre Brokers' arranged 20-30 mortgages of £30,000 each for the sales of flats in that building alone, and I did most but not all, of the work. Solicitors don't see mortgage application or valuation forms. They had other clients who were simply re-mortgaging and raising money on Harrogate properties. I was doing the work, along with three other solicitors, none of whom was ever arrested. From the 'blank' cheque stubs I had to guess what I had done. If in doubt, it was charged to my name. I wasn't with it or anything.

Meanwhile, Peter's new venture took shape on the busy Leeds-Harrogate Road at Yeadon 'Murgatroyds - Britains Finest Fish and Chip Emporium.' This was embarrassing to me - my life training is quiet understatement; reputation is earned over time. He put my name to it all; I must pay everyone - and guarantee everything. Chaos, chaos, chaos - do this - do that - now go away. My mind was a mess and my spirit simple and suppressed. Three 'managers' were recruited and an initial staff of sixty. Anna was selected from THF Group as general manager; Keith was recruited likewise and Carole as an ex-Ramsdens manager to know some of the pitfalls. Peter would collect bundles of cash from my office - 'borrowing' his own mortgage money in my eyes. He had my credit card for his family holiday. I am horrified to say I saw that as no problem. But how much did he get? How much did his business get? Medical experts all will later say, they would have expected me to become 'a pawn in the hand's of others – without realizing and unable to stop it'. I put a few entries on a scrappy piece of paper which came to over £352,000, but that was my money. Drugged up, what I was doing was horrendous, but what was being done to me was surely criminal. Not that a jury would hear.

[I am open to be accused of being in cahoots with Peter, and knowingly doing wrong and giving him funds not due to him. But that begs the question – why should I do that? There was nothing in it for me. The answer comes later from themedical evidence – once adversely affected by these drugs, you lose the right to your mind. I became 'liable to accede to unreasonable demands without demur' - however hard that is to understand. But one is not an automaton. Its just chaos, chaos, chaos and more chaos without being able to see it or stop it.]

Finally in November Murgatroyds opened. As manager Anna demanded the safe keys and custody of the takings. Not clever - Peter got rid of her in the first week. By mid December the Restaurant was flourishing at weekends. Keith told me takings were about £13,500 per week without anyone knowing the place was up and running - a goldmine in embryo.

Peter knew I had Indian clients with stashes of cash to lend; he needed some. I asked Paul Kang - a Sikh for whom I had just done a house purchase, and knew well. One Friday he arrived after 6.30 with £20,000 cash. You can indeed guess where it went! About a week later Peter's wife rang me; she had no money - why wasn't I helping Peter? I sat there baffled - what's going on? - what if the number 10 bus runs me over - there's no receipt for Paul Kang. There and then, I dictated a letter acknowledging £20,000 cash to buy a house, details to follow. I saw my duty as being to Paul Kang - a paradox of confused duties.

In between, there were amusing instances. On my birthday, Graham and Tony took me to the Grillade for lunch. Two glasses and everyone was a blur. On the adjacent table, a large blond cleavage seemed to be sitting on a judge's arm (it was a bunch of crooks) - friends of my hosts. I went to the loo, and returning asked the owner who that judge was seated next to me. He was no judge, but a man who'd met a few. The room was a blur, as I returned and sat down at the wrong table, talking gibberish to two strangers. And in this state I continued my robotic life. Get up, climb into shower, make way to office and shuffle files and papers, visit bookies, give them whatever I had etc. It was easy as all the girls were called Doris – if they dared speak to my silent face. My horde of cash was falling fast, and I cared not a jot. After the office it was go home via Murgatroyds, have a spritzer, cook, eat, horlicks at 10, with a couple of Dalmane to ensure I sleep, then climb into bed. That had been life for the last three years. You don't know you're taking drugs.

I kept a diary list of work I hadn't done. Between 26th –30th of each month I sent a letter to the head office of the Building Society that I hadn't been able yet to complete the mortgage work on that file, and sent a cheque on account of the interest due from money I was holding. Sometimes I sent roughly what was due and sometimes a round figure; sometimes I took cash to local offices. So problems were 'windmilled' - no one must know I'd lost the plot of life. Admit it; you don't admit your failings.

Christmas arrived. Keith told me one evening how many covers Murgatroyds were doing - excellent, he said. It was Peter's business, and he told me to 'stay away'. There were no problems, as everyone was happy. Petrina would be away for Xmas and brought Holly to share it with me as her guardian. I could have two days complete solitude, which most benzo people will tell you is heaven. I set the table for a full house and sat down alone – in a world of my own; completely barmy.

Simon Kaberry

CHAPTER FIVE

A Damaged Mind is lethal…
Confessions - Arrested

Life was about to implode; it was inevitable - over the past three years, gradually and insidiously falling apart. I was a lawyer, unregulated in that time, sedated, and in sole charge of hundreds of thousands of pounds - nay millions. A recipe for disaster.

The day after Boxing Day Keith Brown phoned, frantically seeking help at Murgatroyds - they couldn't cope with the volume of customers. Peter was 'somewhere no one was allowed to know.' I worked flat out, clearing tables and re-setting. You don't need a mind to clear tables and reset them, although I gather I looked like an out-of-work bank manager. Then I sat down and shook like a leaf in tremor - I was actually very ill.

By January 1994 my office staff had reduced to just Jennie and Jean working alternate days. The residual work I had done beyond routine, I'd done badly or half done. I was on auto-pilot, save for one thing - everyone had to be happy, anything they wanted, they could have. I feared everyone.

One Monday morning, Jennie had found the office door wide open. All the Calibre files had disappeared – but I hadn't registered their purchase or sales-off. It would be post trial before I discovered what had happened. Had I been myself, none of this could have occurred, as I later told Judge Hodson; he didn't understand.

Early January and Peter rang for an urgent meeting that night. We met at a restaurant by my home. He explained pointedly that each time I visited, I upset staff. I must stay away.
"I'm sorry. Yes, of course, but I had no idea."
I was mortified. I don't like upsetting anyone. He also explained I needed to sign some more papers. I signed - '*got to help all those with whom you deal in life.*'.......
"Look - and stop talking to people - you nearly cost me the bank"
Lloyds Bank wrote I was overdrawn £400 on my personal account and demanded that I put it right forthwith.

-'Ha-ha - got them.. I haven't used it in months......its in credit'
"No Mr.Kaberry" said the aggressive girl, - "you are four hundred pounds overdrawn - we need you to put this right immediately"
They were all picking on me.

Someone had emptied my account, then back for another £400, paid in cash. With Jennie and police I went to view the CCTV. What got me was that *I felt* like the crook; had no confidence at all. We couldn't recognise him - a man in his fifties. Reading this now, you and I can see the significance - all those blank cheque stubs. I couldn't see it then. No one was ever charged - *not true....* you have already read the start of the trial. The jury was never told - I'd called police in for help.

At about the same time my Client Account, unchecked and unauditted for eighteen months, was bare. I couldn't miss it - what should have held over £8-900,000, was often down at £100,000 or less. Nearly a million pounds - 'missing.' Day after day I floated in a daze from early January onwards. But not only could I not complete the work, there was no money in my account. Logic? - no, I had long lost that. Help - who? I didn't know what to do, so did nothing. I did as I always have done in life - and accepted I was responsible.

Amid that, Keith Brown rang. Carole and he wanted to see me after hours. I went up at about 10.30 pm. as the place was closing down - maybe a Monday or Tuesday. I was nervous but one mustn't dodge these things. We sat in the smart empty restaurant.
"Simon" Keith led the attack..."there's a problem.... just how serious we don't know....."
I interrupted: "Look - I'm sorry. I didn't know, but when Peter told me.... er.... how can I put it.... er... well since then I've kept away.... and don't worry, I won't trouble you again... I'm awfully sorry"
Silence: they looked at one another.
Big Carole in her blunt Yorkshire manner: "What the hell are you talking about Simon. We've asked you here; we want to know why you haven't been here - we want to know what's going on."

Keith took over: "Simon - I don't know who's being saying what to you, although I can guess... but keeping away is the last thing you need to do. Now Carole and I run this place and it's doing very well... exceptionally well. But things are going on......well, how can I put it - that make the hairs stand up on my neck. I don't know you or Peter but I thought you were partners... are you?"

"Erm....umm... well I suppose so, but it's a strange partnership ......er…"

"A strange partnership?..... .Simon you ain't a clue mate. I've taken three anonymous calls in the last few days... *'is Harpo there ... the old con man.....who's he doing this time'*... that sort of thing. And of course, he's not here - he's never here. His wife rings looking for him.... she doesn't know where he is. We know... he's with that redhead all the time. But first, he goes to the tills and empties them of cash, then buggers off. Don't know who she is - but she's got a bloody good body. Then there's the books… his mother takes them home each night. We're not allowed to look. But I did banking twice last week. Do you know he doesn't bank the cash takings; he just banks the cheques and Visas. Suppliers ring up.... cheques are bouncing, yet on a weekend we can take over £15,000 cash. Now you come here and tell us you've been told to keep away." Silence.

He continued: "It happened with Anna didn't it. She wanted to be in charge so he eased her out - you know… ignored her. He won't let anyone look at the books or takings... but we know what they are. This place is a goldmine."

Big bespectacled Carole, in her understanding Bradfud voice: "Simon me luv, you've got to tell us.... he's got some hold on you or sommut like that, 'asn't ee - because this has got to stop or this place will go bust quicktime, and it shouldn't. We need you here..... look we're being conned.... you're being conned.... all suppliers are being conned. Come on.... tell us luv. - what's it he's got on you. Come on.... we know the cash never gets to the bank, so what's he doing with it? He and his mother - are they jointly saltin' it away... what's going on. This has happened before hasn't it?"

I dithered: "umm....er... I'm sure there must be some reason. I'll have a word with Peter."

Peter had warned me not to say anything to these two. This couldn't be true. He only had £20,000 loan from Paul Kang six weeks ago. Much later, Keith told me they thought he must be blackmailing me about some sex scandal!

"Er, well I'm sure there's a simple explanation. I know he had some problems paying Ecsec (the shopfitters) but I'm going to see them for him next week."
"Oh are you.... and why you - not him?" said Keith
"Well he's asked me to… er, he's too busy"
"Too busy!!! - he sits behind the bar with a bottle of Jack Daniels all afternoon - then raids the tills and buggers off for a shag at the Bramhope Post House most days."

I was in turmoil - couldn't grasp it at all. Into February, I scheduled all the money I was sitting on. It confirmed a million pounds 'missing.' This schedule followed me around for the next six weeks. Only one thing was certain - I was responsible.

[I recently saw a Richard Carpenter docu-film on what happened to him after three years on dalmane. By then he couln't 'arrange' or write any music, was often euphoric, but could hardly even sign his name. He got help in a rehb clinic, as his sister went solo. Lawyers don't understand].

The saying is - "a damaged mind is dangerous, because it believes it can survive." This survival instinct, and denial that there was any problem, alternated with a desire to top myself. By rules of life requiring no thought - I was the man in charge; as such I must take full responsibility. The shame of it all. I knew I couldn't o/d on Dalmane. My shotgun had been stolen years ago, so I couldn't shoot myself. My spirits forced my legs to carry me to work each morning - all clients must come first and be safe. I would ensure that above all. I would write to them all - that I was guilty and a terrible man.

I met with Graham and Tony and explained I was in dire straits. Client account was bare:
"Oh god - no… course you are; it's Peter - you've been giving him our money. Now look, you're going to prison, but not for long.... you 'aven't been right since yer father died, you know that dorn't you. Look: you gotta say you took money to gamble - mek up a good story an' they'll believe you.....everyone knows you gamble so they'll believe it. Then we'll look after you. But we need some time to get things straight our end. You gotta get away - Spain, something like that…"
"Me - Spain - but that's where crooks go"

"Simon - I'm telling you straight. You ain't right. You used to be so cool, but look at you man - you're a completely different person from what you were... and Harpo... ee's bin runin' rings round you for the last year... you're to pieces man.... but first you gotta say that you've taken all the money. Do that fer us and we'll look after you. Say you've taken it to races and they'll believe you.... everyone knows you gamble."

Imagine a reasoned mind sorting that lot; and mine, sedated but trying to reason, was anything but sane, reasoned or rational - without 'gut instinct' that comes with emotion.
 - *'Yes, they're right - gambling - that sounds right. Whatever has happened - without me they couldn't have done whatever it is they've done'*
- that was my mindset.

I must fall on my sword - that was the proper thing to do. So, I started to write (in an Evidence Book of all things) in mid February – "pages and pages" sprawled out. Put a pen in my hand and I can write for England - all sorts of credible garbage will come out of a damaged mind, and did.

I began - *"How do I start this story.....where is the beginning?....."*
like a fairy story, I related all my gambling successes of the 1980's - years before the problems of 1993; that was easy, logged in long-term memory forever. There were four long confessions in total, two later finding their way to police and being put to the jury as true, and two remaining in my desk which Petrina moved unwittingly and were never found. The schedule of 'missing and incomplete work' followed me about in a briefcase, forming a template for the confessions.

I told Peter I was in trouble. He looked at me with his cool stare of innocence:
"Well I've done nothing wrong. You can't involve me in any of your problems. But you don't know who you've been dealing with do you – those others? That chap Tony Heatherington - he's part of the Bradford mafia. If you've been doing work for them – and I don't know what came over you - they'll do you"
"What d'you mean - do me?"

"Well let's put it this way. Someone owed them money once. He lived in a bungalow... they knocked it down... I mean.... do I need to spell it out for you ... he was still inside."

I was chilled.

"Now look, first I need you to resign as a director of Murgatroyds so I can distance myself from you.... you're not going to take my little family and my business down. We've nothing to do with you and whatever it is you've done," said he despairingly.

"No....no... of course; you've done no wrong; it's me - don't worry. I'll make sure you aren't involved."

I continued to write and was so sorry for anything I had done which might rebound on Peter - who was blameless.

Clients would be receiving their annual statements from banks, confirming that I'd never finished their work and I had paid interest over. I still did. I wrote to all of them - *"everything is my fault - my punishment will follow"*. That would put their minds at ease, and protect them - they always came first. That act would cost me dearly.

Feelings of desolation were replaced with a determination to admit responsibility for everything - I had taken the money to meet my desire to gamble. I wrote *"all I did was lose, lose, lose"*. *"I am such a greedy man ...... such an awful man"*.......pages and pages of.... I stole it all. I remembered the girl from Law Society - so I wrote *"I've been robbing Peter to pay Paul'* - sounded good.

If I admitted receiving £20,000 from Paul Kang for a house, he would be compensated, so I wrote *"you can guess where that went"*. That I was suicidal is obvious from the content. But just before the end I was hit by tragic news – like being hit in the face by two, not one wet smelly kippers, in place of all this fantasy. At that, I wrote *"today I heard ....(I related the event)... what the hells' happening to me, where is all this money, I've stolen nothing; please someone help me."* My lawyers would never read that. Back home I put two sets of confessions in my big mahogany wardrobe and another set in my desk. And forgot them all.

Law Society noticed I had filed nothing again. Yet another Accountant was coming to inspect.

I met my old friend John Patchett in Ilkley for lunch with his wife Mandy. I started to talk about 'problems' for a good half hour. We had a camaraderie of student days - so they sat in silence, as I tried to explain the inexplicable.

Then smiling and laughing John said:

"Simon - we've known you a long time... er.... how can I put this nicely... er..... politely!!" his face creased in stifled laughter.. "you've finally 'gone'.... completely and utterly puddled....... you're off your trolley.   Come on, we've got an office to run. You go clear your head, then start again.... bye-bye!".

No one could help me. I walked Burley Moor across to Ilkley with Holly when the accountant was there; it's pretty bleak up there in early March.   He left a Note that my legal practice was now 'closed.' By now the mere ringing of the phone sent me berserk – my entire body tensed. I couldn't say "I don't know anymore." You don't admit you've lost it; you don't say - help me.

That evening at home, at about 9.00 p.m. the phone started ringing. I wouldn't answer. It rang for over an hour with rests for seconds each three minutes or so, then it started again. That did me. Next day I saw Graham and accepted his offer - get away.

We know this is 13 March from the visitor's annual passport date, which they took me to get. I must drive to their hotel outside Yarmouth. I did as told. I remember the trip to this day - down the A1, left across England, a straight long road towards Yarmouth, right at the second roundabout, across the next and first left. 'Damaged Memory Man' with a memory! Sorry, I can't explain that. I was still carrying my briefcase with the schedule and office paper and my Day Books of Account.

Thursday: they came to see me.

"Now look Simon... things are hotting up in Leeds so you've gotta move on from here. We've been told something's about to blow about you. Now here's two grand (or whatever it was) and you've got to get away from here. Spain, then see what you can do…. But we can't have you connected to us"

"Sorry - er, yes of course - Can you take this Case back and give it to John Patchett. I've written out all that's wrong".

They set off and re-appeared an hour or so later.

Simon Kaberry

"Simon: We had to open your case and I've read this and you ain't said anything about gambling in here. Come on.... do the decent thing and we'll look after you, and we reckon you still owe us some money, so we need a cheque too" opened Tony

The main admissions were at home. I had a wad of office notepaper and went upstairs and rewrote it. If I admit I'd lost £100,000 on horses that would be enough. My third attempt, this time including a paragraph about the Grand National, and that they had done no wrong, that I owed them and that Peter was to blame, was OK.

Where I went and what I did in the following week, I don't know. One foggy March morning I checked out of a hotel in Evershot, and drove along - going nowhere. I found myself in Puddletown. '*Puddled – ho-ho'*. I went to the red roadside phone box and rang John Patchett.
"Hello........it's Puddled from Puddletown here"
"Yes...very funny... and you're also headline news as missing with a hundred grand of client account"
"Oh dear"
"Anyway, from what you wrote you're lucky it's just a hundred grand. I've had Petrina ringing me all the time; she's very worried about you - and Simon - so am I. You've got to come back - puddled or whatever"

I longed for my own bed and drove north, but got lost. John arranged for Kerry Macgill to be my lawyer - to meet at 7.30 am

I found somewhere to stay, ordered steak and salad and bottle of red. I took my last Dalmane pills and put my head down about 10 pm. Rattled and shaking I never slept a wink, took a bath at 6.00 am, and drove to meet Kerry at a service station on the M62. Over tea I told Kerry something, but was in no mental state, yet probably looked 'normal'. That's the thing about being nuts – no one can see it. My mindset was simple - to admit everything.

He drove me to Weetwood police station, near my home. There we met Det.Con Johnson and a little man with a sharp Scottish accent called Sgt.Clark; strange how shorter people try to intimidate. As we do on a first meeting, I made a mental note:
- "*Mr.Minor Personality Disorder*".

'Calm bemusement' is the only way I can describe the feeling. They had my letter dated 13 March, re-written in Yarmouth, but also produced two of my long handwritten 'confessions'. How had they got those? (it's all on tape). I was then asked to read out the long 20-pager, from the opening - *"how do I start this story…"*word for word. I didn't have to do what I couldn't do – 'think or explain,' - just 'read and admit'.

- '*this is fun… if only they knew - load of utter codswallop*'.

Medical Experts agree I was in no state to be interviewed but years later, clever barristers Oliver Thorold, and MarrowQC would each say: "you made the admissions, so they must be true." Lawyers!

The rules are that your solicitor sits and listens, ensuring no intimidation of the arrested person. But Kerry knew nothing of the truth. By noon they'd enough, and we came out to the crisp grey March weather. I was placed on bail to return in September time.

Kerry: "I don't know Simon... er....well - it's going to take them *months* to sort that lot out, whatever it is you've done. Look, you go home now and come and see me later, in a few days or so".

"Aren't they going to charge me?"

"I'll put it this way. It'll be a year at least before you see any court. It's a nightmare, whatever it is. Quite frankly, I don't think you even know what you've done."

There's no answer to that.

I went home - it was empty; virtually all my furniture gone. I had no choice but to stay at Petrina's in Bramhope. She explained she'd put all into store; I'd apparently told her I was going away. The wardrobes were too big to move. After she emptied it, police arrived and all they found were 'confessions.' Magic! Holly returned from Staffordshire and so started years with my best and closest pal thru thick and thin. We got back into Adel Willows and I sat alone each day, walking the Beechwalk (a two-mile old trek running from my home to a park) with Holly to break the monotony, day after day - thinking.

Question: '*what the hell has happened to my life?*'

All we can do is wait – for as many years as the police want. Again Kerry warned me we were in for a long haul; he said I must just leave it to police. I had to stop this so rang Det. Con. Johnson:.

"Umm. I'm looking for Det Con Johnson please"

"That's Mr.Cabri isn't it" said Mr.Minor Personality Disorder in his abrupt Scots accent - "What's it you want. Mr.Johnson has moved to another case."

"Well, you said I should call if there was anything else to discuss"

"Yes - what is it you have to say?" he snapped.

"I think we need to resume our interview - things aren't as they appear."

"Mr.Cabri - you can't just resume an interview; we've Rules to work by. I will now make investigations and will call you when I need to see you"

"But things are not as they seem." I couldn't shout the odds.

"I'm sorry - all approaches by your solicitor"

"We need an off-the-record meeting"

"Mr.Cabri; if you have anything to say it must be done through your solicitor Kerry Macgill. I'm not having off-the-record meetings with anyone… you know the rules."

I rang each five days or so for the next months April, May and June, then gave in.

I had seen what the *Yorkshire Evening Post* had done to me: 'KABERRY HUNTED" - 'in banner headlines, so had to lie low. PD helped and brought food from Roger the Butcher. I posted a request to my GP with an SAE and received another 30 dalmane and started to use them just twice a week or less, to get some sleep. I didn't know this was the best way to taper off the dependence on the drug - you mustn't go cold turkey. Graham and Tony took me out one lunchtime and left me with another 'confession' to write out - admitting I'd been stealing from them as well.

Whilst away my phone had been cut and I had no money to restore the line (bank account frozen). Lloyds wrote that my account was 'closed' - in Leeds I was already guilty of everything nasty. I was soon selling items off and first to go of real value was my large antique Dining Table which fetched £1,000 from a Harrogate dealer – later that year I saw similar in an antique shop asking £7,500; is there no honesty in life! A replacement now would set me back £14,000 plus.

One morning Graham appeared via my back door:

"Oh hello…. startled me"

"Oh yes hello indeed. Now I'm in a hurry - I need that letter from you" (the confession I had to re-write)

"Umm.....what letter?"

"Don't play silly buggers - you know damned well." He looked and sounded annoyed and continued...."Don't you go thinking you're the only one with problems. We've got us own problems yu'know. We got all those mortgages to pay and no cash. It's all tied up. Now I need that letter... you're not going to do it fer us are you? Well I can tell you that when push comes to shove.... I won't help you."

He was away, never to return. I'd forgotten his letter. And what exactly did he mean – *"we've got these mortgages to pay and haven't any money?"*

The flashman car (a 928) Peter had made me get (so he could have one too) was on lease and had gone, I had no money and the loan car gave in - beyond economic repair. PD loaned me his car many afternoons, so I could get out with Holly into the dales or whatever. My neighbours Ann and Tony were most understanding - bemused by it all I suspect.

The manager in charge at Law Society was called Robin Penson. He would never be available - in ten years. Kerry wouldn't see me. Jock Clark - what was he doing. Letters started to arrive from a lady called Sarah Wade at Law Society Compensation Fund. Word was out that I had stolen all this money, so everyone wanted compensating for my thefts. This fell to Penson, with a man called Neil Rogerson and 'the team' in Leamington Spa to 'investigate'.

By law, the Law Society must maintain a 'Compensation Fund' as part of the package which allows them to self-regulate, to compensate clients of lawyers who 'suffer hardship financially' by reason of a solicitor's 'fraud or dishonestly.' A panel of solicitors rely on this staff in Leamington Spa to collate the information to enable them to decide whether or not a claim should be allowed. This is also housed within Victoria Court, Leamington spa – the same building as the regulators.   So, those who had failed in their statutory duty to regulate me, were in charge of compensating those who had lost out, when I was defrauded and deceived; they needed to get me, to deflect attention from their failings.   They would also be my prosecutors to justify what they were doing

AND they house the press office of Law Society so control all the public know about lawyers. No lawyer would allow anyone else to operate such a potentially corrupt system. Yet Lords Bingham and Phillips and many to follow, will bend over backwards to protect that system - the "Importance of Independence." But it's more to do with conceited self-interest.

Separately lawyers have insurance to cover their acts of negligence (except judges who cannot do any wrong, even when blatantly dishonest); just like accountants and doctors, surveyors and other advisors etc. If the funds had been stolen from me, or the loss arose from my negligence, then the claim would fall to my insurers – called in those days, the Solicitors Indemnity Fund (SIF). This distinction between SIF (insurers for negligence) and Law Society Compensation (for dishonesty) becomes critical later. I would be personally responsible for my dishonesty, but not deception on me.

So, in June 1994, I started a weekly letter exchange with Sarah Wade. She would write to me with details of a claim, alleging that in consequence of my dishonesty, a client (in this case they were all banks) had lost money. Much of this was the mortgages arranged by Calibre and other client's mortgage money which I had been sitting on – but all had 'disappeared' somehow from my client account. The team of Penson and Rogerson allowed every single claim with interest and costs on the basis of my dishonesty – no investigation of the facts allowed. That tab would be picked up by all practicing solicitors - who were being told I had stolen it all.

Constantly I wrote…. "*you need to see me*" I replied I hadn't taken anything, but didn't know what had happened. Graham and Tony had been paying the interest; now they stopped. Law Society started to repay their lenders on the basis that I had stolen the money, leaving them with the cash and property – as I hadn't registered the mortgages. Little wonder men like solr Anthony Isaacs, (head of SDT) Law Society, and Lords Bingham and Phillips would later be so keen to suppress the truth – and did.
Sarah Wade's replies always took three weeks and read:
> "*I thank you for your letter dated….. and for
> the information.*" That's it.

At an early stage I sent her details of Calibre and Howgate House, Dewsbury and Peter Harper and Murgatroyds. I referred to them treating me as '*some sort of money-well*', and '*someone stole all the files.*' Of Tony I wrote – '*he looks and sounds like a crook, but I haven't seen him dancing.*' She and Penson did - nothing.

Some people can only manage just one day alone. Soon it was eight weeks, often dazed and unwell. I started to play all my classical music night after night, knowing all the best inside out; it does help. Then I lay awake, going downstairs to talk to my big 'boo-boo-bear' dog; all I could do was think - what the hell had happened - *what had I really done*? I couldn't have stolen all this money – claims were soon over a million, and rising. After three months, I had to push for something - *make* Jock Clark see me. To kick them all, in July, I delivered statements about Calibre, and Peter Harper and Murgatroyds to Jock Clark; he had to see me.

Keith Brown came to see me at home:
"I told you Simon.... it was inevitable. Murgatroyds' gone bust and Receivers are in" he told me.
He explained how Peter had told him one night to hide the cash takings as they were going into Receivership next day
"He told me not to worry - we'd be back running it soon, but he had to do this first... it's closed, but Peter assures me the 'deal is done' and he's buying it back with these others."
"I see," said I quietly "I know exactly what he's done... it's a simple phoenix job. Anything else... what about Carole"
"Oh she went over a month ago. Peter told her the company couldn't afford her, so for a good week he played the game of ignoring her... he did it to Anna… made life impossible. Then he told her she was being made redundant. She walked out. Minute or so later, Peter was sat at the desk, back to the door, she walked back in and poured a pint a beer all over him and said 'that's what I think of you'. It was good - she enjoyed it."

I explained how a 'lawful' phoenix operation works. The Bank as security for a loan, had taken a 'floating charge' called a debenture or mortgage on all the assets of Northernfolks Limited, trading as Murgatroyds, including the goodwill and the lease of the premises. The company will have breached the loan terms, so the Bank appoint Receivers to recover its money by selling those assets - i.e. the entire business. If anything is left, they pay ordinary creditors, then hand the balance cash back to the owners - in theory. In practice there's never anything left after the professional vultures have divided it up. That sale would 'over-ride' and wipe out all other debts – i.e. so the new owners would not inherit any of the other debts. Hence the 'phoenix'. Peter could run it down, make it look broke, then buy it back with others or alone, through another limited company and no one could do anything about it. It would also wipe out any chance of recovering any money for Law Society - or all practicing solicitors, as I continued to write to the Penson team: – *"as you delay recovering, so those with the assets and cash acquired from me, are making it all untraceable."* They weren't interested

Yorkshire Post published:

> "HONOURABLE FRYER TAKES A BATTERING"
> 'The Honourable Simon Kaberry" had set up Northernfolks Ltd to trade as Murgatroyds Fish and Chip Emporium, intending to rival Harry Ramsdens, but the business had failed and Receivers had been called in..

- *'clever Peter.'*

At 10.00 a.m. on 18 August - five months since my arrest - I attended Weetwood police station. Kerry had vehemently opposed this; so I had delivered him a fait accomplis. I was well that day.

- this would be interesting:

"Right," opened Jock Clark on tape - "this interview is held because you, Mr.Cabri, have passed to us these two statements regarding Peter Harper and Calibre mortgage brokers."

"So - let me get this straight Mr.Cabri. Murgatroyds has been built or funded entirely from your solicitors client account - other people's money - fraud. Is that right?"

"I don't know. I have no idea what anything cost or who paid for it and with what, and much is my personal money."

"But you were an owner?"

"Was I? I was made a director, and I seem to have guaranteed it, but I don't think I had any shares. I have never been paid for anything I did, and have no knowledge of what money went where. I never saw any accounts or figures, nor met any supplier."

"Mr.Cabri - you're a solicitor - don't be silly. You must know!! Now - what arrangement did you have with Peter Harper to repay this money? You had an arrangement - didn't you."

"Umm...er.. I don't think so. We had no agreement or arrangement about anything. You see it was his money... well, I thought it was... or, was it my money? I don't know"

"This is just ridiculous... you were paying his mortgages and paying his debts from client account with money due to his mortgage company. He was giving you cheques for cash, then cancelling the cheques. Come on - why? - why were you letting him do this? - walk all over you?"

"Well.... er... he asked me to and I like to help people"

 -*'this is going wrong.... sounds pathetic Truth is I'm guessing. I actually don't know myself'*

I handed over the scrappy piece of paper - it totalled over £352,000 which I had noted had gone to Peter and the business – but that was just the big bits, I explained.

"Let me get this right, Mr.Cabri - you're telling us you gave Harper over £352,000.... probably more.... and some of it from client account? - money due to his banks"

"I don't know." My quest was to force an investigation.

"*Why* in Christ's name why - you must know!!"

I didn't.

We moved to Calibre work.

"Right, then Graham Carter, you say, was joined in business by Tony Heatherington: when was that?"

"I'm not sure...

"So," continued an exasperated Jock Clark "all these mortgages on these various properties - they're all based on fraud are they?"

"I don't know... what I say is that all the files were later stolen from my office..... I don't know any of these people."

"And, what was your cut? – for doing all this work," asked the officer in tones of innocence, hoping for my confession

"MY CUT?" I exclaimed - "What do you mean my cut? I HAVEN'T EVEN BEEN PAID! I just wanted them to go away – I wanted no part of them."

A moment's silence, and he continued quietly:

"Come on Mr.Cabri, you've got to tell us. *What hold* did all these people have on you. It'll come out sooner or later – what hold - *what hold* - did these people have on you?

Kerry leaned over and whispered in my ear so that the tape wouldn't pick it up

"Simon - obviously you were being blackmailed. That's what he's saying - what was it they were all blackmailing you about".

-*This is nonsense - blackmail? - if only life was so exciting*.

I continued: "Umm......I think you may like to see this."
I took out the letter passed to me by Graham last April. They each read it over. Another confession, but this time in someone else's handwriting. Bizarrely the payments of interest continued for some months after my arrest – so I wasn't the one doing it, was I?

It stood the confessions and March interview on its head. My bail was now extended to return on 28 March – now a year from arrest. I returned home and watched racing from the York August Meeting. Imagine my thoughts, as I watched Petrina Bay taking the field along – just for three furlongs of the five. She had won her last two races as well. I was on bail and being accused of all things nasty, and they were living it up as owners at York. Life.

On 2 September 1994 CPS sent directions to the Leeds and Bradford fraud squads to open separate investigations into these people and warned them *not to delay* further or risk being accused of 'abuse by delay' – a common trait in the fraud squads of England. I found these notes years later, but no Judge will allow the truth out.

By September time, largely off the Dalmane for five months, I no longer walked in fear of people. Walking around Sainsburys, but keeping my head down as you do, I bumped straight into Louise slowly pushing a trolley around.
"Well, here's a surprise" she nervously said - "you seem to have been in the wars if we can call it that."
"You can call it what the hell you like – and I'm in it for sure."

A few years younger than me, she worked as some sort of Librarian, and wasn't my type at all. Bright but too shy and reserved, she was petite and mousy, with shortish curly hair. Quiet and unassuming is one way of describing her; one would never describe her as a trophy girl, if I may put it that way - nor would she wish to be.. She lived alone so far as I knew. Our chat then led to her following me home for a glass of wine. Holly took an immediate shine to her. So started a most unexpected relationship which would be sustained throughout harrowing times between two people with nothing at all in common. She was entirely different to all those with whom I had ever associated. I had high expectations of life; she had none. I would lead a line; she would walk in shadows. But she was a real friend who never believed the stories abounding about me in the Yorkshire Evening Post etc.

I had no way of paying my mortgage and must lose my home. Rationale returned; I had to save somewhere to live. My neighbours Anne and Tony would buy my home for their relatives and I could remain there until my troubles were over. We agreed what I will call a 'very favourable price' (to them). The sale swept through in September – I wouldn't get any proceeds as that was charged as security for Murgatroyds as well as everyone putting charges on it. But I loved my home – my roots of life; I'd lost it - you grit your teeth and accept it - a 'no-choice' job.

On 17 October I sat alone flitting TV channels over dinner. It was World in Action, discussing drugs - '*boring.*' Some men were pontificating, when I heard one of them clearly say

- "*and I've known someone take Dalmane one night, and next morning whilst driving, being told to turn right at a roundabout, and promptly turned right against all the traffic; that's what they can do under the influence*"

I scrawled out Prof.Ian Hindmarch from University of Surrey. John Patchett would write for more info. Meanwhile, Louise came to take me to the Lakes on Thursday and the following Thursday, and weekends and so on. Sometimes she didn't leave until midnight, and sometimes not at all. But oh – the screaming cramp which came with recovery and attacked at all sorts of times!!

Into next year, and on one of many walks with Louise in Studley Royal I suffered what I later learned was a panic attack - part of recovery; other effects - tinnitus and sleeplessness continue ten years later. I made an appointment to see my GP for a check-up.

Needing help I rang brother Andrew in Wetherby, who reluctantly called one afternoon. We sat in the bay window, both in overcoats, as I had no money for fuel for a fire or gas tokens for the central heating - so cold my nose turned blue. Knowing he would do nothing, I phoned and told his secretary he had agreed

that his company agreed to install a phone at my home – "OK, I'll get onto it straight away". At the beginning of February, after eleven months incommunicado, a phone-line was connected.
Bingo - my lifeline.

On the morning of the 6th February John Patchett rang:
"Simon - now, this is serious.   I've just been talking to this professor Hindmarch for you.... you bloody fool"
I was cold and shivering as he excitedly explained Hindmarch may be able to help me – there had been cases about these drugs. He spoke at me for about two minutes. I'd be 'like a zombie trying to work things out – liable to do anything.'
- '*what the hell have I done to myself*' - my eyes watered in sadness and I felt my heart pounding - blind panic went over me. Down went the phone and I walked sharply across the hall to the kitchen - '*quickly, have a cup of tea - relax.*' As the kettle boiled, a mug flew across the room and smashed on the wall - I was shaken, with anger within - what had I done to myself?

Same day, I attended my GP noon appointment; I asked for, and got more dalmane - no problem! I was setting him up. Then, I told him I had 'problems' - so he arranged for me to see a psychiatrist. I left surgery with a prescription for a mind-changing drug I never needed, a clean bill of health and an appointment to see a psychiatrist (I later gave the prescription evidence to my lawyers). Welcome to Life in modern England.

At 7.00 am on 16 March Det.Sgt Clark and his team descended on Peter Harper's lovely country house. One may ask why they didn't arrest any of the individuals in the Calibre scenario.   You may ask indeed. But no judge will let anyone answer.

Clarkie had traced some of my client account cheques.   Some had gone to pay Peter's debts and the debts of his companies. Even I didn't know that. I later got a copy of these interviews...

> "So, Mr. Harper help me with this would you. Mr.Kaberry didn't finish the re-mortgage work on your house and so he had just under £100,000 sitting in his

client account; he was short, so couldn't finish it, or something like that"

".....er.....I can't really remember

"And you were setting up a new business and would take him cheques, and he would give you cash from his client account – is that right"

"Well he insisted in giving me cash......

"So you gave him cheques and he gave you cash?

"Yes"

"But I've got a series of cheques here from you to him, and you later, having got the cash, cancelled the cheques - they weren't honoured were they"

Confronted with the cheques before his eyes....

".er......well one or two..."

"One or two..... there are scores - it means that you were taking client account money due to your building society. Mr.Kaberry couldn't repay your bank, because you already had that money. Then you were taking more…?"

He produced other payments I seem to have made for his business - payments I knew nothing about.

Clarkie had him in the palm of his hand.

After some more ramblings (from the tapes I have)

Clarkie: "It seems to me Simon Kaberry was like ruddy Father Christmas visiting daily"

Reply: "......er.....well........."

Clarkie again: "Forgive me and I'm maybe a big cynic, but it seems to me he was just an '*easy touch*' for money for everything...whatever you wanted, he paid ...from 1991 onwards.... now you tell me, why should he do that"

Reply: "well, er... you could put it that way. He became utterly eccentric. He'd come to my house in a morning and stay all day. He just took control of my life and helped my family. He was our guardian angel in difficult times you could say"

"But you must have known he shouldn't give you money from client account?"

"I thought it was his…. I assume you know about his gambling successes. I even acted as his runner on some occasions as he wasn't allowed to bet. I mean, I could travel a hundred miles from Leeds, go to Willie Hills and hand a bet over, only to have it refused 'cos he's barred for winning too much. They know his style or something like that"

"Oh yes, what kind of bets – what sort of money"

"Well, always only small stakes – £10-20 each, never more than a hundred pounds in total"

"Yes... I've heard all about it. Tell me this; what arrangements did you have to repay all this money due to his client account"

"Well, you see he was just helping me out as a friend. When I refinanced the business I was to repay what I owed"

Clarkie and CPS had confirmation if needed - the confessions of February were nonsense. What is stunning on this information is the way it was later used by lawyers and judges. Top men you are told to trust blindly like Lords Phillips and Bingham won't allow you to know the truth.

Peter was released on bail whilst CPS considered how to proceed in such a peculiar case.

On 28 March Kerry and I presented ourselves at Weetwood police station at 10.00 am for my third interview. Clarkie had the police in-house Accountant Mrs. Scott as company. I waited, apprehensive that there may be something I knew nothing about, that incriminated me. There was nothing.

 Soon it was lunchtime.

"Right, Mr.Cabri – you go in the cells whilst we have lunch"

Refusing to accept that this was happening to me, I stood to attention 'Bridge Over River Kwai' style in the centre of the cell. Alone, shoulders back-stomach in, on Parade mode in the middle of the cell for forty five minutes.

- *'these buggers will never get me down for sure'*

- *'bet anyone watching would say – 'you've got a right idiot in cell one'; but what the hell. They'll never beat me'*

We resumed but there were no admissions. The Scotsman seemed tired of it all; nothing made sense.

"Right Mr.Cabri. I've got to do a Report and someone is going to ask me where all this money is - there's over £600,000 here on these cases we've just discussed alone, and much more than that – *millions* we're talking. Now I can't find it, and my accountant Mrs. Scott here - she can't find it either, so you must know – you tell us"

- *'gottcha; you know.... and I know you know... exactly where it is and who's got it....and you've got an accountant and she knows'*

Against Kerry's instructions, I now told him of my discovery about the effects of the sleeping pill.

"Well maybe it could explain and I'll have to tell CPS who are in control of this case".

"Well, I haven't any of this money, nor have I had any of it"

- *'got that in on tape........one day, could be relevant – another denial'*

The interview finished. Over a year, sitting and waiting – soon someone would realize it wasn't me, and the nightmare would be over. Beyond that, you can do no more than accept you are 'in the system,' then keep faith that all would be well, however uncomfortable.

Simon Kaberry

CHAPTER SIX

'The Sting'
- *the power of the Legal Establishment to destroy anyone with impunity*
- *the world of self-regulation at work*

Police knew from the signed cheques and my bank accounts I had none of this money. They had admissions from Harper. And presumably, they were well-on with Calibre investigations. CPS were thinking who to charge, and with what.

Sarah Wade continued to write with compensation claims; as ever, she ignored all my replies. I would write - *"someone has been paying the interest until recently - who?"* I'd already told them who. Yet I found myself walking the Beechwalk day after day, shouting at the silent trees
- *'why won't someone listen to me and stop this nonsense'*

A habit continued each Thursday that Louise would take a day off work and take me into the countryside or coast - I'd become a day-tripper. Often I'd sit in her car for miles on end in complete silence; what was I doing in this tiny car with a strange woman, behaving as someone I didn't know. I should be at work. A strange relationship was emerging between two people from entirely different backgrounds, with entirely different expectations of life and views of it, and nothing in common. Jane Austin may have written of her that she lacked the confidence to hold herself forward as a person of significant consequence. Louise wanted to be outgoing and happy, but didn't know how - or was that my terrible effect on her. She had no ambition; we could walk in shadows together. But Holly would greet this stranger who always had hidden goodies for her on the shelf at the front of her car, as it arrived at the front of the house.

I rang my old pal Donald Coverdale - what did he know of benzodiazepines?
"Simon - how good to hear from you…. and how are you coping. All this flack they've been giving you; it must be awful" came the compassionate opening from an old friend. I told him I may need a barrister and he suggested his neighbour Aidan Marron QC.

"I'll think on it - like the sound of his name."

"Look Donald - now something else. Have you come across drugs called benzodiazepines"?

"Oh yes, but not so much as Coroner. There's been a lot of litigation about them, but it fizzled out. I had a woman who was on one of them... Ativan I think... she says it ruined her life"

"Never heard of it. Mine was called Dalmane...

"What - you were taking them!" came the exclamation... Then he gave me the name of Freeth Cartright Hunt Dickens in Nottingham; a man called Paul Balen - he'd run the litigation.

"Donald. I owe you - thanks."

I made an appointment to see Paul Balen on 28 April next. I could ditch Kerry. Steady... I would get out of this shit.

Keith Brown came to see me again, baffled, jobless and penniless. Murgatroyds had been back up and running again for some while, just as before. 'Someone' had bought it lock stock and barrel for something like, as rumoured, £100,000. The phoenix operation had been implemented simply. A business which must have cost half a million pounds to set up and flourished, had closed, apparently bust, but never was, now re-opened without paying its debts. Keith wanted his money back (he loaned too) and his job.

"Simon" he said... "Carole (O'Neil) rang asking for a job and the man in charge is Peter. I mean... what the hell's going on. There must be something you can do to stop it."

Keith told me Peter claimed to be a 'mere employee' of the new company Castmark limited, and so couldn't give him his job back. I was later told the £100,000 was loaned by the bank as before, so the 'buyers' had nothing to find to 'buy' it. This is Leeds??

The phoenix had also created debts guaranteed by me. I had guaranteed the bank and the trading account to John Smiths. Somehow Courage (owners of John Smiths) had given supplies unpaid of £30,000, now held judgment against me for that. With all the other problems, I hadn't really read the writ – just assumed it was for supplies I had guaranteed. Yorkshire Area Conservative Clubs of which I was trustee wrote Courage demanded my resignation or would cut off supplies. Peter had told them I had stolen from the business - so they were after me.

Weeks flew by; the sun shone as spring headed for summer. As Wade and Penson were plainly useless, I extracted the name of Mohammed Quasimodo as Clarkie's contact at Law Society. *Wait*....

I reached the offices of Freethcartright (they've a new name) in Nottingham, taking a 'draft discussion statement' over several pages as background. Having been told by Hindmarch I should have been told never to drink any alcohol, I took a draft that my GP knew from the 1980's that I could drink as much as 2 bottles of vino sometimes (boys night out job), but said I then found 'just one glass and I was tipsy' at lunchtimes, but often had 2-3 glasses of wine with dinner (recorded by the GP for medicals in 1991&2).

In Paul Balen I found a younger and more cocky man than me; he lacked charm. We didn't gel and I wasn't at ease:
"What's interesting about your case, Mr.Kaberry, is the time when you were being prescribed this Dalmane. You see, anything before 1988 and you can't do anything but after that date... well, no one should have been left on repeat prescriptions as you were."
He explained something of the group claim - claiming fault lay with the Legal Aid Board, but my prescriber case was different.

He scanned the Hindmarch letter of advice, and continued:
"Well that's quite interesting as Prof.Hindmarch was actually *against* us in the group claim, but he seems to support you now, so I'll have to consider him as expert advisor, but that comes later."
[That's not quite right, Hindmarch had said that problems arose on overuse - the drugs are not generically dangerous, as Balen/ Thorold had claimed. Their pleading was flawed.] He told me the best expert was Professor Lader at the Institute of Psychiatry.

Balen would now get Reports from a doctor on the prescribing, then an expert on causation of injury; it would take a few months. To get legal aid to fund them, you have to show a 'prima facie' case, and I certainly had that. Balen assured me I would get the best of everything, including, in a man called Oliver Thorold - the best benzo barrister in England. I was in the right place.
"Now, these criminal matters" he said "we've got a criminal team here and it may pay you to have a word with them - chap called Mike Thurston's in charge and he's got time to see you"
"Er - but does he understand the effects of these drugs?"

"Oh yes, Mike consolidated the thousands of claims - he's very much up on it all." I was in and out in about 30 minutes.

He introduced me to Mike Thurston. This one was clearly ex-public school, self-assured and charming, ready to put his client at ease. I sat there feeling so foolish, watering eyes - man of integrity, accused of theft of client funds. I was with him an hour and returned to Leeds quietly pleased - all was well; these lawyers were the tops. Louise took me for a pub meal and as ever I let her pay - shame and pride gone.

Within days, on 4 May I received a certificate from the LAB that funding of £7,500 was issued to Balen to obtain experts reports, then for counsel to advise in Conference on bringing a civil claim for compensation. Now I could focus on those idle so-and-soes in Leamington Spa. Mr. Quasimodo turned out to be called Qasim.

"Mr.Qasim - Simon Kaberry in Leeds here. I assume you know all about me from Sarah Wade, and Robin Penson"

"Yes Mr.Kaberry - I work within a team here and am aware of your case"

"Well, as I'm sure Jock Clark will have told you, this is very complicated. So I thought I'd call you directly, as I think you're in charge of recovering these monies."

"Yes I am - go on."

"Well, you know all about Calibre and Harper. Now there's a new development"

"Well...not exactly, but go on...."

 - *'what the hell's going on here – he must be playing'*

"Its set out in my letters to Sarah Wade which I assume you have seen... scores of them...well there's a new development."

"I probably have, yes, and you say there's a new development?" - *'this man clearly knows nothing about any of this...'*

"The explanation is sleeping pills - a pill called Dalmane and I've been given legal aid to start a claim for being put in a condition when I was taken to the cleaners..."

"Go on Mr.Kaberry...

"Have you heard of a group of drugs called benzodiazepines?"

"Mr.Kaberry - I'm going to have to stop you there. Yes I know all about Valium and things like that.   My sister (or did he say girlfriend) is a pharmacist and there's nothing wrong with those drugs.   Yes they make you a little giddy, but that's it. All claims were withdrawn.... Pull the other one Mr.Kaberry"

- 'yea gods .. this is another waste of time'
He hadn't read any of my letters, wouldn't see me and didn't want to know, save I could write to him.

Frustration mounting I wanted to scream, but penned him a letter. He responded he was taking a 'second opinion.'
- 'second opinion..... what tosh these clerks write!' I was learning
- this world of self-regulation.

Courage issued a Bankruptcy Petition on the £30,000 judgment. I needed to see someone at their nearby office in Tadcaster. Kit was in Kent, so I sent a message to Andrew – would he help? PD brought the message back – "you're on your own." As his brother was in trouble, he'd run away, but in fairness I knew he could never be a line-leader. I'm sure he has other qualities.

I lived in solitude, save for my best mate and my limited contact with the outside world. Now I was surrounded by the uncertainty of what police would do, the hope of a civil claim, the incompetence of Law Society, and now bankruptcy threatening. The drugs had robbed me of the ability to appreciate the joys of a mature garden. Rather like life passes an alcoholic by. For the first time in years, I saw the colours, and smelt the shrubs - lilac was powerful and two large aged mock oranges to the far end and side of the lawn were sweetly pungent. Salvaging my home was the best move I made, but each day - that thought - where will all this end? How would you have coped? – not the odd day alone, but now it was thirteen months.... and you know you had very powerful opponents saying nasty things about you.

Moneywise I was selling off thisthatandtheother - tables, chairs, ornaments, books retrieved from fathers collection. It hurts, so you say - "its only possessions." Louise was taking an increasingly active role in my life. She had savings from earnings; I'd never encountered these people but there are thousands of such sensible types. I admit it - I've never budgeted in my life; there are loads of prats like me.

The Bankruptcy Petition was served. I filed an affidavit at court that I hadn't been served properly (no statutory demand) and 'this was in nobody's interest.' The lawyers refused to talk to me.

Victoria Court, in Dormer Place, Leamington Spa is a grandiose white-stonefaced building by the river; it houses, the home of the Law Society's self-regulatory arm (now called S.R.A.).

Here, manager Robin Penson worked with Sarah Wade, Neil Rogerson, Mhd Qasim, and another I had not yet encountered Susan Head. These clerks have power enormous power (above their station?) and no one has 'the will' to do anything about it.

By now they had over 100 letters from me. They knew I was suing the doctor. They knew Peter Harper was on bail, had client money, yet he filed a compensation claim with them. They knew of Calibre, yet they were repaying the loans to them, whilst they retained the assets, and held a claim from them as well. A decision was made how to deal with this situation - to justify what they had already done – ie to cover their backsides.

Penson wouldn't see me or recover any of the money. He had something in mind for me to protect his bum. But the assassin would be a third party – *finito SK*

"But he can't talk... he's on bail. Who're you going to get to do it?"
"You got it - it'll be a doddle - give it to Geoffrey"
"OK - you're the boss," said Qasim. Welcome to the world of "the Importance of Independence" - lawyers at work.

The June sun continued to shine, and I was in limbo. I couldn't sleep, often felt like a withdrawn zombie, but conversely, often calm and well. I tried walking off the pressure each day. The Bankruptcy Petition was for hearing in Leeds Courts. I didn't think I had any defence in law – so why humiliate myself.

A humdinger from hell hit home on 20 June. A letter from Cardiff solicitor Geoffrey Williams contained an Application by him on behalf of Law Society that I attend before Solicitors Disciplinary Tribunal (SDT) on Hearing 26 July. He alleged that I was unfit to be a solicitor. The principal ground was failing to file Accounts and withdrawing from client account in breach of Rules. Those are 'absolute' offences - so I had no defence. I started to flap - if they did this, I would be ruined yet everything had to be kept 'sub judice' - nothing done publicly, or the knock-on effects would be horrendous. Surely they must know that.

I rang my 'mate'(his choice of speech), Kerry Macgill, but he was away learning to be a judge. So I rang Tribunal Secretary Susan Elston - "This must be stopped... I'm on bail... two complex police investigations are ongoing – anything said will ruin them"
"Oh yes, that often happens. What you must do is agree something with Geoffrey"
"But I can't agree something with him – he's Law Society and no one will talk to me or see me."

This is the comedy of self-regulation. Susan Elston is employed by Law Society - but pretends not to be. Tribunal is made up by members of Law Society, but pretends to be independent of it; its duty is to protect the name of Law Society and solicitors, but it says it acts to protect the public. This is a pretend world – protected by the judiciary, who are similarly self-regulated. Geoffrey Williams was instructed by Law Society and troughs with the SDT judges. And they all pretend they are 'independent' of one-another. Ordinary people would see this as a natural home of deceit and cover-up whenever they want. But our Lord Chief Justice and Master of the Rolls, who oversees them - openly say - this is "the importance of independence." Utter and absurd nonsense. But Judges are similarly unaccountable to the public, and if lawyers were made publicly accountable, then next stop would be our judges.

I wrote to Mrs.Elston, who replied that Tribunal has a legal duty not to do anything with *would 'muddy the waters of justice'*- words spoken by Lord Bingham, surely a highly duplicitous man on the evidence you will read - but you judge if I'm right later.

So I rang Geoffrey Williams. He played the charade that Tribunal is not the Law Society. I explained the ongoing police investigations and that I was still on bail. No decision had been made what to do and who to prosecute. I then explained I had just been granted legal aid to sue for being put in this impaired condition. I didn't yet have all the evidence, but couldn't present it even if I had it:

"So, you see my problems. Can we agree an adjournment from 26 July?" said I. He was adamant he couldn't.
"That is not how Tribunal works.... I can't agree anything with you about an adjournment. Look - write to me and set it all out."

I sent him chapter and verse. His reply was that he would explain my position, but he was in a position to proceed and prove his case. That was double-dutch - it was duty not to muddy waters.

Things got worse. On 6 July the Bankruptcy Petition fell in the Court of my old foe District Judge David Gavin (I had once appeared before him in a civil case, doped up, and not knowing what I was doing). How he must have relished signing the Order. Now I was bankrupt. Years later it would come clear it wasn't the Murgatroyds trading account at all, but a loan to Peter. I should never have been so adjudged. That would cost me far more dearly than I knew that day. The sealed Court Order lay on my doorstep two days later.
 - *'oh Jesus, help me – what else is coming my way'*

I knew Bankrupts lose their assets and are limited in other ways; for example they commit a criminal offence if incurring credit. I couldn't have a bank account, but by then all were closed. I had no assets left - home sold the year before, and most items of any value were sold from my home. A phone call caught Kerry Macgill at his office one morning. Like police, he told me, just to wait. As to Law Society and Tribunal he responded-
"So, you've agreed something with a Welshman have you" in hurried jest
"Er.... what's wrong with a Welshman?"
"Englishman, Irishman, Scotsman...and Welshman... you know"
"Umm, no...?"
"They're Welsh.... clot..."
"No - I mean.... no, he wouldn't
-*'of course. welsh, they welsh!'*

Early July I rang Geoffrey Williams a second time.
"Er... I have your letter, but I thought we'd agreed you have to adjourn in the public interest."
"I said no such thing."
"Well, can I agree something with you...? you're a Welshman... is that a problem?"

"Don't be ridiculous. I said that I will explain your position to Tribunal, and that I will do…"
"But I can't even get there, and I'm bankrupt. I have no money and can't afford representation, and even if I'm there I can't speak – it'll ruin two police investigations as I told you last time. All I ask is that you agree to adjourn."

The pressure was there. Instead of Holly circling my bed and leaping up, I'd come down at 3.00am, talk to her quietly as she lay flat out on the best settee, always that sleepy doggy smell, and thumping guilty tail to greet me. I rang that nice Mike Thurston; we agreed to meet on 19 July. Another letter from Qasim, who once again thanked me for offers of help, but he was still 'considering matters'. I stood calmly by my desk
- ' … are they really as incompetent as they seem. '

On 18 July I rang Williams a third time. He would explain my position to SDT. I made a Journal entry - "Williams is OK." Lord Bingham later made a ruling on that entry - it is 'evidence of nothing' (and none is allowed) - *you couldn't make it up!*

I took Mike Thurston the Complaint and my unsent seven pager to Tribunal, which explains why it must adjourn until I could defend myself. I told him of my calls with Elston and Williams, had over an hour with him and signed a 'green form advice', which would entitle him to claim for an hour's general advice.
"Now - you told me that you've had thousands of benzo cases… What kind of cases, what happened to these other people… No names. But what sorts of things happened to them?"
"Er…. well, one I remember quite well. A professor at some university got hooked on one or other of them… Ativan maybe. He stopped caring… didn't bother with life, his family, his career and would have lost it. Then his mother died… he couldn't cope and topped himself. Before the addiction he'd been fine… a professor. But you can't compare yourself with him or anyone; they're all different.… these drugs have destroyed so many lives"
- ' this man can help me… once he grasps the facts. ' I liked him.

Mike would write to SDT, and call Williams. I was feeling good as I drove down the drive, just as Louise was walking Holly round to the back. They stopped: waggy tail thought - 'great, my daddy's home - that gets me off that ruddy walk, and if she's here, they'll be going out and bring me his liver, chips and crunchy onion rings.' Clever dog.

Saturday, and my hopes faded. Mike copied me his SDT letter.
- *'oh my god..... solicitors... utterly incompetent?* It read:

> "We are instructed etc..... Mr.Kaberry has long suffered psychological and psychiatric injury as well as plain ill-health... he well understands his position.... and is co-operating fully. We have an expertise on the effects of benzodiazepines, and have recently been granted legal aid to investigate a claim for compensation for him, arising from the drug's effects.

- *'this is ruddy awful...'plain ill-health!!.. I've never been ill'*

In no time I had drafted a letter to Tribunal:

> *Adel Willows*
> *Leeds 16 8AF*
> *24 July 1995*

Dear Sirs,

> *I have read the copy letter to you from my solicitor Michael Thurston dated 19 July.... That you must adjourn: but..*
> *1. I (think and hope) that prior to the prescribing of Dalmane I was as sane and rational as the next man or woman. The effects of the sedative are...... etc*
> *2. There has been no personal gain – quite the reverse..*
> *3. To act judicially, you must give me chance to defend.. and not effect police ongoing inquiries..*

What happened to me could happen to anyone, even someone reading this, who, like me, would say it couldn't happen
... Tribunal must adjourn until I can attend and speak...

[you later read a magical ruling from Lord Bingham on this letter requesting a trial – *"I don't understand what he is trying to say"*]

The following Wednesday, the day prior to the Hearing I rang Mrs.Elston again. She cut me short – didn't want to know.

So it was straight to my desk to fax another letter

ADEL WILLOWS
LEEDS LS168AF
26 July 1995

Dear Sirs,

"I refer to my letters and requests for an adjournment until I can defend and answer these proceedings. I wish to make it plain that absolutely nothing must be said in public in an open sitting of Tribunal about these matters.

Concern is *already high* about the conduct and failings of Law Society"

- that should ruffle a few feathers.

The events which follow are largely taken from the chairman's notes and newspaper reports; some must be speculation.

In the morning of Thursday 26 July Geoffrey Williams attended the Solicitors Disciplinary Tribunal in London. I had to attend a course in a Leeds suburb for the unemployed; if I didn't, I wouldn't receive 'Job Seekers Allowance' which I needed for basic living costs. They would teach me how to apply by phone for a job as a waiter – I kid you not; this is what goes on. Mrs. Elston put my fax before Tribunal chairman, a solicitor from Cheltenham called KIB Yeaman, and told him of my phone calls.

Yeaman will have been appointed, like the others, by the Master of the Rolls (then Lord Phillips) to chair this 'court.' With him sat another solicitor Anthony H Isaacs, who plays a key role later, and the public offering - Lady Bonham-Carter (by marriage, aunt of an actress and in politics). Prior to the 'Hearing' Tribunal Clerk send these 'Judges' details of the cases they are to hear. The three judges sat at a table in their courtroom. Mr.Yeaman told Mr. Williams he had my letters. They would know one another quite well. Media reporters sharpened their pencils.

"Have you, Mr.Williams, seen the latest – this fax received from Mr.Kaberry this morning?"

"Yes sir, and I have also spoken with Mr.Kaberry and his solicitor Mr.Thurston"

"Right. Mr.Kaberry seeks an adjournment until he can speak and defend. What is the Law Society's position Mr.Williams?" said the member of the Law Society.

> "Sir. The Society's position is plain and simple. We oppose any request for any adjournment forcefully. I say there is nothing to indicate that Mr.Kaberry has been or will be charged with any offence. If he is to be charged then that is well in the distance and steps could be taken to ensure that nothing which happens here would influence any court.
>
> Sir, this is a very serious case and I allege serious misconduct over a period of time and dishonesty by Mr.Kaberry. As you know there is much precedent that Tribunal has a public duty not to delay in cases of this type. I am in a position to proceed and prove my case."

- *'I will explain your position'* - my bottom he would.

They'd done nothing in four years.... why the sudden urgency? – any normal person would ask.

"Well, Mr.Kaberry has asked that nothing be done in public, so we will retire to consider the adjournment."

A few moments and the trio were back:

> "We agree with the submission by Law Society. This Tribunal has public duties to proceed swiftly in the interests of the public. Please proceed (in public) with your case Mr.Williams."

Geoffrey Williams stood to address the Tribunal of three on behalf of Law Society, meeting its public duty.

> "The accused had been admitted a solicitor in 1974; he had been in private practice ever since, and with his own practice since 1980. In January 1991 he had appeared before Tribunal for failing to file Accounts on time and in March that year Tribunal had imposed a fine of £2,500 and ordered Accounts be filed each six months. He had filed none ever since. In spring 1994 an Accountant for the Society inspected his books and found funds were missing. Mr.Kaberry then 'abandoned' his practice, in March. Subsequent investigations revealed a catastrophic shortage of funds – initially thought to be in the region of £200,000

"Sir - further investigations were made and a letter found in Mr.Kaberry's office in which he admits taking client account to gamble on races like the Grand National...

"Sir - I allege a course of extreme unbefitting conduct – the worst I have encountered... theft of client funds to gamble"

He then handed in the letter written in Yarmouth, now published to media as found in my office and true. He then went over a couple of cases where I had stopped work and paid over the interest arising; the innuendo was obvious. Then he called an Accountant to 'prove' that there was money 'missing.' They accepted his brief evidence. The Society had so far paid out 1.9 million pounds for my dishonesty, Tribunal and media were told. That should make good headlines, one would imagine Williams had considered.

They retired. A few moments and they were back:
"We find the allegations proved. Mr.Kaberry is 'undoubtedly dishonest.' We order that his name be struck-off the Roll of Solicitors. Our full reasons will follow later. Do you have any further applications Mr.Williams."?
"Yes sir for my costs - I ask you to fix them at £10,000."
"Granted" said KIB Yeaman. To his right sat solicitor Anthony Isaacs - part of the team. He would later ensure complete cover-up of this legal kangaroo court, and protection of Williams.

From media reports I am told it took little over ten minutes. Newspaper boys followed Williams outside for his further comments:
"Yes, it's true" said Williams to a reporter from The Times – "Only the Society, in meeting its public duties, has done anything about Kaberry - he remains uncharged by police." – said the man in whom the public put their faith not to deceive them

Job Done - *'finito, Simon Kaberry... for life'*

Let me digress on what Williams, Yeaman, Isaacs and Bonham-Carter had just done in law. They knew two complex police investigations were ongoing, one man had been arrested and was on bail, whilst police and CPS decided what to do. They knew I had a prima facie clinical negligence claim pending for being put in that condition. Many hours of police time had been spent so far, and my evidence could be critical. Nadine Milroy-Sloan caused police to waste hours by falsely alleging Neil and Christine Hamilton had raped her. She was sent to prison for three years for wasting police time, and trying to pervert the course of justice. Inevitably, I would be subject to horrific vitriol then and for years thereafter in consequence, and two police investigations would inevitably be hijacked. Geoffrey Williams knew from me directly, and as an experienced lawyer not to do what he had just done.

These false allegations would be reported and accepted as true; pose this question - how would you have reacted to reading their 'Verdict.' You'd revile me, wouldn't you - just as people still do.

Section 1 Contempt of Court Act 1981 reads: *it is a criminal offence to....*
> *....interfere with the course of justice with particular regard to legal proceedings regardless of intent*

Sub judice rules are quite simple. The letter, which Williams published, was taken from an ongoing police investigation. If a newspaper takes such evidence and publishes it, the Editor and Reporter are likely to be sent to prison for contempt as the accused could not get a fair trial, or justice is perverted. That must be right as one of our principles of justice.
So - what would you do to these three lawyers?

I could no longer be any prosecution witness. Set the scene at court by each defending counsel
- *"and it is true Mr.Kaberry, is it not, that on 26 July 1995 you personally were convicted by the Law Society of gross dishonesty and struck off for stealing all this money alleged to be held by my clients...*
  - How on earth do you expect this jury to believe such a man."

If a surgeon is reckless, his career is over. Not lawyers or judges - until they lose the right to self-regulate. Williams had just blown hundreds of hours of police time, and saved three men from justice, whereas Milroy-Sloan caused them to be subsequently wasted. The principle must be the same. What do you think they did to Williams, Yeaman and Isaacs? When men like Lords Bingham and Phillips read of what he had just done? It will surprise you...

Would our 'independent' judges allow anyone to expose wrongdoing by lawyers and Law Society?

Apprehensive of evolving events in London, I returned home at lunchtime. Should I ring Tribunal? Strange isn't it, but we often don't do things when we don't really want to know the answer. Another super summer day of sunshine and I watched racing from glorious Goodwood. Holly sunbathed until too hot and came in.

At about 4.00 pm a car slowly came down the drive and pulled at the front. Two men got out, one carrying something that looked awfully like a camera - *'Something's happened'* - I panicked and in a flash, sped out of the French window round to the side veranda, Holly in my slipstream, thinking we were chasing Mr.Fox. You see people standing sheepishly by front doors and I wasn't going to fall for that one. I was caught in the killer of uncertainty, waited a good fifteen minutes, then walked up to the top wood, and ambled the seventy yards down the shaded gravel drive to the front. No car but a man was waiting for me:

"Oh, Mr.Kaberry, can I have a word with you about this morning's case in Solicitors Tribunal?" said Garry Finn from Yorkshire Post.
"Oh yes – it was adjourned wasn't it?"
-*'stay calm…. don't flap'.* My heart was pounding
"No, I'm afraid - you were struck-off. I'm looking for your comments on the allegations. You are said to have stolen millions from clients to go gambling all over England"
Garry later told me he watched as I physically changed colour.
"What!!… well - I can't comment. I need to know exactly what's been alleged. As you may know, I cannot speak anyway…."
He had some papers faxed through from Tribunal or press association so far as I could see. I continued:
"…and where am I meant to have taken all this money?"
"To the Grand National." Tribunal had a letter found in my office admitting it; the Hearing had taken about ten minutes.
"Umm, I need to make some calls. Come in…"
I tried to keep my cool and not alienate him. Michael Thurston was meant to have ensured that just this didn't happen. He'd gone home. I went calm and quickly sorted things out in my mind - say nothing until you know what's happened. My only comment was "I'm amazed by everything you have just told me".

Garry was a pleasant man, but he was a reporter with a good story. We parted and I accepted he would slaughter me.

PD took me for dinner at Stuarts Wine Bar. For sure I wouldn't be showing my face anywhere after tomorrow. At the end of dinner I told him what seemed to have happened and to expect the worst. He dropped me back home and I was amazingly calm before the storm. I heard him putting papers through the letterbox at 7.30 am. – 'take a deep breath before reading them'

I opened The Times and found it on page five

Gambling Lawyer struck Off

> There followed a report of what Williams had alleged and found proved, and his comment that I was still uncharged and only Law Society had done anything about me. He said I had taken vast amounts to gamble on the Grand National and other races

I was shafted nationally. Then on to the Daily Mail:

Gambling Lawyer Struck off
Same story

My stomach was churning as I turned to the Yorkshire Post - big bold front-page and continued on another page

Lawyer struck-off for gambling clients cash
This time the story was much more detailed with, as expected my family history. The figure was now 3.5 million. People would all believe Williams. At the very end came my rather feeble statement – 'I am amazed by everything you tell me.'

At 9.05 the phone rang:
"Simon - it's me - **what the hell's going on**", snapped my lawyer, now in his Bradford office, "I've had Jock Clark on the phone already... have you seen the papers, **I can tell you heads will roll for this.... police are livid**"
"Er... I don't know Kerry. I haven't seen yet..." I lied.
"Simon, we're meant to be having a proper police investigation here - you told me you had all this in hand with those Nottingham

people. Who is it in charge at Tribunal - I'm going to have real words over this - **they've buggered everything**"

At lunchtime came the one I knew to fear - our nasty monopoly rag - the *Yorkshire Evening Post....*
The **entire Front page** of a broadsheet

'SHAME AND DISGRACE'
PEER'S SON STRUCK OFF
FOR STEALING MILLIONS FROM CLIENTS
Then a sub-heading and pictures of me (with hair) and my home and office

> Then followed the entire letter dictated in Yarmouth, now published as a voluntary and true confession found in my office. The story filled the entire page.

I could do nothing about any of it, save keep my head down. The 'easy touch' was now an easy target for anyone to pot at.

Meanwhile that Friday morning the phones were hot. It rang at in North Yorkshire.
"Morning Peter. It's me... are you smiling?"
"Umm... why... should I be?"
"Haven't you seen today's papers?"
"Er...no - not yet"
"Right. There's been a trial of Kaberry by Law Society yesterday. He's been found guilty of stealing over two million from client account to go gambling"
Silence for a moment.
"I don't understand - what d'yu mean."
"Just that. Solicitors Disciplinary Tribunal yesterday struck Kaberry off the Roll, and found him guilty of stealing millions from clients to gamble. It seems he has admitted it all."
"You're not having me on are you... and where's this leave me? I mean - I'm on bail"
"Don't worry. I'll get on to police right away - just thought I'd have a word with you first. It'll be a formality. After this, realistically they can't charge you with conspiracy, fraud or

receiving, when he's already been convicted of stealing it to gamble by Law Society. So - there's nothing for you to answer."

"I don't quite follow all this…."

"Frankly, neither do I"

"So what do I do?"

"Smile. Well - you can laugh if you want… next stop Law Society are going to have to pay off your mortgages, compensate you and meet my costs."

"I don't think I can take all this in yet"

"Just sit back and it'll happen. Go have a coffee now."

At lunchtime, across at their office in North Leeds, Graham Carter and Tony Heatherington poured over the papers strewn across the desk.

"'Ere… look at this will ya"

"Yeah – 'Shame and Disgrace'…. and a letter of confession found in his office…" and with a big grin "..think I've seen that letta somewhere before," followed by loud cackles of laughter

"'an d'yu know - 'ee was paying interest on mortgages to cover 'is thefts"

"Terrible… wot 'ee done" - more cackles

"Who'd 'ave believed it… not in me wildest dreams could I 'ave seen this….. Law Society publish that letta…. a confession found in his office!!"

They laughed on a while. Then Tony suggested Graham get away to avoid any immediate investigation.

"Makes sense - bitta Spanish sun would be good…"

"Gor right away - Mundi - and keep outta wey in meantime. I'll 'old things whilst your away."

"Right – I'll get the wife un kinds set"

So Graham left for two weeks sunshine. But things would not be so simple for him.

Louise called in after work:

"It actually had me in tears - how could they do this to you. I thought people were meant to have trials first." I held my hands up in despair – we are powerless against these types. Roger the butcher's Range Rover pulled up and in he walked:

"Here… thought you might welcome this" - obviously a couple of steaks

"Thanks - I don't think it would be too prudent to show my face just now… has anyone said anything."

"It's great - beats talking about ruddy weather with the old ladies all day. I can tell you - they all hate you - knew you were no good. You've been fucked mate - good and true - by your sort - Law Society." And he was gone.

Had I been on Benzos, or not as strong as I am mentally, I may well have topped myself at what they'd done. How would you have coped and reacted? Remember - you can't shout as no one, but no one, would listen.

I had a vow – to beat them and bring them to account before an honest court.

-'*I will never give in; I will return to fight you bastards for this…. one day… however long it takes… I will have my life back*'

Until then I knew I had to wait.

.

Simon Kaberry

C H A P T E R   S E V E N

'Charged'

The brutal Law Society-inspired media attack shook me - vilified by the nastiest published untruth. I plotted cold revenge - I'd get them one day - however long it took. Friends would be in short supply and my own family was silent.

By Monday and Tuesday it was all change. Police and CPS had to react to the Williams account that I was uncharged. Kerry rang - I was to be charged. I looked for the best from the worst - at least something was happening! I was still mulling my options when the phone rang again.

"Simon. Right - I've just spoken with Clarkie and agreed we'll attend at Weetwood at 10.00 a.m. in two days - on 4th (August) to charge you…"

I boldly told Kerry I wanted to do this alone - no lawyer at all.

"Don't be silly - you can't... I'm your man for this... I've years of experience."

"Sorry. I've made my mind up." No one else was to be charged.

"Well be it on your head."

- *'don't panic…. smile at adversity and it will never win'*

4 August: 9.55 am. I walked stoically into Weetwood police station - calm and alert, but deeply apprehensive. What could the charges be? I could hear Clarkie in the back room, muttering. He didn't agree with this, but CPS give the orders.

I knew the routine. I was being detained so the Charge Sergeant had to be involved and he would hear the charges put. Clarkie had a sheaf of papers. He formally read out in detail the fourteen Charges - it took a while. There was nothing in there which I had to fear. Without any facial expression I said to myself:

-*'I can beat this lot - but why Kang?'*

Then came the formal caution at the end of Charges.

"Do you have anything to say?"

He started to write 'No Comment' as I said…

"Yes. I have a statement to make…would you be so kind as to write this down please". I was firm and dictated slowly:

"I trust you acknowledge.... that I have been as helpful over the last fifteen months...as you have permitted me to be"

I like plans and traps; one day Clarkie would have to tell a court what that meant, when my counsel put it to him - that would open a can of worms.

Actually I felt sorry for Clarkie - *'he's been had - the two of us'.* - but - *'he's your enemy'* kept coming back. I was like ice - I don't often do panic, even as the roof collapses. Then you go for fingerprinting and mug-shotting – a highly demeaning experience; it was pre-DNA days. The Charge Sheet put me on bail to attend Leeds Magistrates Court on 9 October.

- *'Say nothing – but why two months away? It should be next week ... they're not ready are they?'*

"Come on, play the game. You go and see Mr.Macgill, and get weighed off"

"OK, OK - see you in court. Bye bye".

I set off walking back home, waving to him.

- *'That'll fox him - let him think I'm still the village idiot'.*

Charged with theft of over £600,000 – and there was a spring in my step; the rest would be 'taken into account' he told me. The uncertainty of the last fifteen months was gone. By the time I had walked back home, the decision was made to give Kerry one last chance. I couldn't risk all eggs with Freethcartright.

I lay on my bed to unwind, overlooking the sunny lawn, roses, garden with graceful lime and beech trees beyond. In the silence, reality struck home - I held the charge-sheet. Me - man of pride, trust and honour charged as worse than a common thief. *'SK... you're completely alone.'* What about Holly? I had promised her a good life, but I had let her down; would I miss her death - she needed me. Lying flat on my back, breathing slowly, a tear ran silently down one side of my cheek; they'd finally got to me. I didn't know I could do that! How would this nightmare end - would it end? A piercing headache sprang from my eyes across front to back of my head. I lay there a good hour until Holly wandered in to see where I was. How would you have reacted? to whom do you turn? One thing was certain – you would find nature's natural power to survive. We're all fighters really.

Next day I travelled to Kerry's Bradford office. Transport was no longer a BMW, Mercedes, Porsche or anything smart. As I parked up in Roger's butcher's white delivery van I thought
- '*holy humility, but at least I'm not wearing a white coat*'.
I signed the legal aid papers to fund Kerry's time and work.
"OK.   Now… I'm away for two weeks from tomorrow and I know you want an expert about these drugs.   I use Peter Wood here in Bradford and Judges listen to him - he tells me he knows all about them - been involved in several cases."
'*Peter Wood? - never heard of him in any of the mountains I've read about these drugs at Waterstones*' It can't get any worse.

"Well Kerry, if you say he knows benzodiazepines… that's fine. I'll give him a go."

The following Thursday at 10.30 in the bright summer sun again, I presented myself at Peter Wood's Consulting Rooms in Manningham. I was calm, relaxed and at my naughty best, ready for the worst.   I met an awfully nice chap about my age and height; flat thinning hair, neat and relaxed. I reckoned he had a wife and two children and small dog.   Conversation flowed readily. Calls himself a forensic psychiatrist, but…

He had read 'all about me' in the Yorkshire Post. And '*Kerry has filled me in*' – with what? We were together about an hour. I was smiling, thanked him sincerely and drove home where Louise was waiting; we had planned a day out to Lake District. Holly was sunbathing on the lawn, too lazy to greet me, save for the thumping tail on the grass, as she heard my voice. Louise always has that sheepish timid look of no confidence about her; she had been waiting without complaint - she was always waiting then and for years. I kneeled to play with Holly's silky ears and big tummy.

"Well then?" she offered – "it obviously went well?"
 "Oh yes; it went spiffingly well.   Fantastic…" - a smug look over my face
"Go on"-she knew that look. We sat on the lawn
" 'Well you see' " and I started to mimic my expert - 'I've got my reputation to think of. If I think a man is guilty I shall say so. I appear before these judges regularly - they've got to trust me to tell them what. I've seen people high on temazepam, rob banks, know nothing about it… but they're guilty. You probably ran out

of money in troubled times and helped yourself. These drugs affect memory, so you may not know. Racing you know - I've had experience of this - you can't win'... Nice chap - just what I needed - to remind me of who I don't want. He couldn't be worse for me - and he's the selected expert....." I was grinning as I stroked my best friend's tum-tum

"So why the mood?"

"Well - just think...consider my position - and of course I'm very well today - which helps"

I continued quietly, stroking Holly's floppy silky ears –

"I've just been made bankrupt for another mans debts under a guarantee I know nothing about. This house where I have lived all my life is no longer mine - I'm a guest. I have this beautiful big dog, who I adore, but can scarcely support. I have lost my career - proven guilty a thief. I have no money - selling off whatever I have left bit by bit to survive. Law Society - that wonderful august and honourable institution has published to media that I am guilty of stealing millions from innocent clients to go gambling all over England. Everyone simply accepts that lie, because it comes from them. I have no family - my friends have all gone; I walk in shadows because of it. I use a false name if I go to the dry cleaners. Now I'm charged with stealing over six hundred grand for starters – part of the two million. I am completely alone - my lawyers have done sweet FA to help me. I can't sleep and am often very ill, but I'm going to prison so that doesn't matter. The one man who could possible help me says I'm guilty without even knowing what it's about. So yes... I'm OK - really happy"

"Come on then... why the big grin – why the delight?"

"Don't you see. Surely, - *surely*" I emphasized – "I'm at rock bottom now... it can't get any worse, can it. From hereon it can only be up. So let's look forward to it. Come on let's go before the sun goes. I'll tie Holly up so she can wander in and out of the French Window and sunbathe on the lawn - fetch her water bucket. Chop chop. Let's go".

I shoehorned myself into Louise's little Peugot and we travelled over via Skipton, having a pub lunch on the way. Then up to Windermere, through the must-visit Kirkstone Pass and along the side of Ulswater, stopped for Afternoon Tea at Sharrow Bay – the lady took one look at my crumpled trousers held up by a dirty belt, etc and suddenly 'afternoon tea had just finished'. I was no longer a smart well-healed professional, but riff-raff; a very poor man. Then back via Angel at Hetton for an excellent supper. I was blind to reality, save Holly always came top - having called Ann earlier to feed her. When I got back, Petrina had been and taken Holly.

Back from his holiday, I spoke with Mike Thurston; I needed to lodge an appeal against Law Society and its Court.
"But now you're charged you'll never get legal aid for an Application to the High Court"
"I just want to lodge an appeal, and leave it outstanding"
"Well, you'll need legal aid and you won't get it." No help there. [His advice was wrong, but I didn't know that then. I'd left him with the Rules, which provide I could have appealed for free.] He assured me that if acquitted it would be plain sailing.

A letter landed on my mat from a new name 'Sue Head' at Law Society. She wrote that it was a criminal offence to hold myself out as a solicitor. My blood was boiling, as I rang her...
"I have a letter from you today about the fiasco in SDT and this ruddy welshman Williams - you know I was set up don't you? He lied like a trooper in Tribunal ... who instructed him?"
"You're offensive" - *Slam*, and the phone went down on me.
- '*my day will come... I'll get you bastards one day for this*'.

My weekly letters with Sarah Wade continued a few months yet, but my responses were now harsh and angry. In one vicious two page reply, I wrote of Williams (letter 25 August 1995) that I'd be in a witness box one day, and have him, but 'never sink to the depths he reached with such ease.' [Lord Bingham later ruled my letter was 'evidence of nothing' and none would ever be allowed]

August and September flew by. Kerry's promises to start work didn't materialize. Often I was very poorly. Paul Balen told me to 'wait' for an expert's report on the prescribing – now five months gone. I paced that Beechwalk every day, then up and down the 34 paces of the front lawn, exasperated. I was a powerless cog in the legal machine, selling off whatever I had left - by then it was books, all which I had planned to read in my older years at leisure

----

"Honour Among Thieves?"
Graham returned from his sunshine holiday. He went to their office in north Leeds - all was quiet. There had been over £100,000 in the bank; the account was now empty. At lunchtime a man appeared at his desk. Scruffy, short, aggressive looking aged mid fifties, with curly matted dark hair – not a nice man. He was wearing a long raincoat in summer weather.
"Hello Graham"
"I've seen you before - it's Frank isn't it?"
"Whatever - we have a message for you; you don't have business here anymore - right?"
With that he undid his coat and placed a sawn-off shotgun on the desk before him.
"And just to let you know, we know exactly where your kids go to school and where your wife works. It's time for you to go home. You don't have any business here - got it".

Graham was involved in something above him; ashen white, he shot home then straight to the local CID. He described this man 'Frank' and repeated the threats. A senior sergeant showed him some mugshots
"Yes - that's him"
Suddenly it was serious. I don't know 'Frank,' who is well-known to police; he dined out on stories of how in 1960s he was a henchman for the Krays. His surname ('K') is on the list of 'buyers' of flats at Howgate (found later) - a Bradford lawyer, called Fitzpatrick who later disappeared with millions 'missing' from client account, acted for him. That lawyer has never been found. The police sent Graham away for the weekend. Alarms were fitted directly to the station; armed units would be there within minutes. Tony owed men from way-back; they had got word he had money - much of which I was accused of stealing - as I was to discover only years later. This was later set before SDT, Lords Bingham and Phillips - who covered all up - "no evidence allowed in any case involving Simon Kaberry." – the greater good is to protect Law Society. "Independence" or Corruption and Deceit? – *you tell me…*

Sarah Wade wrote that any decision about Peter Harper's claim for compensation was 'on hold'. Truth was his claim was nodded through. Later I took what they had done to a Council Member of Law Society, Roger Ibbotson, who refused to consider any complaint about what Law Society had done; now he's a Judge. It's a big closed shop - worse surely than the church. I would expect members to skin him if they knew; I would!

August and September passed, and I was due in the Magistrates Court. Some days I was dead to the world and just had to write that day off – exhausted and tired, spinning head. Provided I could get three hours sound, continuous deep sleep, I was up for it. Still police hadn't served their papers - I didn't know what I had to answer. Kerry demanded I agree an adjournment.

"Sorry Kerry - they decided to charge me, so make them get on with it. Truth is, they'll never be ready."

"Come on - you know how it works, they're only going to ask for more time… and they'll get it." He agreed an adjournment to 2 January, and still did no work.

My mind was turning. Kerry and I were going nowhere together; he told me I'd be pleading guilty, so it made little difference. But I was reluctant to put all eggs in one legal basket with Freeths.

Paul Balen finally had a report from expert GP Dr.Scott. Having given hopeless instructions – he got a hopeless Report. I got him to re-do them.

I had scarcely enough money to keep warm as winter approached – times were not good; and nothing to do but think what would happen. Mike Thurston was a nice chap, but so laid back he was horizontal; I found Balen useless. Kerry's promises to start work weren't materializing – this was a big fear. Dr.Scott, now with additional information, concluded that my prescriber was completely in breach of his duties of care to me - 'top end stuff.'

Another TV programme reported on benzodiazepine problem. From their researcher Jim Booth I got the name of an organization in Liverpool called CITA. Someone called Pam Armstrong the Director may be able to help, as the expert lawyers were… umm?

I concluded that if I didn't sack Kerry, I'd be going where all his other clients were - prison! Kerry objected so the court clerks refused to transfer the legal aid to Mike Thurston. My Appeal would be before the Stipendiary Magistrate Mrs. Wright.

Just prior to Xmas I went to the Leeds Stipendiary Magistrates' Court. Humiliation, but 'needs must.' There I appeared before a tiny shrew-like woman peering down at me, snapping with a woodpecker's voice. She wouldn't 'let me delay this case anymore.'.. "You have an excellent solicitor in Mr.Macgill, who is well-known to us." I wanted to revert to my youth and shoot her off the telegraph line she was sitting on, with my air rifle. What a complete buffoon – she's not allowed to chose my solicitor. We argued for five minutes - no way would she 'allow me to delay this case anymore' - I must keep my lawyer.
"Madam. I have dismissed him. You cannot select my lawyer"
- *'this cow is trying to humiliate me'*. That'll shut her up.
"I have not. You selected him and he remains your lawyer"
"No - I have dismissed him. Only I can make this decision"
"Your application is refused. Legal aid must remain with Mr.Macgill. He is your solicitor"
- *'Don't demean yourself with this silly woman SK'.*

I left court fuming, walking, head down in seething, boiling anger, out and towards the bus stop - passed it… never stopping and all the way home. It took over an hour and a half. Time and drizzle had soothed nothing in my frustration. I left a message with Mike's secretary:
"….Tell Mike to threaten the cow with a Judicial Review. That'll stuff her. I'm sorry Theresa… I'm mild-mannered, but very… very, very….. angry. That bitch wound me up"

Christmas was just three days later. Out of the blue a good friend called for a chat and cup of tea. As Jim left he offered an Xmas hand to shake. As I put mine out, he stuffed a very large wad of notes into my palm – "here you are mate – try and have a better Xmas – things aren't too good for you, are they" and off he went. Tears welled up but didn't come out - I'm not very good at receiving. I went back inside and leant against the cold radiator, chin wobbling - £200: did I deserve such kindness.

2 January: Louise dropped me in town at 8.30 a.m. at the top of the walkway to the courts to ensure I missed cameras. The shrew had retracted - 'funding was transferred.' CPS finally served their bundle of 'Committal Papers.' The three lay magistrates duly 'committed' me to Crown Court.

[the system has since changed so that the cases are transferred to Crown Court much more readily and quicker - before committal]

Michael and I returned to Adel Willows to read over the papers - I was excited and needed to explain what there was in them for Michael, but quickly he took control

"Right - well I've got quite some reading to do" said he, pointing to the bundle of papers before him.

"Yes, but I promise you - you won't find what this case is about in any of those papers - I assure you."

He didn't want to know; no discussion allowed.

As I waved him away - I had a real fear within; had I leapt from frying pan to fire?

Simon Kaberry

CHAPTER EIGHT

Facing the Courts of Justice

It was the end of January - three months short of 2 years alone most days. By phone, Michael re-assured me he just needed to 'grasp the case' before seeing me, then starting investigations. But the truth and facts were nowhere to be seen in the papers.

Likewise Paul Balen knew nil of the facts in nine months - save, he'd read Law Society 'Findings.' We awaited Prof. Hindmarch's Report. 'Needs must' - I rang and told him a little of the real case. Pam Armstrong would also see me. But what I still couldn't follow was why they talked about tranquillisers – my problem was sleeping pills; I hadn't taken tranquillisers.

Waiting for both lawyers, I travelled to Liverpool to the 'Council for Involuntary Tranquilliser Addiction' (CITA). In a crotchety old building in a suburb of Liverpool, up some rackety stairs, I found this powerful individual with her super Liverpudlian accent and manner. Gingerish or auburn hair, in her late thirties, and full of an energy and vibrancy, yet able to listen. Some people you instantly take to – and she is one such.
"Well if you're looking for help about Benzos you've certainly come to the right place. But you tell me you've problems with police?" she said both snappily and with understanding - in that scouser accent.
I explained the brief history and the charges I was to answer.
- "Well don't go thinking you're the only one. There are *thousands* of people – awful cases. I don't know about civil claims, save that GP.'s need taking to task, but no one will do anything."

She continued in that sharp but warm scouser snappiness, inflected with tones of both incredulity and friendliness. She looks at you as she speaks; and you feel you can look back. As a lover this woman would be demanding I thought - '*stop eyeing up every woman you meet SK'*. She listened, understood, communicated, laughed, cried and joked with people – a real person with whom we connect quickly. She knew the subject - worked at it every day. This woman radiated warmth, giving me a confidence I had never had with 'expert' lawyers. She could talk to normal people using normal words. She knew all about Paul Balen, Oliver Thorold and their civil claim - 'they're a bit of a waste of space.' I was learning.

This was my expert. But she came with a major problem - no professional qualifications. I stayed some forty-five minutes – leaving with the 1988 Committee for the Safety of Medicines (CSM) Warning and Direction to all GP.'s not to prescribe any benzo longer than two to three weeks – thereafter one is addicted. They can make you confused and suicidal. I asked why there were no Dalmane cases and no work published on Dalmane.

She replied - sort of, was I dumb? Peter Ritson, co-founder of CITA, had published a book on how Dalmane had ruined his life. I wasn't alone. I'd met the real McCoy. And I liked her definition of a benzo person - "*it's as if all the lights are on - but there's no one at home.*" People could understand that.

Back home, Louise continued to spend her hard-earned savings on me. I didn't like it, felt awkward, but let it happen. I was on top of the world - I would win through. I phoned Ritson who warned me - "Simon - I must caution you: I've had grown men crying down phones to me... they're in prison and would never have done wrong... they lose it and become aggressive... you really have a battle... lawyers don't understand." - Freethcartright and Thorold are not the experts they claim to be.

February: Michael, without seeing me, sent me the CPS Case Summary, written by a young barrister called Robin Frieze in Leeds. I'd stolen all this money and admitted it - simple as that. Should I laugh or cry? Mike accepted it as true, and got my suitable comments, but did - zilch.

Professor Ian Hindmarch's did a 'first shot' unsigned draft Report supporting my civil claim fully. Dalmane is so long acting it '*puts and keeps the working mind asleep'*. Exposed to the drug for so long, could "*have had effects not dissimilar to dementia.*" At work I would not have been able to concentrate, and would have been '*divorced from reality'* – unable to see if I was being swindled.

When interviewed by police, in March 1994 – *"he would not have been able to give a good account of himself"* – that explains the confessions and police interviews. His conclusion was that the wrongful and continued mis-prescribing of Dalmane *had 'major and profound' effects on my thought processes, my ability to reason and understand reality.*
Now Balen arranged to see Thorold with me, in Conference.

The week before Crown Court of 16 March I attended the York Chambers of Aidan Marron QC. You have 'Consultations' with QC's (c/f 'conferences'). As a senior QC and head of Chambers, Aidan Marron cut a good enough figure, a few years older than me. We sat around the table:
"May I say this first" opened my counsel "and I direct this at you Mr. Kaberry, how sorry I am at these events. It must be quite sad for a professional man - a man from your background - to find himself in this position"
-'don't worry boy, soon you'll be expressing your horror at how I've been set up'
"However I must make this plain from the start... having read the papers... that the intention to plead not guilty does not seem to be well placed. I mean the chances of success must be so remote as not even to rate a mention on the Richter scale. However, I understand that is the present intention, and we must review the case. Now you're first time up next week, so time is not vital"
- 'oh Michael - what on earth have you been given my man in his set of Instructions?"

I hadn't seen Mike since committal, so they talked in circles for over an hour; rather like discussing the intricacies of a cricket match with a Scotsman, or curling with an Englishman. I referred them to my Report from Prof.Hindmarch - "but he is not a forensic psychiatrist" - said Michael.

As we finished, Marron took out some books:
"Now - I have researched a little on sentence guidelines - I don't want you to be shocked later at what happens; you must know what you are facing here."
He read from the head-notes: - "Professional man, breach of trust - £700,000 - eight years, another - ten years. Solicitor 3 million - twelve years." The warnings were starting - 'you're going down

boy - for a long time.' I was looking at 10-12 years in the opinion of my own lawyers. I smiled; well, what else does one do.
- *'oh dear SK..... what the hell have you done...this is worse than it was with Kerry.'* But - it could only get better.

My appearance in Leeds Crown Court arrived. Humiliation big time. Michael's friend from Doughty Street Chambers - Nicholas Paul - a colleague of Oliver Thorold, would represent me.
"Don't worry... I've put word to the Judge's Clerk that the Judge needn't read the papers" Michael re-assured me the night before. The Crown Court complex is in a precinct between the General Infirmary and the Headrow. Louise dropped me at 8.35 a.m. at the top, about eighty yards from the main entrance. I'd hatched a plan; I espied the cameras ahead of me. Heavy overcoat and flat cap on head, I walked as if going to work in the building behind the cameramen - opposite the court. They didn't know exactly what I looked like. Then a swift turn at ninety degrees, and I approached from behind them, at speed, so all they got was my backside passing them. *'Job well done'* said I.

I was before Mr.Justice Collins - a visiting High Court Judge. The place was busy with people I once knew, pretending not to know me. We moved up for a coffee and chat. Nick Paul was a man about fortyish, thin sallow face, straight shortish hair about 5' 9" with a quiet voice. One could not dislike him.
"Now they've put you before a red judge, and we've been told not before eleven o'clock. I understand you want to plead Not Guilty, and I gather Aidan Marron has advised you of the problems" said the man who knew nothing of the case or me, but was my mouthpiece; it's the system. As ever, I listened attentively. This was really happening to me, but I was cool. I had promised Holly I would be back for lunch, and she was well accustomed now to a nice piece of grilled chicken form Roger the butcher for lunch.
" 'Venue' - Michael tells me you don't want to be tried in Leeds"
"No. I'm already guilty here - no chance of any fair trial in Yorkshire." But of course they hadn't seen anything.
"OK. I'll raise it with the Judge. Again Mr.Marron has told you the chances aren't good." I put chances at 9/10.

There was no time to feel the humiliation as I made for the Dock in the big full court. I sat – the robed red Judge in my direct line the other side of the court. *'I wonder if he slept well? – stay calm -*

don't flinch' The clerk called out the case number and my name. I espied little Robin Frieze, with his papers spread out before him, ready to mislead the court. Over to my left, Clarkie sat with his superior officer. Next, four media boys and girls, waiting to pounce. I was enjoying this.

My man Nick Paul stood to address the Judge:

"M'lord, I appear for the defendant. I have an Application – possibly two Applications"

"Yes Mr. Paul" said Mr.Justice Collins.

"My lord the defence is not yet ready to proceed. This defendant was committed to trial just three months ago and we need time to prepare his defence, but especially to obtain a report from a psychiatrist"

"Mr.Paul. I have read the papers in this case and cannot see how a psychiatrist's report can possibly help you. I mean it may help me, but only as to sentence on this man."

I sat in my familiar unmoved straight-faced manner, wanting to shout out – "*I'm Not Guilty – this is one big set-up*".

My man continued: "My Lord - this is going to be a fight. The defence needs time to obtain a psychiatric report on this man's mental state at the time of the allegations."

I switched eyes left. The media boys smirked - 'he's already been convicted by Law Society; he's going to try to say he was nuts', Clarkie turned ashen - the last thing he wanted.

"Oh - a fight is it?" said the startled Judge

"My Lord yes, and it is accepted that this defendant has had the chance to enter pleas and has declined"

-'*oi - like hell I have declined - I want to*'

"And further My Lord, there will be an Application for change of venue for trial on the grounds of prejudice to the accused in Leeds."

"Right Mr.Paul. So far as the prejudice is concerned, I direct that Application be made to the presiding judge on this Circuit in writing. And I note that opportunity has been given to enter pleas, but the defence requests time. These reports should be obtained and served by the end of June. If you need more time, you must make Application. Bail is extended to the next Court to notify the defence." It was as quick as that, and I was out.

We retired to a small room; Mike's assistant Caroline took notes. Michael would arrange legal aid funding for a 'forensic' report from Prof.Lader and for me to see him in Consultation. Michael would also make application by letter to the Presiding Judge to move from Leeds. This would go before Chris Holland QC, now Mr.Justice Holland, who I knew as a thoroughly decent man.

As we left, a cameraman caught and filmed me all the way to the car; they dropped me home. I sat in silence to unwind; late afternoon the phone rang:

"Simon - it's me" said my sacked solicitor - "I was in court today... people are laughing; they say you're fighting this. Simon - I'd have had this finished weeks ago, so you could be planning a new life." (from prison)

"Well Kerry, that's why I had to leave you. I really am going to fight this... and beat it"

"Simon - you haven't a prayer mate, but I wish you well"

As soon as my lawyers started work the case would collapse.

The last two weeks of March passed. The lawyers did - nothing. Then lovely April started to fly past - still nothing. Will I ever sleep properly? Many days I felt like death warmed up - spinning head, tight chest and exhausted. Progress arrived; Balen told me a Conference with Oliver Thorold was arranged for 20 May. 'Yes, we are arranging for you to see Prof. Hindmarch as well' – 'No we do not need to see you'.

This is no way to run civil litigation or a criminal defence. Michael was instructing Prof.Lader, but refused to see me. What I hadn't had with Kerry was any 'quiet contemplation' – and I wasn't going to get it with these lawyers either.

A forensic report is based on a careful examination of the facts. No one knew them. But I had some peace of mind and was starting to notice life itself; things I hadn't in many years. My local blackbird perched on the finial above my bedroom started to sing before dawn - his pal was about a hundred yards away in a big oak tree and would sing back. April is a wonderful month – warmth and promise of things to come, the colours of the tulips and the greens of the tree's leaves as they slowly open. Drugged up I had missed so much - people and their ways. I grew to love the big lime tree forty paces to the back of the lawn behind the rhododendrons. It's leaves slowly open over three weeks, until the sky behind is blocked out, and then it stands there gracefully to autumn, flanked by the beeches, aside and beyond. To the front the chestnut trees come first and block the road from view, and me from it, by the end of April. One day this nightmare would be over.

Holly and I had our routines; each morning at 6.30 I would hear her coming up the stairs, and across the landing, whoosh my ajar door open, then I would stick my feet from the end of the bed, and she would rub her back all along, wiping the sleep from her eyes on the valance, appear at the side of my bed, for her ears to be fondled - then out to spend a penny and back (to bed). The start of each day. During the night I would lie there, feeling a little lost, and sneak down to talk to my best friend. They listen to all your woes and offer nothing but comfort.

At the beginning of May Prof. Hindmarch was visiting Leeds to lecture doctors, and met me at home. A very approachable man, we discussed things for over two hours. My inability to play chess, plan a campaign was important and typical – 'exactly that sort of thing would happen.' - "you wouldn't be able to plan a strategy or see what your opponent had in mind for you." Missing weekends would not give enough time to excrete the dalmane.

He told me of the sad cases in the 1970's of women, unable to cope with sad lives – who would see the doctor, and be offered valium. All it did was make them even more unable to cope, then beat up the demanding kids in exasperation, and find them taken into care, with mother blamed for being violent. 'Mother's little helper, was anything but…'

Mr.Justice Holland transferred my trial to Newcastle. I must attend on 16th July to enter formal pleas. First, Louise took time off work and drove me to London where we could stay with my friend of bygone years Elaine. I could sleep on the floor – *oh the joys of poverty*. On 20th &21st May meetings were arranged first with Thorold and the experts, and the following day with Nicholas Paul in the same set of Doughty Street Chambers.

Oliver Thorold joined us…early-forties, full crop of hair, nothing special to him. – *'this man?'* - there was something about him not right. I didn't like him; and I'd been warned by others.
My plan was simple - *'sit quietly and listen - these are the experts… let them help me… don't try to rule the roost'*
"Mr. Kaberry" said Oliver Thorold - "You back racehorses"

- '*are we in for a joke? ....maybe he does as well*'

"Umm.... yes; I've backed them all my life, or as long as I can remember. It's my hobby...."

"And in that habit, you have lost a lot of other peoples money"

-'*I don't like this man*'

"No"

"We'll see," responded my counsel quietly in obvious disbelief.

- '*You odious man ... but sit tight and watch – when he knows the truth...*'

"Dr.Scott - you advise that the prescribing by the doctor was negligent."

"Yes; initially I was a bit 'iffy'. But greater investigation shows, and with the supporting evidence, that the prescribing was constant, and there was no attempt - ever - to take Mr.Kaberry off the Dalmane. It was a clear breach of the recommendations by the Committee for the Safety and Medicines, and at a time when there was so much knowledge of the dangers associated to these drugs. I would say it would rank at the top of the spectrum of breach of duty of care to the patient."

- '*and he hasn't even noticed that my records were marked that I had an aversion to Dalmane in 1980*'

"Well, so far so good" offered my stone-faced counsel - "but what we have to consider is whether non-negligent doctors would also have tried to wean him off the sleeping pill."

-'*that's a barmy thing to say; he's just been told a non-negligent doctor would have been negligent!*'

Ian Hindmarch joined in. "I can help here. We have been warning for *years* of the dangers associated with these drugs and Dalmane in particular. At the very least he should have tried to put him on a shorter-acting pill, which could have avoided these events - maybe the shorter-acting temazepam, and find out the reason why he couldn't sleep. It seems there was no attempt to do anything"

"Thank you. I see. But there is this over-riding problem that when Mr. Kaberry was on Dalmane before, there was no stealing of money - in the 1970's - by him and other similar conduct"

- '*What the hell's going on....*'

"But there hasn't on this occasion either... I haven't stolen anything"

"But clearly, in your own words, you have admitted stealing it to gamble - you were windmilling client funds by your own admission - and skillfully covering up your thefts, robbing Peter to pay Paul" said my counsel.

"But… I thought, when writing that, that I was doing right – actually I thought perhaps I had, because that was what I was told I had done. But if one examines those confessions, you will soon see they are impossible."

-*'Jesus.... and this is meant to be a benzo expert...sit tight ...'*

It went round the houses for over an hour. Hindmarch said my actions could be explained by my attempts at 'firefighting' problems, but Thorold was determined - I had stolen millions to gamble.

- "To resile from your own written words will not be easy. Plainly, you did not suffer the common affect of amnesia, as you covered-up your thefts with care, by paying interest."

"There is then your alcohol problem. You were drinking two bottles of wine a day…. you have an alcohol problem, and we know how the courts view that"

"But the GP has accurately assessed my alcohol consumption at 2-3 glasses of wine a day and ½ a pint of beer. Look it's on my records - in 1992 for insurance purposes. I don't think that is excessive. Some days I never had anything at all to drink. It is properly recorded… I wasn't drinking anything like that…"

"No Mr.Kaberry you were drinking two bottles of wine a day"

"No I wasn't…. I wrote (in the draft given to Balen) that I used to sometimes drink that (in 1980's when having a boy's night out), but the GP has checked my real alcohol consumption accurately at 2-3 glasses of wine a day - its recorded in his handwriting. If one glass sent me tipsy – how could I drink two bottles – and when?"

-*'help me Jesus, this man knows nothing of me – stay calm… '*

Again, Ian Hindmarch joined in forcefully to help me:

"Mr.Kaberry never drank at lunchtimes, just after work at home with and before dinner – and he only drank top growth clarets. There is nothing in that to suggest he was some kind of wino – if he was, he would have drunk anything at anytime"

But Thorold would have none of it. "He was stealing money and windmilling"

"No I wasn't."

"Clearly, you are a racing loser with an alcohol problem"

-*'Gordon Bennett - couldn't I even be a womaniser too - a gambling, alcoholic womaniser - please!… this is <u>my</u> counsel!!'*

"Now, there is the problem of Limitation." A personal injury claim must be brought within three years of the '*date of knowledge*' that there is a claim.'

He then concluded that as the constant prescribing started in 1989, so did Limitation, and I should have sued in 1992/3 – when no one knew anything about this.

[The Limitation Date is actually April 1998 – three years after Balen told me I may have a claim, or even November 1998, three years after the Scott Report confirmed it.]

"As I see it" continued my counsel "you are going to have to establish at trial, that the Dalmane was responsible for your conduct, and to such an extent that you were an automaton."

-'*this is complete nonsense..!*'

"Now if you secure acquittals at trial - ***things will look very different***, and it would be good reason to proceed with this claim - which clearly will be costly but seek substantial compensation. But it seems to me that you will use the drugs' effects as mitigation of sentence only, and in that event, we will have to look at the Judge's comments after trial. The evidence of guilt is compelling. I am going to recommend that the files be closed, and we look again after trial and see where we are."

Hindmarch protested, but it was all pointless with this barrister. Concluding -

- "I have a duty to the Legal Aid Board not to proceed at this stage" - '*ah-ha......that's the problem..... you're frightened of taking any benzo case after wasting 35 million.*' (makes sense)

Pose this question. What would you have done in my shoes – and you're not allowed to say 'go top yourself!!' Or – is it that sinister feeling again; how can one barrister be so completely wrong, yet be called an expert.

[*Note*: this Conference is confirmed by Balen's notes - ie. it's not my version alone. This actually happened.]

I left Oliver Thorold, who then sent a three page 'Note' to trial counsel Nick Paul, which I found two years later.

A Summary of that internal secret Note is:

1. Clearly Kaberry should expect a lengthy sentence

2. The effect of Dalmane is no defence – he stole the money and wasn't confused, and cannot resile from his written confessions, which aren't explained by drug effects
3. The claim against the prescriber is already time-barred as my date of knowledge would be about 1989-92 – i.e. I knew Dalmane was dangerous – and kept taking something I knew was injuring me (the reverse of human behaviour).

No judge would ever let me take him to task for such incompetence. But this was just the start.

Louise took me out for supper in Kensington. I got enough sleep - maybe three hours on the floor. Next day I returned to Doughty Street Chambers for my noon Conference. No sitting back this time, I entered all guns blazing, very much on top form.
"Now Simon... reality time... I've spoken with Oliver. I'm not an expert, nor is Mr.Marron – so we must be guided by him"

I smiled at them. Big beaming smiles mean mischief's about when they come from me. I was on top form:
"For my part I want this to be clear and understood. An examination of the facts will show that - when someone does some work - these charges are nonsense. Yesterday I sat through a meeting with Oliver Thorold which was a fiasco... an utter waste of everyone's time and I'm not sitting through another one...Mr. Thorold hadn't *the faintest idea what this case is about*.....and what's more, I don't think he even understands the effects of benzodiazepines..."

I continued in my attacking and friendly manner, -"Williams...and the rogues in Leamington Spa... need shafting. I've told them I'm after them come trial" I was just into second gear. No way were they going to brow beat me as I was yesterday.
"Now - Simon; we're here to help you. We, as your lawyers want the best for you" proffered my junior counsel. "You mustn't blow the best chances you have; it may well be best to plead and blame the cause on the drug... for making you do as you did. If you fight it, you won't get any discount when convicted – you must take that into account" he continued.

It was hopeless. We moved on to 'expert for trial' and I was told Prof.Lader had agreed to see me. For the rest of the meeting they talked round in circles. Witnesses? - no, no need to discuss that. Accountants' report? no, no need either, until we know if the expert supports me. Tracing the money? - no, no need to do that. That I had no gambling accounts, nor been anywhere since 1990 - not important. There was no need to do anything.

PD hired a car for me to get to London to see Lader, but I had no money for fuel and other costs, and was due there at 2.30 p.m. I agreed a 'job lot' sale of possessions to my neighbours for £500 - a fortune to me. With the cash late arriving, it all went so wrong - for the most important meeting of my life. First, I put petrol in the car; it was a diesel. I spluttered down the M1. I arrived hot, flustered, dying for a cup of tea and a pee at 3.35 pm, just over an hour late. A pleasant elderly gentleman, slight of build but not small, with smart rimmed spectacles beckoned me straight in to his room. I was full of apologies, for a meeting with a stranger who may save my life, late, smelly, gasping, and bursting for the loo.
'Compose yourself... no one wants hard-luck stories... don't complain – be nice, outgoing and positive – be yourself '

"Now Mr. Kaberry" offered the extremely polite man, aged over sixty or more, "I received your fax (not to read anything) , but in the time waiting, I've read the papers sent by your lawyers."
I could see them – the confessions, case summary, and my draft statement that I can drink two bottles of wine a night.
-'Yea gods - try to get out of this one SK...'

I gave him an epitome of the facts and my knowledge now of the effects of these drugs.
"May I be clear - there was no way I could get away with what I was doing" referring to the fact that I was giving client money away without realising - "the pit wasn't bottomless - I like helping people and it seems my better nature took over. I am not a fool, normally and would never have done it - I had no chance and am clever enough not to have tried."

He made notes as I spoke, which later appeared in his Report to the Court. I smiled a lot and was completely at ease on the basis of presenting myself as a nice chap, but this was a losing battle. I dare not criticise my lawyers - he would report back any criticism I made of them.

"Well Mr. Kaberry - I'm not too sure how I can help you?"

"But I've given away my life for no reason, without even knowing."

That struck a cord with him. After forty minutes, I was out. *'Don't give in – it can only get better'*. Plan 'H' would have to be activated – I would return to Ian Hindmarch for trial as well as for the civil claim. Was I in a fool's paradise? Could anyone beat this kind of power?

The report was copied to me. It was written on an acceptance that I had done as alleged – as my own lawyers were telling everyone. I read it over a few times: the promising bits were in the conclusion:

> "*Mr. Kaberry would have fallen into a hole from which he no longer had the mental ability to climb...and...*
>
> .... "*There is a verisimilitude about Mr. Kaberry which just convinces me that... he was adversely affected by the Dalmane*"

"*His mind would have been like that of a chronic mild alcoholic, constantly under the influence of 2-3 units of alcohol*"

[Lader's real report comes later]

But this had to be tempered with:

> "*He told me he couldn't possibly get away with it*" and "*he says his better nature took over*"

Another meeting was arranged at Mike's office on 2 July with Prof. Lader. I was on top form, but quickly realised it was pointless - '*ruddy Nick Paul's here!*' At 3.00 pm Prof. Lader arrived, and I was asked to leave as three people who, between them, knew nothing of the facts, nor me, discussed my defence. Despite my protestations, the Report would now be filed, as drawn, with the Court and CPS for the Hearing on 16 July. Mike added a new pressure - who did I want as my counsel? Did I want the QC who said I should expect 8-12 years, or did I want his chum Nick Paul - who... was surely worse! - the mouthpiece of Oliver Thorold.

'*Umm ... thanks Mike, quite a choice?*'

With Mike filing a medical expert report that would condemn me, I spent the next days in quite some turmoil. The good was there – with a Report like that, CPS didn't need their own - mine did me.

Days later Newcastle Crown Court beckoned. Louise took time off again and drove me to Newcastle the night before and paid for our stay at the Copthorne, just along the quayside from the courthouse.

Deeply apprehensive, I reached court at 8.35 am; no cameras or media. Aidan Marron arrived just after nine and we spoke for a few minutes on the empty concourse of the court.
"Umm...can I mention that Report and the problems within it?" I then explained how it had come about.
"Mr. Kaberry, between you and me, I am sorry to say... that Report should never have been filed. It actually makes things worse for you."
- *'Glory be.... well, this is a start'*

Caroline Coles arrived and we then discussed any Directions and Witness orders. I told him I needed my August Interview – the Calibre interviews, the Harper Interview and my other 'confession.' He made Notes and repeated that the Lader report should not have been filed. Into the Dock and a thug of a prison officer took me into the back to frisk me for weapons; he refers to prisoners as 'scum'.

We were in and out in ten minutes. I formally pleaded Not Guilty to each Count. Trial would be 'later' - sometime. Louise and I drove back via the coast road to Scarborough and inland to Driffield where Petrina was then living in an attempt to revive her life in a relationship doomed to fail. She had Holly who was over the moon to see her daddy, but so was Petrina - things were not working out. Back we came with big happy dog in the back of tiny car. I had much to be happy about - things had gone as well as they could. Best was to have my dog back - my chum. Now I had to 'do something' about that Report.
What would you do? Come on...? think...

I attended a word-processing course in Leeds city centre, overlooking Millgarth police station – the home of Fraud Squad and Jock Clark. First day, just gone noon, I saw him walking up the Headrow...
- *'Got it... '*

It was a hairy long shot but for the next two days, over lunchtime, I walked up and down that stretch of the Headrow. Day three and I accidentally bumped into. Clarkie who stopped for a polite chat.

"Well, well" said I - so surprised to see him - "it's a small world isn't it"

"Hello Mr. Cabri and what are you doing down here."

"Learning ... learning - you know... life's tapestry. I'm at school over there (pointing). Anyway, as you're here, do you know when we're likely to have a trial?"

"You'll have to talk to your lawyers Mr. Cabri - not me. You know the rules"

"Well it depends on your witnesses - come on, any idea?"

"Next year - probably April time - that's what I'm told....

"Oh god - that far... anyway, it'll give us time to sort out the medical report. What did you make of it?"

"Don't know what you're talking about"

In précis I said - "Go on... you must have been shown a copy. Anyway, it's a load of nonsense. Let me tell you how it came about. I borrowed a car, but put petrol in a diesel... then I got lost and delayed and arrived an hour late – so we never got around to talking about the real facts... it's a nonsense report - he had no brief of the case!"

"I've no idea what you're talking about. Anyway – got to get on. See you about"

We had chatted for about three minutes. He had been walking uphill, away from Millgarth. He left me turning back to his office. I would live in hope.

I sent seven witness statements to Caroline. Best was Joanne who had worked for me since she was a little office girl in 1986 - I told her she wouldn't understand:

"But Mr. Kaberry... after I stopped working for you, I had trouble with my husband ... the doctor put me on Valium ... and when I went back to work, I couldn't work. I was still taking Valium. I would sit down and say 'right – do a search' – but I couldn't. 'Your mind just hits a brick wall, doesn't it?' So that's why you were giving us all the work to do ... you couldn't do it!"

 -'*Oh Joanne - you little angel...* Now, say that in court.

Simon Kaberry

CHAPTER NINE

'The strategies of a legal defence team?' -

Planning for your own trial is actually quite exhilarating. Well - I had something to do at last. August passed, and my health was steadily improving, although still losing many days. Since March, my lawyers had done – nothing.

I took statements from ten witnesses in all, which the competent Caroline Coles had typed up, speaking by phone with a couple only. Finally on 2 September 1996 I presented myself again at Freethcartrights offices at 11.00 am. for our 'strategy meeting' with Aidan Marron, Nick Paul, Mike Thurston and Caroline Coles. How much would that cost the taxpayer? – all day job. I was assured and up for it - my quiet determination and pleasant demeanour very much to the fore. At 12.15 they had finished "a lawyers conference" and invited me in.
"Now Simon" started my solicitor. - "before we address the issues, we have a serious situation of your indiscretion to address first. You have been talking out of turn and it has caused a major problem" in slow, exasperated but firm tone.
 - *'Look contrite - you know what's coming'*.

My well-conceived but highly improbable plan had hatched in spectacular fashion. I hid my glee, as Michael Thurston explained that Jock Clark had recorded all in his Police Pocket-book… 'The medical Report is a load of rubbish etc.etc.' CPS sent a copy to my team.
"You do realize what you have done… you have undermined the credibility of your expert witness."
 - *'Brilliant…could this have been better - act simple'*.
"Oh dear - I'm so sorry, but perhaps we can fall back and call Professor. Hindmarch, as you said Michael"
"I said no such thing. You can't have two experts in one trial"
 - *'Don't flog it SK - at the moment its mission accomplished'*
Then I suggested calling Pam Armstrong as expert instead
"You can't do that; she has no professional qualifications."

We had lunch nearby and reconvened the meeting. I was asked to re-appraise my determination to plead guilty. My only defence in law could be an intention, however improbable, to repay the money I stole.

"Your only case - you intended to repay the money," said my QC. *'this is nonsense - first they have to prove I took money, then that I acted dishonestly.'* This was the result of the lawyer's discussions. -*'wait... do it my way later - stay quiet for now.'*

But I did persuade Aidan that Prof. Hindmarch was needed as expert to 'set the scene' so that a jury could understand me when I said I lost the ability to work. He would give a 'general report' on the general effects of Dalmane. To fund his time, Aidan would write 'an Advice' for LAB. Malcolm Lader's report was never discussed again.

In a criminal trial, the defendant is now required to disclose 'the nature of his defence in a written Reply' to the Case Summary, but prosecution can still be taken unaware. The only Defence Witness Statements that the prosecution is allowed are any Expert Reports that may be called. But defence gets all the prosecution statements. In this case, CPS held Prof.Lader's report but there was nothing for them to rebut - it concluded I may have been 'made reckless' - they were perfectly happy with that. My 'team' didn't grasp that that mental state explained the written confessions – made recklessly. We finished the 'strategy' - no need to see witnesses, or trace cheques.

"I reckon we're all up to speed now" concluded Mike. I smiled - *'Yes - up my bottom at speed Mike.'*

September and October passed; no one did any work and I broke my leg; Louise pampered me. I posted my detailed 'Answers to Charges' to Mike. He thanked me - and did - nothing. By December I was fretting on crutches - we'd lost a year and just three months remained. Hindmarch hadn't been instructed. To all problems there is a solution - do it! I rang Pam; I would get her there. By Christmas 1996 the uncertainty and dark days weighed me down. The human spirit has its limits of endurance – I was going to lose. Could I sack them? How could I do it alone? No one else could possibly take over at this stage.

My state of mind was exasperation. Christmas Eve was spent as ever for the last twenty years with good friends and their family, but I was an outsider to everything normal in life - what did they know of life and its problems? Louise came for Xmas day lunch which was as good as ever; even a bottle of Corton Charlemagne, funded by my sales – as if to prove I was in a dream world. This could be my last Xmas as a free man; I knew that.

I started to prepare my speeches in court, as I lay sleepless yet tired, and as I walked each day up and down the Beechwalk. Had I gone quite barmy by then – three years on my own; one thing was with me each day – *'I'll get you one day Williams'*.

Finally Prof. Hindmarch's excellent 'general statement' arrived. Again there was nothing to concern CPS as it wasn't specific to these facts and me. I wrote Pam's Witness Statement based on her book – 'Back to Life.' Peter Ritson could come over from Spain, and explain to the jury that I was far from alone. Lawyers should have done all this; now – how do I get them to call these witnesses? On 5 February, I made a Journal entry that I felt like shooting myself – I had flashbacks of events and of the lawyers meetings. These are not experts.

Eight months on, Oliver Thorold finally wrote his Opinion, dated 25 February 1997. It reflected all his misunderstandings of the facts and me – *and the effects of the drugs.* The Opinion concluded 'only *acquittals would be good reason to proceed.*' But I was an alcoholic gambler! I sent a stinker of a letter to Paul Balen - 'Thorold was "wasting my time." It did me no good.

Mike finally agreed I could see the Marrow on 4 March with just 4 weeks to trial left. I took a 3-page typed complaint of all the work that hadn't been done, and setting how my counsel should present my case, cross examine police and expose the The Law Society Sting. Hindmarch must give evidence about the drugs before me, so I had a jury verdict on their effects.

Louise dropped me in York at 9.20. This was a vital meeting. Aidan Marron took control and my momentum was lost. I was being told. He maintained that my defence was an intention to repay the money I hadn't stolen - my only defence in law.
He threw one allegation at me
- "You stole the money and fabricated false entries in the ledger"
 - "No, I didn't... I have never stolen anything"
 - "...then where is the money - what is this entry?"

- "...I don't know... I guessed and guessed wrong. I asked Mike to find that cheque – it will tell us a lot"
- *'Help me, they don't understand.*
If they read the client file they'd soon see it is an open book - I wrote telling everyone I hadn't redeemed and why.
- "Well it's your books - your handwriting.... you must know"...

I kept my cool, as we toured on, getting nowhere. As lunch approached, I put two copies of my complaint on the table whilst Aidan continued to question me. Mike started to read one. I saw him turn the page...
"Hold it-hold it-hold it..." he snapped in angry tone. "I'm not standing for this one moment... Aidan you'd better read this... something Simon has produced" and handed him a copy, but swiftly turned on me....
"I'm not standing for this one minute... don't you go setting me up Simon.... that's what you're trying to do isn't it" he barked.
"No... I'm setting out my concerns as any client should, so that his lawyers understand his position".

Moments of silence as each lawyer read my complaints – about them. They stood and paced the room, as I remained seated. Aidan, still reading, guffawed:
"Huh... he even calls me incompetent here..."
"No - I say that you don't know the facts as you don't have them."

Silence as they both read on. One circled me as the other paced the room. Two angry professional men criticised by their client. Snapping with a lawyer's indignation Mike came back shouting:
"I have told you time and time again – you cannot blame Law Society" – as he read of the Sting of July 1995. (what had my own lawyer agreed with Williams that fateful day I left it to him?)
Aidan boomed at me –
"For god's sake man – *take responsibility in life*. You weren't fit to be a solicitor. Law Society has *every right* to do as they did."
I remained seated as they paced about me, in no position to force this. They each had flushed cheeks in anger. Mike wasn't done with me:
"It's no good saying – 'I'm an honest man, I wouldn't steal anything from the man on the corner shop.'... and then quietly think 'ah but helping myself to fortunes from banks and building

societies is different - they aren't human,' - we've heard it all before Simon; it doesn't work… the principle's the same."
-*'Oh you bastard Mike…'.*

'My own quiet way' was no good with this lot. Quickly that old rule of life took over - *'Don't fight a battle on their terrain - retreat… wait… your time will come… back down… 'Conciliate':*

The battering continued all afternoon - 'Why did you write that' – 'why did you do that' - 'why did you pay the interest if you hadn't stolen the money' - 'what do you mean, there weren't any accounts?' – 'Don't be silly, you must know what happened' - 'you had an arrangement with Harper didn't you?' - 'Well, that's your only defence - an intention to repay'…. 'don't be silly, you must have had one.'

"Er… Simon wants to call Mr. Kang as a witness, you know!"
At 6.00 pm we parted, each one of us exasperated by the futile meeting. Michael dropped me at a Little Chef on the A64 between Leeds and York, where I had arranged Louise would pick me up. One hell of a mental beating had been taken by SK. Tears filled my eyes for I was so alone - my hopes were pipedreams - I could not win. They hadn't looked at one single account, any file, and traced no cheque.
"You look dreadful." I hadn't seen Louise arrive and was sitting with a blank expression, staring at my tea.
- *'Don't let her see they've got to you – have some pride SK'*
"No - I'm fine."

A quick pint of Tetley's, followed by mixed grill, and I was back on song. Knackered, I slept a fantastic four hours and arose ready to recommence battle. Next day….. faxed to PD

5 March 1997

Dear Simon,

"As you know I was considerably concerned by the contents of a document you produced… (At yesterday's meeting)… That …criticised both counsel and this firm, you repeated that criticism and went further. …you have indicated that you do not have trust and confidence (in us).

"After conference...you told me you were frustrated. That may be right, but you repeated the criticisms in conference. This must be resolved. I must warn you that any retraction may not be enough, if you wish counsel and me to continue to act; you must countersign this letter and so confirm:
a) That you wish us to continue to act; and
b) You withdraw your criticisms and verbal comments and criticisms, explicit and implied, that counsel does not understand the case or see your point of view, that I did not see your point of view and have continually thwarted you, and that I am responsible for the fact that your poof of evidence is not yet prepared

> *I retract my complaints and wish you and counsel to continue to act for me*
> ....
> Simon Kaberry

If I would not sign a retraction of my complaint, Freethcartright, and counsel Marron QC - four weeks before trial, would walk out on me: I signed, now holding evidence for an appeal. Three days later, I rang Michael with the hope of mending bridges. He'd gone on his annual skiing holiday.

With the cat away, this mouse could play. I posted Pam's Statement to his secretary, for filing at court and with CPS. Expert Statements three weeks before trial are not generally allowed, but one lives in hope. On Saturday mid-afternoon, two weeks left only, the stress of it all finally got to me; I just keeled over, dead to the world for five hours. I awoke re-charged; was this really happening to me. If I 'lost it', I'd lose.

Mike returned. The Harper interview was typed up (but not the critical one of August).
"It's cost us £700 to have that done, Simon, and there's nothing in it which can help you."
"How do you know? I haven't even seen it yet."
"I sent a copy down to Nick Paul. He's gone over it in fine detail... a complete waste of money."
"What about Mr. Marron – what's he got to say about it?"
"We don't trouble leading counsel with worthless information."
I changed tack...

"Pam Armstrong... now, you'll have seen, she's signed a Witness Statement and she's willing to attend for free, I just have to know she'll be called if I get her there."
"Yes I've seen it... and I've served CPS and don't foresee any real problem." Again, it was non-specific.

I needed funds or would have to spend trial in Durham prison during trial. I tried my brother, Andrew, for help but hit silence again – 'you're on your own' remained the message. Without hesitation Kit arranged funding for me to get to Newcastle and stay and be fed for three weeks; more than I needed. Years later, I haven't had the ability to repay him.

Your lawyers should examine unused police material and evidence months before trial; it can throw up all sorts. Mine couldn't be bothered, so I went alone. Clarkie had closely dissected my personal Lloyds Bank Account statements, and paying-in books, looking for evidence that money had been paid in from client account or the like; no it hadn't. He knew damned well I'd had none of this money. Among my personal files, I saw a copy of my winning bets of August Bank Holiday - over £100,000 for a £70 stake – that was the source of my admission of losing £100,000.
"If there's anything in there that you need for trial, your lawyers must make formal requests and it'll be there." They didn't.

Thursday 27 March before Good Friday, Louise dropped me in York for our final meeting. Mike brought a new girl Kate Moyler who would attend trial as their representative. I had received a copy of the Harper interview, littered with useful information... I was *'like Father Xmas visiting daily'*. ... I became *'quite eccentric'* and ... an *'easy touch'* for money. Vital stuff for the jury to hear. Why hadn't he been charged? What about the others? "No-no, there's nothing there to help us" said re-assuring Michael to Aidan Marron – "Nick Paul's been over the interview for us with a fine toothcomb." I had wasted their time demanding it and likewise my interview of August, which they never got.

Louise took me to case Newcastle - important to pick a convenient hotel. Then Richard Aston loaned me a Polo car, and I drove to Newcastle in spring sunshine of Monday 7 April. My spirits were high for no one could stop my reaching that Box, arriving at 4.00

pm for a Conference. I was there to talk and win, but what a way to go to trial.

- *'Chin up; keep smiling - never let the buggers get you down'*

CHAPTER TEN

No Ordinary Jury Trial

Having done nought for three years, this was exciting. My chance to expose the Sting. Yet I also had an enemy within to defeat - my own legal team. Adversity brings out the best in us, and my health was A1 as I arrived for the Conference.

Over that famous bridge; left, left and left again, under it, and I was parked up on the quayside, diagonally across from the Crown Court. The Grand National had been postponed since the bomb scare on the previous Saturday. It was to be run at 5.00 o'clock that Monday.

"Right" offered a cheerful Mike "where can we watch the Grand National? And come - you're the expert - who's going to win?"

"Well, I've backed Suny Bay and doubled it with Sleepytime for the Guineas.... but I'm not so sure now after this delay…"

"Why - what's the difference in three days?"

"Fine weather and about 15,000 people walking and rolling the course from good-to-soft to firm."

They looked at me - '*idiots going down for years and he's had a bet for a race in a months time!!*'

We left all the papers and retired to the adjacent pub to watch the race. Suny Bay came second. Then they all left for their various hotels. Silly me for expecting a trial and strategy appraisal.

The following day proceeded as I have already related - go straight to prison without passing 'Go.' The gaping hole in the prosecution case was there for all to see; there isn't often real evidence of something that didn't happen.

Day 2 - Wednesday and again I was in court for 8.30 am.- cameras would never get me. But I'd hardly slept and felt dreadful; confidence replaced by pain and exhaustion. My team came later at ten o'clock, but had nothing to say. I had read all the prosecution witness statements, and admitted all bar Law Society and Paul Kang, who had done as I instructed him initially, and said the money was to buy a house; that had now backfired on me, save Law Society had paid him £20,000 plus interest. Defence can 'admit' a witness statement in which event, the prosecution can simply read the uncontested statement as evidence, or call the witness and risk cross-examination of that witness. There are tactics here, as oral evidence has far greater impact - but then the witness may dither, or say things in cross-examination best unsaid. If a defendant thinks he may be able to get something useful from a prosecution witness, he will call him. I admitted all the prosecution witnesses, bar Paul Kang – and the Law Society and Clarkie; all three were actually my witnesses – if questioned properly. That presented prosecution with a problem – how to interest the jury.

Hatton was to call a number of Building Society staff to prove I received the money, and two of my clients who I felt may help me. Not one accountant - surely my 'team' could understand? Then *'Hang on… there's no Paul Kang in this lot to be called - what's going on?'* My lawyers had admitted his statement – against my repeated instructions. Hatton, having taken the jury over their bundles of papers and statements and bank accounts, now had to prove his case and allegations. It was quickly boring; listening to managers confirming they sent me money and evidence to show it being banked - correctly - nothing hidden. From the corner of my tired eyes I reckoned the jury was bored as well. He was proving what was readily admitted. I had done nothing wrong; save he said that paying interest on six accounts meant I was 'covering up my thefts.' But - what thefts? He showed how the balance in the Accounts kept falling, but never showed where any of it went.

Day two finished. I beat media on day three as well. But I had slept, re-charged to fight:
"Can I have a word with Mr. Marron please?"
My team joined me in the small consulting room outside the court. I wore my dumb look.
"Yes, what is it Mr. Kaberry"
"Well, I've been going over this schedule of prosecution witnesses - there's no Mr. Kang. When's he being called?"
Exasperation sighs all round again.
"We've told you many times and you agreed. He isn't to be called. You admit his signed statement"
"But I don't... I have said so many times. I do not admit it"
- 'Keep your cool SK; anything different is pointless… look dumb - you know you're good at that'

"But you've been warned - Mr. Kang will say he gave you 20 grand in cash to buy a house and you admit that. You then stole it. Surely - can't you see that challenging that evidence will only make things worse for you? Your case is that you were confused, and somehow came to take it as yours" stated my QC.

Nick Paul nodded in smug disbelief.

- *'Keep cool... hold your ground... ignore these buffoons'.*

"But I've told you... it's in my answers to charges - he was not buying a house. He had just bought one. How many houses does he want!! What house was he buying? Where is the file? Why didn't he ask for his money back in seven months? - no one gives a lawyer £20,000 for seven months – and never says a word - this was a commercial loan to Harper. I can't admit what isn't true. Look – I wrote to him that he didn't want anything in writing... how can you buy a house with nothing in writing?"

The allegation sucks.

"But you've admitted it ... the jury have your confessions" stated the hopeless Nick Paul again.

"As I've said so many times, those confessions are meaningless... they don't fit the facts... I've admitted all sorts that isn't true"

"But you wrote them..."

"And they're utter nonsense - I was suicidal - cared not a jot.... they can't be true!"

I was required to sign formal instructions to have this prosecution witness called up from Leeds, against professional advice. I signed and wrote instructions that Marron QC must ask 'which house he was to buy' etc. I was then sent back to Coventry.

Next witness up was Barrie Mayne, the Law Society 'Fraud Investigation Officer.' I've no idea who he is, or what he knows of the truth. Formally, Barrie Mayne told the Jury I had been admitted a solicitor in 1974 and in March 1991, I had been fined £2,500 for failing to file Accounts in 1989/90 and ordered to file Accounts each six months or not have a Certificate to practice. He omitted the June 1992 Inspection when there was nothing missing. In March 1994, my practice had been closed after non-filing of any Accounts since 1990 and then 'shortages' were found in my Accounts. In July 1995, I had been struck off the Roll of Solicitors and was 'disbarred.' The jury had no detail beyond that plain fact.

Marron QC stood to cross-examine him.

"Mr. Kaberry was fined £2,500 in January 1991 and ordered to file Accounts each six months thereafter, or have no Certificate to practice?"

"Yes - that's right"

"So... he would have known and understood... as any intelligent man would realise.... is that fair comment... that at *any stage thereafter*, Law Society could call to examine his Accounts... and if they were wrong... he would lose the right to practice. He was on a *'Final Warning'* in 1991 - fail to keep and file proper Accounts, or do anything wrong - and his career is over"

"Yes; that sort of thing"

"So... he should have filed Accounts... first in January 1991... then...in July 1991...in January 1992... in July 1992...in January 1993... in July 1993... and in January 1994... that is on *six or seven separate occasions*, yet he filed none... and the Law Society... did nothing... is that right...and, as you agree, he must have known that *on any day* in those years, your office could have rightly closed his practice? And he would have lost his career - bizarrely, an intelligent man simply ignored a serious final warning... and indeed, things got worse"

Before he could answer, Judge Hodson joined in....

"Mr. Mayne: what on earth was going on in the Law Society?"

"I don't know sir"

-*'Aidan - I like your point..... I must have been nuts not to give a toss, but come on, finish the poor man off – The Sting.'*

But it didn't happen.   No one knew of the 1992 investigation that there was no shortage then. Judge and jury would never know the critical evidence of 'The Sting' in July 1995, and the consequences - why I was on trial, not those with the money. Marrow sat down.

More boring Building Society evidence was called to prove the admitted. We all dozed. Early afternoon and Mr. Kang stepped into the Witness Box. A little man with a big turban, wispish beard and great heart. I like him. This would be tricky. If he told the truth, he would be in bother for not keeping to his signed statement – that's perjury. If he didn't, I would have a problem. There had to be a half-way house. He wasn't fazed by the experience at all. Hatton QC questioned him.

"Mr. Kang - you are an Inspector with Bradford Metro?"

"No sir - I am not"

- *'you old goat... I know this trick'*

"Oh – I'm sorry…er…I thought…" Hatton started to fumble…
"No sir…I am *Chief* Inspector". He got his laugh but only from the jury.

Hatton then took him through the signed statement. In November 1993 he considered buying a house, so took £20,000 in cash, to my office (no one knew it was 7.00 pm in a brown paper bag and he didn't even get out of his car!). A week later I sent him a receipt by way of letter. The jury had it - two paragraphs only. It reads that he had given me £20,000 but didn't want a receipt and I wasn't to write to him. It identified no house or price and set no time scale for when this would happen. Paul Kang's evidence then was that I had no permission to use that cash for any other purpose; it was his money. The inference was that I had stolen it. It wasn't banked in client account like all the other money. So this was different to all the other charges. That concluded his evidence.

My man stood to cross examine him. I prayed - in vain. Mr. Kang agreed I had been his solicitor over many years and we had worked together, but he said I had become 'forgetful in recent years' (I hadn't done anything he had asked). He agreed that I had mentioned a fish and chip shop and that a friend needed a loan. But the £20,000 was for a house - not a fish and chip shop (he had to say that, or be done for perjury). My man never pushed or raised my instructions - nothing about why had he instructed I could never write to him about the house, why it was delivered at 7.00 pm, how the price would be raised, or why he had never, in six months, contacted me at all. His 'file' sat in CPS papers – there was nothing in it bar that one letter – nothing one would expect. None of them – Judge or jury were allowed to know this.
- *'Jesus, help!'*
It was not going that well for me; Paul must have sensed it. - so he threw this line in:
> "If Mr. Kaberry wanted money for anything all he need do was ask… he knew that - not just twenty thousand - maybe forty thousand…. whatever he needed, all he had to do was ask - and he could have it - he knew that", for he trusted me.

My man left it in that unsatisfactory manner. You read about barristers destroying witnesses - not in this trial.

Suddenly - good news. The Almighty had answered one of my Prayers. My lawyers said Prof.Hindmarch could not give evidence before me, scuppering my trial plan. Without warning, Kate Moyler told me that Prof. Hindmarch was arriving in Newcastle that night, to give evidence tomorrow. He had to go abroad to lecture and was not available next week. It's tactics - the order you present any case can affect the result.

So as an independent expert and officer of the court, he would give evidence during the prosecution case, of the general effects of Dalmane. Judge and Jury - maybe even my own lawyers, may just then understand my evidence. I saw him for a most enjoyable evening chat after dinner, but, quite properly, he refused to discuss the facts. Another Merlot arrived; I declined; he did it justice. Thorold would say he was an alcoholic.

We discussed how drugs work: - changing the brain computer
"No this is general... but a benzo doesn't just go to part of the brain. It sedates all parts and goes all over the body. So, in your case, its primary purpose – the reason you took it – was to send you to sleep, by sedating the brain as a hypnotic. But Dalmane and a number of others in this group don't stop working when you wake up. It keeps the working brain sedated, so it affects the daytime processes... so you can't work things out, as you would have done before. The processor is changed - sedated; thus your 'responses to information' or 'conduct' is not as it would have been. Your reaction time is changed... you can't react to information as you would have... the computer has been changed for - you can't process the information as you did before"

I never slept, just lay there trying to rest. Next morning he brought a short Supplementary Statement with six copies for the court.
It reads:
"Mr. Kaberry regularly took 1-3 pills (15-45 mgs) of Flurazepam (Dalmane) each weekday for a number of years. In those circumstances, it is my Opinion that he would have been in a constant state of drug induced intoxication...... synergised with the ingestion of alcohol with dinner.

"Under the general effect of such intoxication, Mr. Kaberry would undoubtedly have been confused and somewhat detached from what was happening in the "real world". Most importantly, his

cognitive abilities (including memory, intellectual functions, comprehension and understanding) would be severely compromised, <u>although he would not necessarily be aware</u> that such a devastation of his intellectual competence and judgmental abilities had taken place. Further.... he could well appear unreasonable or, conversely, <u>accept other persons' unreasonableness without demurring</u>"

Drained, I arrived at court at 8.30 to miss the cameras, followed by Ian Hindmarch at 9 and my learned QC at 9.45 – his only meeting with my expert. I suspect my man agreed with Hatton that this vital supplemental evidence could not be heard because it was not released in advance; it just 'disappeared' - more defence evidence on the Cutting Room floor.

Into court and Marron QC took the professor over the original Report. I précis the judge's version in the Summing-Up in the next chapter. I reckoned, despite my spinning head, that Judge and jury got about a third of what I had wanted.
 - *'Was it enough - why the hell drop the vital Supplementary? '*
We all are powerless; once you pick a barrister, you are in his hands. Just like a surgeon I suppose - we have to have blind faith. I was resigned to having to rely on my secret weapon – Pam.

Hatton stood to cross examine:
"This is all well and good. But how did these drugs affect Mr. Kaberry – *if at all"*
"I don't know. I cannot tell you. I do not pretend to link anything he has done, with Dalmane. My understanding is that he has dealt in strange ways with large sums of client money. But what he has done, I cannot say. My Brief is only to give this court a general Report on possible effects of Dalmane"
"So, you don't know he covered up his thefts – the thefts he wouldn't have known anything about?"
-*'Jesus; help - this isn't cricket '*
"No. As I say I have no knowledge of the intricacies of this case, only that money went missing"

His evidence was finished and court finished at noon. My legal team departed, leaving me to thank my expert.
"I'm sorry Simon... I feel I've just been torpedoed by our own side" offered my expert once we were alone.

Once the cameramen were gone I drove down the A1 back to Leeds in the VW, so exhausted, and in real physical pain, I was holding my eyelids open as I drove in the April sunshine. It was Friday and court would reconvene on Tuesday – someone needed Monday off. I was losing. Back home, I rang Michael at his Nottingham office.

"Michael; I'll be straight - I'm not happy. Nothing's going right"

"Oh dear, I'm sorry you feel that way – but you were warned. No - you insisted to do it your way. I heard about Kang... but I gather there wasn't the disaster I feared" said the laid-back-as-ever solicitor.

I explained no one would talk or ask the right questions.

"Look - write to me, and I'll see what I can do"

I turned on Split Ends for her 6.00 o'clock Calendar YTV Report. She was actually better than the evidence in court. She reviewed some of the limited evidence - it would change the way I saw things - make me liable to behave irrationally.

Petrina called in. My beloved dog was staying with her parents. With a smile she offered:

"Sounds to me from that, as if Dalmane made you steal loads o' money to back sedated horses!"

"Great.... thanks - just what I thought"

Knackered by the events, I slept deeply, maybe 4-5 hours, to find my batteries completely re-charged on Saturday morning. By 7.00 am. I was looking over the peaceful lawn from my desk and drafted a three page letter for Michael, setting out numerically all that was going wrong, and, still holding Richard's car took it to a typing agent to type and fax. It was a hard-hitting letter.

Then I drove to Liverpool to see Pam Armstrong and meet Peter Ritson - as personable and forthright a man as I could have needed. Peter feared the worst - "Simon... I'm sorry, but we've had this before. Lawyers don't understand". I was lifted by the pessimism; my judges weren't the lawyers. These two were open people, good witnesses, who I had to get to court.

Life goes on even when on trial - Sunday was for country walking with Louise. Monday, I packed the house up and she drove me to

Newcastle after her work. I arrived first as ever on Tuesday morning at 8.35, on top form – calm, assured and in control. Aidan Marron arrived. *'Oh that look!'* He stayed in the Robing Room. Kate and I sat in silence. I couldn't love her however hard I tried. If she called me her client once more, I'd throttle her. But far from my complaint making him talk to me, I was now in Coventry. Nick Paul arrived late at 10.40 and we all went into court. I was cool as a cucumber and strong enough to lead a battalion, but smelled rats. The Judge came in.

'Aye-up – no jury; summats afoot... Marron had obviously put word through... he's going to walk out on me '

"My Lord" said my man - "I am obliged to you for this moment. I am afraid, my Lord that there has been a communication from the accused which causes me, and junior counsel Mr. Paul to have to consider our positions. And this is not the first time this has happened. Either we must resolve this - and *now*, or we must withdraw. May I seek Your Lordship's indulgence for time with the accused to discuss these matters and see if we can continue?"

"Mr. Marron. I understand. By all means have as long as you require and I hope very much that matters can be resolved. Shall we say – what – all morning?"

-'Oh well – nothing quite like telling the sentencing Judge your client's a difficult wanker '

We went into the Consulting Room outside. I needed to defuse this:

"Look... may I just say that the one thing I loathe is being difficult; in fact I'm surely the easiest going person you could meet. I always listen, weigh advice up and decide... but you won't talk to me... I don't know what's going on and I'm not in control... "

It did me no good. If looks could kill I would be dead. He took out a wad of letters - all from me to Michael.

"Mr. Kaberry - I thought we had finished with this nonsense last March. But no - let me read these to you... this one -after the Conference at the end of March.....*'Mr.Marron is on the motorway, whilst I am still on the scenic route'* and it goes on – *'there is still so much to do and so little time'*. Mr. Kaberry... it's never ending!'"

147

"Now I've another. *'No one will talk to me'*... you don't like the way I called the Professor's evidence... you don't know who is to be called to give evidence... you complain documents and evidence isn't here... then the ever present cross-examination of police ... you complain about Kang ... the Law Society..."

"But if I knew the answers, I wouldn't ask would I? I don't know what you're going to ask Clarkie. I don't know what you're going to ask me - there's no proof of evidence..."

"Mr. Kaberry" he interrupted, in a firm tone - "I have more statements from you than I have ever had from any client. Now, what I will do is take you over everything once briefly. Then I will do it again in more detail a second time going over each individual charge."

'don't fight back.....don't give him chance to walk..... stay cool ....'

We spent some time on my evidence. He didn't know me - who I am, what I stand for and believe in. He didn't want me to give evidence about the effects on me in late 70's, - because I hadn't stolen millions then! I made it plain I would give evidence of what had happened to me in the late 1970's. That was met with resigned sighs of silly me. He didn't know I had no gambling accounts, and hadn't been to the races for years.

"Now what's all this about the cross examination of Sgt. Clark?"

"Well, first he will agree with you this is unique... a case where he has, initially, all these apparent 'confessions' in writing"

"Yes, he certainly can agree that!"

"But you haven't got any transcript of the August interview, have you – when he suggested I must have been blackmailed. So, you will ask him how much money I stole... how much I received...

Nick Paul did his best to stifle his silly grin at my stupidity, whilst Aidan Marron scoffed at me - "and he'll say *all of it*... I can't ask him that!!.... What do you want to do... make it worse!"

I persevered in my way of old; this is as intended last March:

"No - you see it goes like this. Surely you have all realised what's missing from this prosecution?

It was my turn for the pause as they considered ... and I continued -"...there is no evidence I stole anything - none whatsoever"

Nick Paul interrupted: "Simon.... you admitted it... they don't have to prove it... the money has gone, and you have admitted stealing it to go gambling," he smirked.

- *'Ignore him.... don't lose your cool SK*

"Well, if you read those admissions and compare them to the real facts and evidence, you'll find, first that I write in them – 'they're not true', and then, from the evidence, you'll find the two don't match." Beyond admitting taking £30,000 from an account which had nothing missing, to a Grand National that never was, there was actually no specific admission. I hesitated. I daren't mention he missed the Hindmarch evidence that I wasn't fit to be interviewed.

"But you wrote the admissions..." he repeated

- *'ignore him'*. I paused and continued:

"Yes, and by August they knew they were nonsense. Now.... two weeks ago I went alone to view the unused material at the police station. Clarkie and his accountant have thumbed over all my *personal banking accounts* and statements... looking for some evidence I had any of this money... *my entire personal bank accounts*. Forget about Gambling accounts - there aren't any. Now, there is only one specific 'admission' in my confessions ..."I stole the Beales money to take to the National - there never was any money missing from the Beales account, I've never been to the National, and there wasn't a National in 1993. Remember - it was void. Now... Clarkie and his accountant can't find any evidence - as it never happened ... so you ask him... if there is evidence... why hasn't he brought it to court - there won't be evidence of something that never happened."

I was on form that day. He must put it all to Clarkie that the allegations cannot be true - then expose Law Society and get details of those with the money - Calibre and the Harper interview. Marron took a deep breath and slowly said:

"So... you want me to put that to Sgt. Clark... that he can find no evidence you received any money from client account according to the evidence of signed cheques and your personal accounts?....yes, and there are no gambling accounts?"

"Yes. Then you progress from there... he can't lie, as you'll then ask him *why*, <u>if he has evidence</u>, he hasn't brought it to court. Then you move on... on to my August 1994 interview.... he thought I had been *blackmailed*... to his arrest of Harper and the seven tape interview – which you do have."

Nick Paul interrupted: "No: I've read it. There's nothing in that to help us"
- *'for god's sake... I'll clock him soon*
"Then you move on to Law Society involvement"
"Now Mr.Kaberry we've been there.... you cannot blame Law Society for what you did."
-*'don't fight this battle here, do it in the box later –*

It was pointless. If Marron couldn't take the first part on board - that I never had this money, then I had no chance with the second bit - the set-up.

What would you have done in my shoes – sack 'em?? Well you can't. Well, you can, but you won't look clever if it backfires.

I went back into court, steeled by outward serenity, smiling at the lovely blond as I walked back to the dock. If I flipped, I would lose. We re-started. The residue of the day was spent on more boring evidence - proving the admitted arrival of money. Next day it was the crucial evidence of Jock Clark.

Det. Sgt. Clark gave his formal evidence to Hatton. The Jury got little of the history; prior to my arrest, he explained, that they had been to my home and office and 'recovered' files. At my home, they had 'found' my written confessions. The letter written in Yarmouth, published earlier by Law Society was handed to him by John Patchett. No one thought to ask where John Patchett got it from. He presented no evidence I had ever stolen or received anything. *Surprise, surprise.* Parts only of my interviews were read out – but not a word said of August, nor of Calibre or Harper. Then, with little Frieze, he recited extracts from two interviews

Marron QC stood for the cross examination.
"Officer: as an experienced fraud officer, may I suggest to you that aspects of this case are 'unique'. Have you ever experienced anything like this? You have three, at least, detailed written confessions from the defendant in which he takes total blame and responsibility for everything?"
"Well... er... not quite like this"
"Unique - you may agree. But further, the defendant read them out. He seemed to want to take all the blame. Would you not agree - at least at first? That must be unique?"

"Yes unique - I accept that. Mr. Kaberry seemed anxious that he should take all the blame."

"But I think it is right also, that shortly after that March 1994 interview, Mr. Kaberry started to call you. In fact he called you many, many times - wanting to continue and explain"

"Yes: I accept that also. He wanted to talk informally – 'off-the-record'. But I cannot do that. Everything had to be formal"

"And he continued – calling you didn't he? And still he kept ringing you... he was making a nuisance of himself seeking off-the-record conversations"

"Yes I accept that ... He kept ringing but I couldn't have off-the-record dealings with him"

"Then you interviewed him again in August 1994?"

This vital aspect of my defence was uninvestigated by 'my team'. So Aidan couldn't put it to him...

"Yes that is right"

"And in that interview he withdrew his confessions. Later, in January 1995 he had sent you long letter – over twenty pages - telling you, as best he could, what had happened. Then he kept ringing you again... in that letter, he wrote that it was 'not safe to rely on anything he had written in his 'confessions'?'"

-'bugger it – he's flown past the critical interview....'

"Yes that's right. But I could not proceed on what he said. I had to make my own investigations and they confirmed that large parts of what he had written in client account were correct. I checked the receipts of all the money and they are correct. He had received the money. We considered an in-depth investigation to trace the money but didn't make such"

'Aidan, you've got him – now remind him about his in-house Accountant Mrs. Scott and KPMG?'

Nothing - the fact that he had an in-house accountant was never mentioned.

"I see. I think it is right Sergeant Clark, that you have had access to Mr. Kaberry's personal bank accounts as well as his business client account... access to all cheques he signed on client account. They are in unused material – you have had chance to look over them all? And access to all payments made to his personal accounts?"

"Well - er... yes... and I am satisfied that Mr. Kaberry had no money"

'Aidan that's not good enough... I beg you...just do this little thing for me... please answer my prayers once more...I'm sitting here begging...then its nearly over...please'

But it wasn't to be. He put none of the questions I needed
"Thank you officer"

He dithered, looked down, unsure what to do; he had a partial admission - there was no evidence I had ever stolen anything.
"I have no further questions", and he sat down
'Oh damn, he's blown it..... Sack him now...no, it's too late....'

That was it. Still nothing about Harper or Murgatroyds or Calibre - the admission in someone else's writing - that I was charged within seven days of The Sting, forgeries, Harper's interviews etc. That ended the prosecution case. Court continued without the Jury

What should have happened next, had I competent lawyers, who had exposed the truth, is this. Marron QC should have successfully submitted to David Hodson that I had 'no case to answer.' There was no evidence I had stolen or received anything, and my bizarre confessions couldn't be true; medical evidence confirmed why I couldn't work or explain what was what. Hodson would have dismissed the charges, and directed investigations into solicitors Anthony Isaacs, KIB Yeaman, Geoffrey Williams and the Penson gang. Some or all of them would then have been prosecuted for perverting the course of justice, and contempt of court. Further, enquiries into police and CPS – why had they brought a case which had no chance of success.

Instead, the case took another bizarre twist.
Marron: "My Lord, my submission relates to the last Count – No. 14. The allegation that the Defendant stole £110,000 from the Building Society, mortgage money duly banked, intended as a loan to assist a client in a re-mortgage. My submission is that the Defendant has no case to answer on the evidence
- *'Aye-up, what's going on here. If I've no case to answer on this, then the same applies to all of them'*
He continued:
"My Lord, the charge is that the Defendant stole this money. The evidence is that he applied for it and it is accepted that when it arrived at his practice, it was properly banked under the correct

client name in client account. That My Lord is the only evidence. There is nothing else in evidence."

- 'Oh Aidan - that's the same on all the charges'

And he continued: "My Lord, when the Defendants practice was closed a few days afterwards, that money remained there in client account. There is a balance standing in client account of £120,000"

- 'I really don't believe this... some dumbo at CPS has stuck a '1' in front of the closing balance of £20,000, someone typed it up ... no one has checked anything. It simply is not true...'

I sat there with my ever-stony face - in a comedy of errors.

"I see Mr.Marron." said the Judge... "All the defendant has done is bank the cheque, stop work and then been charged with a theft that never was. The money was still there - in client account. Thus there is no case to answer. Any comment Mr. Hatton?"

"Well yes My Lord. One must look at it in the whole light of everything. There should be over £700,000 in that account – not just £120,000"

"I agree with Mr.Marron. There is no case to answer on Count 14... I will give the appropriate Direction to the Jury"

The Jury returned and he directed them to formally enter a verdict of Not Guilty to Count 14

- '14 just happens to be my lucky number – leaving 13 – another lucky number! Take heart SK... what a holy mess'

I was well, calm and up for it as I heard my man say:
"My Lord, I call the Defendant"

I had waited for this moment for two years since the Sting. I walked from the Dock at the back of the court to the Witness box opposite the jury, twelve pairs of eyes on me

– 'don't fluster - appear as you are, a thoroughly decent man without pretensions... now – where's he going to start?'

"Mr. Kaberry: now you are likely to be giving evidence some while - how old are you?"

-' I don't know how ruddy old I am – what a start...birthdays have never meant anything to me or our family'

"Er...umm.... well, I was forty in December 1988..... so I must be er.. forty five.... no six...er...yes"
Hodson gave me a look - *'was that a filthy look?'* - And it just got worse without being terrible. I never knew quite where the questions were coming from. We identified that I was admitted a solicitor in 1974, but all he asked was that I agreed I was now "disbarred," without any detail of The Sting. I had no chance to get the truth in; he controlled my evidence. At an early stage we identified Dalmane and that I had been prescribed it to help me sleep. But it was a battle to get things in; Aidan kept saying 'thank you very much' to shut me up as I rambled on, getting as much in as I could from my prepared speeches.

I explained that in the late 1970's Dalmane had made me so ill that I couldn't work and tried to top myself. Then we identified my lifelong love of horse-racing and my successes 1982/3/4/5/6/7/8. That I had no 'Gambling Accounts' didn't go in - but that I won a lot of money in 1988 did. Then my second addiction to Dalmane in 1989 onwards and my mental decline. I called it my 'scrambled brain' - so I couldn't concentrate and started to sit on work I could no longer do. We identified Peter Harper and his business Murgatroyds. Out came the 'Note' I had made and given to Clarkie in August 1994. But that only came to £352,000. What was the real figure? And wasn't that my money? - Judge and jury would never be told. Then we identified Calibre, Graham and Tony - but no detail of his prison history. Clarkie should have been asked all this. It never came out that Harper had been arrested by Clarkie, and jointly they agreed I became an Easy Touch for money; neither that he was let off with Cautions after Law Society damned me. It went in that I was bankrupt, but that's all: I saw a woman juror turn white at that. If I'd stolen two million quid, how could I be bankrupt for a £30K guarantee?

Judge and Jury left. A press gag was placed on reporting of any of these people by name, as judge was told they were yet to be charged - with what, thought I. After three years waiting, to report would be a contempt of court - well unless you're called Williams, Isaacs or Yeaman. I needed to talk to the Marrow:
"Mr. Kaberry... you know the rules; no one can talk to you until your evidence is concluded."

I never slept and early morning knew I had a 'lost day.' I can't function properly on those days. Confidence, guile, insight, and all I needed to succeed was gone for this vital day.

I would be able to hold my own, but progress nothing. Court resumed promptly at 10.30 and my evidence in chief continued. I was uncertain. My mind was spinning in exhaustion. Complaining would make me a wimp, but that's what I said – "I'm no wimp, but I'm not up for it today." Hodson looked at me in disdain. Not a good witness for myself, I didn't know where my counsel was coming from in his lines of questioning and gave extended answers. Each extended answer had the put-down 'thank you very much Mr. Kaberry' to stop my rambling on.
He asked me openly if I intended to repay the money. To answer honestly would require me to fight my own barrister before the jury – then I would be bound to lose; you never do that in court or when standing for election. I found myself, shrugging shoulders and saying 'well - er - yes, of course' – but that wasn't true. .

My case was never emerging. Marron never asked me where the money was. He asked nothing about Heatherington and thefts of my cheques and forgery - so judge and jury never knew. We reached the Confessions. I said I was suicidal when writing them and thought that was the thing to do - take blame, as the man in charge. He asked me to read one out word for word. I knew that if I did I could break down - was close to it already. I told him I declined. He read it out for me. Plainly, its tone was that I was contemplating topping myself when I wrote it. But it wasn't the one which said – "god help me… I've stolen nothing." But he did refer to the letter in someone else's handwriting: save my lawyers had lost the original! You couldn't make it up. The crucial evidence of The Sting wasn't asked. We broke for lunch and I went walking. I was not well at all that day; never let anyone know you're wounded. I was losing and powerless – unable to get many of my rehearsed lines in.

After lunch, Marron was soon finished with me. My critical August interview and the *'you're being blackmailed'* never went in. Appreciating he was running down, I gave longer answers. As he sat down, I raised my arms in despair. My wits weren't working fast enough and confidence too low to sack him there and then. I reckoned the ladies on the jury felt for my plight.

Everyone remembers the Stefan Kiszko case. His 'legal team' demanded he admit he had done what he hadn't because he'd admitted it; they wanted to excuse him on the basis of his state of mind. He served sixteen years before it was plain he couldn't have done it. My plight was not dissimilar, save I was going over the heads of my 'team' and playing my own cards whilst they tried to control me. I knew I hadn't played enough of my own hand, as the Marrow sat down.

Time to pray hard, as I looked at Hatton - *'please Jesus.... if he says "no questions My Lord - I've lost.'*
I watched him. It was slow motion – *'I'm here... a sitting target... a dead duck... go for me.... please.... Jesus.. p<u>lease</u>.... just don't let the whatnot sit down... go for me, mock me....'.*
I'm not a salesman, but had to sell myself. He was standing:
"Mr. Kaberry...." he started. I would get the missing evidence into cross-examination – just spin the day out.
'- thank you Jesus... thank you, thank you, thank you forever.'
He was speaking clearly and slowly:
"...what would you say... is the purpose of a Solicitor's Client Account
-'...we're headed for an Elephant Trap....'.
I'd prepared for just this. He got a wonderful extended reply - more than he expected - client account is sacrosanct; the sum total of all individual ledgers must equal client account at all times. Then he wanted to know - to each question, whether what I had done *'right or wrong?'* Rather than set it out here, the Transcript is on the web. Essentially, we spent the next twenty minutes or longer, with Hatton walking headlong into my first prepared question and answer session.
And for ages he got the same answer:
"Sir - it wasn't right and it wasn't wrong; I did what I thought was right, but had I had my own brain and mind, I'd have seen it wasn't right...'
To which he would say – *"so it was wrong?"*
And I would say: -" *it was neither right nor wrong – I was on auto-pilot with my scrambled brain"* (but no one quite knew what 'it' was – what had I done?)
Finally this was extended to: - *"I'd never have done it, but it was wrong in hindsight, but I didn't see it that way as the person I had become, whatever it was....*

Later I said I never did it anyway - what was he saying I'd done?
"So - if it wasn't you Mr.Kaberry - who was it?"
'It certainly wasn't me', was my answer; I wouldn't do wrong. I held my ground. Without proper evidence against me, he needed my Admissions – but got none. There was nothing I couldn't answer. But I wasn't taking the battle to him as I had planned.

4.00 pm approached - Judge Hudson
"Now: it's getting on Mr. Hatton. I think this would be a convenient time to adjourn for today"
I was playing some of my prepared lines, but not as planned. Tomorrow I'd be well. I walked Newcastle to physically knacker myself, then to my hotel and lay on my bed. Dinner adjacent to the hotel, and, exhausted, I went to bed at 10.00 pm - and slept. At 6.00 am next day, with batteries fully re-charged, I was singing in the shower.

Court for 8.40 as ever and I waited, full of it. Calm and assured, I was myself. I would get my evidence in somehow. Time to be positive. I ignored everyone: 'focused' - I think they call it.
'*Don't get cocky… don't let them dislike you*'

Hatton QC resumed my cross-examination at 10.30. He didn't know it, but he had a different witness in the box; he was confident. I was even more so.
We started and I replied that I didn't know what was going on because of my muddled and scrambled mind:
"Oh yes…. your 'scrambled brain' you call it." he snapped - " But that claim was withdrawn" (i.e.'there's nothing wrong with these drugs')
"The pharmaceutical industry is more powerful than government, sir" said I firmly.
 - '*that'll strike a few cords…. nice one SK*'
On he went, getting sharp clear replies. I had done no wrong and stolen nothing.
 -'*what do I do now - destroy him? Ask him why he has made allegations he had no intention ever of proving*'
I discounted that in my mind, as I gave evidence. I couldn't risk the jury feeling sorry for Hatton.

An excellent line surely was the one rehearsed time and again. It didn't fit the question but in it went, in reducing quiet slow tone…

"Sir, you see, I've been on a coach trip to the suburbs of Hades (on these drugs) and I'm ringing the bell 'cos I want to get off..... I know where the bus is going...(pause)... and I never wanted to get on in the first place."

-'*golly SK - you got it in quite neatly.... make a few hearts bleed that will'.*

Hodson gave me one of his filthy looks - and the jury looked at him - then me. I'd won with that one again.

"You have no remorse... you feel no sorrow for the people who have lost money?"

- *'you fool - what a thing to say of a man who plainly was suicidal from the events and had taken all blame.'*

Silence. It didn't need a reply; a bullet to his own tummy. An hour and a half on, he was beaten - stuck, he was on his last shot

"Mr. Kaberry - you admitted it before and now in court you don't have the integrity and honesty to admit it all again?"

I had prepared a long ten minute reply to just that very question – 'honesty and integrity.' I would destroy him. Then I made a snap decision not to give an answer which may make the jury feel for him, not me. Instead I gave a short quiet answer:

"But I'm not a dishonest man, sir." That was the issue - could the jury, normal people, accept that. They'd heard and watched me for three days – ample time to appraise anyone. Had I sold myself? That's what you have to do in life.

What was he hoping - that I would break down and admit all the false confessions were true! Hatton sat down; we all knew he had scored '*null point'.*

Aidan Marron told the Judge my witnesses were not there, so court finished at 12.30 pm. We went to the Consulting Room outside. I did - I heard those little words from the Marrow:

'Well done, Mr. Kaberry'. Yes... he said it.

It was agreed I could call Pam Armstrong on Monday and some witnesses. Your lawyers should do this for the defendant well in advance of trial. I was on a high but unmoved visibly. If only I had been like this yesterday. One big question - had I got enough in? Now the cavalry was coming - but would he let them in?

I returned home to Adel Willows - not my home anymore, but it felt good. Petrina brought Holly to stay with me. We well knew I may never see my best chum again; these are the words no one would speak. If I lose, my best pal would be dead by the time I got out - frightening, this English justice system. I arranged for Split Ends to come and film me on Sunday for YTV. She was going to report something, so I may as well get my spoke in.

I had no choice but to limit witnesses. Giving evidence would be a gruelling experience for anyone; was it fair of me to ask anyway? I would call just Richard Aston, who being a natural salesman would take it in his stride, and Petrina to show that I was quite normal until 1990 - and I knew they'd like her. Then Peter Ritson to tell them I'm not alone - refer to his book. Would that be enough? I had another ten I could call.

Split Ends came Sunday afternoon with a Yorkshire TV film crew. She didn't like me, and I wasn't going to tell her I was winning. Worse still, she didn't like Holly – so I didn't like her. Her questions were meaningless.
"What would your father think of all this?"
-'*Well really! What a question!'* I'd blobbed in asking for the interview; pointless.

Monday morning to Newcastle with Petrina and Richard arriving at 9.30. Pam and Peter arrived together at ten o'clock. I was embarrassed; all these people to help me, how could I ever thank them. I took them all into the empty court, and made each stand for a few moments in the witness box, to get the feel of the place. I indicated where each barrister would be and stood over by the jury benches. Of the jury I repeated the obvious least it be forgot:
"*They want to know, they want to hear you..they will be with you – but if you don't tell them, they won't know. Treat them as friends waiting to hear good news.*" (all witnesses should be told that)

Aidan Marron saw Pam in the consulting room for a few moments, as Kate Moyler took some form of statement from Peter Ritson. The Marrow would have to try to make the most out of the statements made by Petrina and Richard. Hope still sprang eternal.

So into court we went and Aidan took Pam over her general statement. She was exactly as I had expected – forceful, interesting, informed and to the point. She had Judge and jury in her hand – listening. She even had chance to make the odd joke,

bringing sex into play - you don't really want it. [I'll give you one of the present jokes - doctor treating patient who wanted viagra, but he didn't have any - so gave him valium. Why? 'so he doesn't give a …. if he doesn't get a ….']
From the corner of my eye I observed the jury; they related to her. As with Prof. Hindmarch, Hatton QC moved to cross examine:
"And what effect did the Dalmane have on Mr. Kaberry?"
"I don't know - he came for help long after he was off the drugs"
"And if memory is so affected, how was he able to remember to cover up his thefts"

We broke for coffee. After fifteen minutes I joined Aidan Marron walking to court.
"Very good Mr. Kaberry. Now - I don't want you to undo the good she has done you. I don't think you should call any witnesses at all - you can't risk it"
We went into court. I approached Kate.
"Tell Mr. Marron to call my witnesses in this order - Petrina first, then Peter, and finally Richard", I said firmly. It was simple logic. Pam and Ian Hindmarch had explained what might have happened. These witnesses could say it did happen. My counsel surely by now knew it was pointless arguing with me.

I set the evidence in the Judge's Summing-Up. It didn't take long, with three witnesses left wondering why they hadn't been asked enough questions.

Defence over. The judge, jury and lawyers all left the courtroom. Trial was over, just Speeches by the two counsel, and Judge's Summing-Up to follow. I could now relax for the simple reason that there was absolutely nothing I could do.
- *God help you, if your trial was like this.*

CHAPTER ELEVEN

The Jury's Issues and Verdicts

The rules for the completion of a criminal trial are quite simple. It's been our system for centuries and the courts are full of injustices, right and wrong for years, but you tell me a better system. First the prosecutor addresses the jury on what they have heard and puts it to them that they must convict – the evidence means they can be sure beyond doubt. Then defence QC speaks and draws their attention to the evidence he thinks important and tells them why they can only acquit – they can't be certain he is guilty. Finally the judge goes over the law and some of the evidence and sends them to decide.

Hatton QC started at 10.30 am, as ever, hardly anyone there. Nick Paul, the bag carrier, had gone before my evidence, but would play a critical role later, held out as 'trial expert.'

Things had changed a little since the Opening. Hatton had adduced no evidence at all that I had ever stolen anything; police had admitted they had no evidence I had ever received any money; there were no gambling accounts. If only the Kangaroo evidence had gone in – but the eggs were long since scrambled. Hatton now concentrated on the fact that the money 'had gone' and I was solely in control. My confessions, he said, 'had to be true.' Give him his due, he did as well as he could:

> "The fact is, ladies and gentlemen, that this man was left in control of all this money, and it has gone – where doesn't matter. It has gone where it shouldn't have gone when he was in control and he is responsible. That is dishonest, for he has covered up what he was doing by paying interest, as he admits and as you have heard."

He told the jury the medical evidence could readily be dismissed – not one of the experts knew anything of the facts.

> "Ladies and gentlemen - each expert has told us the drugs affect memory; so how on earth, if Kaberry was affected, could he remember which payments to make, to cover up his thefts!"

And as to impressive witness Peter Ritson: "Mr. Kaberry is no Peter Ritson." I liked that, and wrote a note for my counsel: '*No - Peter Ritson is no Simon Kaberry.*' My man couldn't see it.

But overall Hatton made a good and persuasive argument. Solely in charge and all that money 'gone.' I must be guilty – my confessions were true. I was living a real risk - I may well lose.

At noon, he sat down. Now it was my man's turn.
"If it please you, my Lord... I may be some time in addressing the jury in this case."
Without warning, he was on the Road to Damascus – a convert. How many times had I told him I would never self-destruct, but that is what I had done, for no reason at all; that is fact.

> "Ladies and gentlemen" he said slowly... "Do you remember in the war, those Japanese pilots?" Pause again for effect. Then raising his arms he illustrated as he continued..: "They wrapped a white band around their foreheads, tied at the back of head... Marked the front with a red circle... they bowed to one another... then flew their planes into the enemy... To kill themselves... And they did it for the love of their Emperor and country"

- '*I love it Aidan... just keep going and finish it*'

> "Ladies and gentlemen... You have heard the facts in this case... you have heard the evidence... You have heard this defendant and his witnesses.... they stand opposite you for that purpose... So that you can see them and assess them... You make of them what you will. But can you find anything that this man has done which makes even the remote sense of what those pilots did - if these allegations made are to be judged true. Just as those pilots self-destructed, so this man has - of his life and career... but why? For what reason?... can you find any reason – just consider all that he has told you and all that you have heard."

Another pause: "There is no reason. Nothing makes sense, does it?" He was still proceeding slowly:

"The reason, ladies and gentlemen, for this defendant losing his way and doing as he did... has to be... can only be... because he was operating under the severe effects of Dalmane on his mind."

My counsel was inviting them to accept that I had done as alleged, because of the drugged mind. He'd threatened it since first we met. This early 1997 – about a year before the public understood or even heard of the effects of rohypnol. However, the moment wasn't lost as he then considered how a normal man would have acted and reacted in my shoes at that time. Under threats from the Law Society, I'd acted bizarrely. I peered from the corner of my eye – the women understood, even if my own counsel didn't.

Quarter to one came quickly. Judge Hudson:
"Mr. Marron. I think this may be a convenient time to take a break for lunch. Shall we say 2.00 o'clock?"

I was alert but disinterested from thereon. Mid afternoon he sat down. The Judge's turn: the Judge 'impartially' reviews some of the evidence and directs as to the law, and tells the jury what they have to consider when reaching their verdicts.

Hodson started:
> "Ladies and gentlemen - what I propose to do is this. I will remind you of parts of the evidence.... I cannot do it all, then I will turn to consider the medical evidence and issues, then return to what the evidence generally tells you about this case and this defendant. I may emphasise something, but that is my emphasis, not yours. I may omit something which you may think is important. I cannot review everything."

- *'fair enough.... but do you know half of it is missing'*

He told them he and they cannot change the law. He would direct them on that, and repeated they couldn't change it either. If he got it wrong in his Direction, then someone would put him right, but they must follow his direction as to the law. Their duties were to try the case on the evidence. Witnesses and the defendant stood opposite them – what did they make of each of them? That was for them entirely:

"Above all, sympathy must play no part in your verdicts. You may have sympathy for this defendant – but sympathy must play no part – it is irrelevant" – he said forcefully.

He then reminded them that I was a solicitor, unregulated by Law Society at the relevant times, and the evidence of Barrie Mayne of Law Society – that I should have known I was on a last warning, yet did nothing - indeed got worse and filed no Accounts 1991-2-3-4:

"One really wonders what the Law Society was doing in this time… this defendant seems to have been indifferent to his position, even when given a final chance to put matters right. Of course, this is his case – that by reason of the effects of the Dalmane he was indifferent about everything."

He then moved on the address issues of law for the jury to consider. First he explained what 'property' is in law, and to make out theft of 'property' I must have (a) taken it dishonestly and (b) had an intention to deprive the owners of it permanently. The 'property' was mortgage cash in the bank – 'missing,' presumed stolen. Then he told them that not only must that element be proved – the acquisition of the money, but also that when I did that I acted 'dishonestly.' He assumed they would find I had taken it. But of course, I hadn't.

"The prosecution have two hurdles to jump. First that what the Defendant did was, by ordinary standards of ordinary and honest men and women, dishonest. By those standards, I don't think you will have much difficulty in deciding that he was dishonest. But if, by those standards, you decide he was not dishonest, then that is the end of the matter and he is not guilty.

But if, by those standards, you conclude that he was dishonest, then you must consider the next aspect. Is it proved by those same standards that this defendant knew that he was acting dishonestly?

"So – there you are. There are two tests**. First is the objective test of honest and reasonable people. Next is the subjective test – did he know, by objective standards that he was acting dishonestly, and it is in this context that you may consider the effects of Dalmane, if any, upon his appreciation of what he was doing and acting dishonestly generally."

-'oi, but this isn't fair... no-one but no one knows what I did. I don't even... but I reckon some of this jury are with me.....'

[** this test for legal dishonesty was set in 1982 in R v Gosh]

"Well, you must be clear about this. This defendant asserts that he would not have committed these offences but for the effects of Dalmane. Taking Dalmane is no defence. It is irrelevant for the two reasons I have given... He cannot say – 'it was Dalmane made me commit these offences' – I hope that is clear to you, ladies and gentlemen. If the ingredients of each offence are made out, then he is guilty and must be convicted. But if you are not satisfied that all ingredients are made out, then he is Not Guilty."

- 'but I've never asserted this... damn, but my counsel has!'

Then he progressed to explain what false accounting meant in law. Deliberately falsifying a document with a view to gain. Having reviewed the law and that I must have done whatever they think I did, with a view to gain, it was not 4 o'clock:

"Well there we are ladies and gentlemen. That is the law. Tomorrow I shall review the evidence... So tomorrow at 10.30 please... I remind you again not to discuss this case with anyone else and only to discuss it together when you are all together. Thank you very much"

He directed the usher to take them out.

-'Aye-up – summats afoot. He's got something to say to my man.'

"Mr. Marron. It is at this stage in a trial that I generally review my bail decision. In this instance I shall not be continuing your client's bail. He can be brought back to court tomorrow morning."

He stood and left the court, giving no chance to anyone to question his decision. That's not right – a man must have a right to be heard before his liberty is taken. In effect Hodson had concluded I was likely to abscond. That told me he hadn't grasped anything.

I was so cool I amazed myself.

-*'treat this as a special moment SK.... saviour it; you're going to prison... part of that old tapestry'*

A guard took me through the back to the cells downstairs. I treated it as a joke – but, '*my god, PD's car was parked at the front on the quayside.*' That was my only concern. In England decent people don't allow someone doped up and robbed to be sent to prison - but plainly lawyers do.   The law is no ass, save when lawyers like these are in charge. Minutes passed and I was told to sit on a bench. So I stood, observed and listened to the clanking of large gates at each end. They were looking for somewhere to put me. Maybe ten minutes and I waited -

-*'Will I be able to have a shave...? .... Judge is a buffoon'*

But before they took me away, the girl Kate came down from the court above. Hodson had spoken with Marron and been told I was at court each day before 9.00am and wasn't going anywhere. So he'd changed his mind.

-*'Bugger it.... I'll never have this chance again'*

I walked out and away to the car, speaking with no one. Life had come to this - I smiled as I drove in the April sunshine down the clear A1 towards Leeds, as I mulled the event:

-*'Always look for the best..... Now he's played his hand, Hodson won't dare to give anything but a fair summary of the evidence... there's much good in what the buffoon has just done.'*

But it would have been nice to say I'd been in prison!

Back home, I had put everything away in the attic - just in case. Holly was staying with her maternal grandparents in Staffordshire.   My photo was all over the papers, so going out wasn't an option; in Leeds the press-gag and limited reporting meant I would always be guilty.   Roger, as ever the helpful brought me steaks and Louise a bottle of red, some salad and pudding.   No one dare say the obvious – I was going down, on what they'd read. I just smiled a lot, with my thoughts to myself.

I admitted to Louise: "I've a big problem. PD needs his car and I've no way of getting back to Newcastle tomorrow."

"Well, it just so happens that I'm due some holidays and I've taken tomorrow off... and the day following. I suppose I could take you up there."

Lord Luck seemed to have taken a shine to me. More to the point, Louise'd become my rock to turn to for help. We travelled up together next morning and she dropped me at the side to avoid media, who weren't there.
"See you later - promise" said I on getting out.
I stopped: "OK, jury will go out about lunchtime; I can't see how they can sort this out in two hours, but we'll see" and I was away.

His Honour Judge Hodson continued where he'd left off. He went over each Count charged and related the evidence. He never once mentioned the missing evidence – that is, any evidence that I'd ever even taken anything. Bits were horrible, and that certainly included the charge I had stolen £20,000 from Paul Kang. I feared that charge. Of the Confessions he said:

"What do they tell you, ladies and gentlemen? They seem to be free and frank admissions of what he had done. But he tells you they are not true. Then you look at his interviews with police."

-'... against my knowledge Nick Paul had doctored them, so vital parts were missing, such as Clarkie saying neither he nor his accountant Mrs. Scott could find the money – so where is it?'

Then he moved on to witnesses:

"Det. Sgt Clark is the investigating officer in this case. Exhibits 3, 5, and 7 (my written admissions) contain the Defendant's own words and are 'unique' in his experience as a police officer.... 'This Defendant was anxious that we should have them,' he said, and he agreed also 'that the Defendant was anxious to take all blame for this chaos and mess,' and Sgt Clark agreed that was the theme throughout those documents and in his first interview of March 1994....

"He said as far as the interviews are concerned – and you have half of them – and in those Mr. Kaberry said – 'I'm totally and solely to blame for all this.'"

[Hodson never mentioned the August critical interview]

"In January I received a long 26-page letter from Mr. Kaberry... I accept he also made a nuisance of himself – trying to speak to me. He made over twenty calls wanting to talk 'off-the-record', but I can't do that....

"He had written of his confessions – 'I don't think it is safe to rely on those. My actions do not appear to have been at all rational. It had taken 6-8 months to return to the state of mind I had in the 1980's.

"He (the Defendant) gave some indication as to where the money had gone. And Sgt Clark has told you there is an ongoing investigation into that and other people

"BUT, ladies and gentlemen, Sgt Clark said he had no doubt as to the reliability of the documents. The money showed as received in the books of account was correct. What he could not do, was find out where it had gone.... He said 'I have had the Defendants bank accounts and I accept the defendant had nothing in his bank accounts.' He said he had not been stealing, and would repay anything wrongly taken

-'*Bloody hell; I didn't say that.... how the hell can I have had an intention to repay when I never took anything...*'

This is England, and our justice system at work. Now you have a slight insight to the vital importance of men of common sense – juries. I will say this many times – '*lawyers are not as clever as they claim and think, and you hope.*' (this story is only half way)

He paused to allow the jury to digest his misleading comments, and then continued:
(*I recite the Court Transcript again*)
"Well, ladies and gentlemen – Dalmane. You are going to have to assess what you have heard about this drug. Consider the extent to which this defendant was taking it... *you are going to have to consider the effects, if any, that it had on Mr. Kaberry....* on his attitude and perception of things at the relevant time....

-'*Yea gods, he's got it... those are the right words to use... and if I win with this direction, the civil claim is won at the same time.*'

from the Transcript...
"First you heard the evidence of Professor Hindmarch, who referred to them as 'the Benzos' in the trade. They all have five properties – sedative, anticonvulsant, anti-anxiety, muscle relaxant

and amnesic- to remove events from memory. He told us that Dalmane has been researched extensively and about its pharmacokinetics – that is, how it distributes itself about the body, and its pharmacodynamics – the effect on the individual user, and this can vary from one person to another. Its half-life – the time it takes to be excreted from the body is between 23-36 hours. [Actually detailed research puts the figure at 240 hours] - It is a strong sleeping pill which acts on the brain, and is known for its impact in a number of ways – memory, tiredness, the ability to reason, the anticonvulsant and similar. It affects 'cognitive functions' – the way the brain works and thinks. It affects short-term memory, judgement and understanding. Dalmane is one of the strongest and most powerful benzodiazepines; that effect increases with dosage and frequency of use – a disproportionate effect. He told us it has an active effect in modifying the cognitive processes of the brain. It affects short-term memory, judgement and understanding. He told you of the pharmacodynamics – it increases with dose. So, as the drug is used, its side effects increase. If you take double the dose, it has more than double the effect on the brain; that is disproportionate and exaggerated. He told you of dosages – a dose of 3 pills (45 mgs) (which this defendant took often as recorded by his GP) has no place in medicine – that is suitable only for hospital use – a specialist dose.

"He told us that where a person takes these drugs there is no over-manifestation in conduct, although a close companion may notice a change in the user, but it is not readily noticed by others.
"Routine work is not affected much but there could be a big impairment when a person is asked to make a judgment or decision. It is possible to continue routine work as before, but learning a new experience is impaired and difficult. Judgment is adversely affected, by the short-term memory damage, and impaired understanding of what actually is happening. 'People do not seem able to get their thoughts together.' A dose of 45 mgs (3 pills as I was told to take them) can induce total incapacity if taken on a regular basis.
(transcript continues)
"But these, ladies and gentlemen, are general effects, which you may have little trouble in understanding. The question here is - what effect did they have on this defendant? The prosecution says you cannot know because Professor Hindmarch had no access to the facts of this case or medical records – 'My instruction was to

give an expert opinion on the general effects of Dalmane.' He has no details of the charges that this defendant answers. – 'I do not know the manner in which the money disappeared' he said and 'I would not presume to link what the defendant did or did not do to with Dalmane. I say only that it can impair judgmental processes. People can make errors of judgment, but I cannot make any judgment in this case.'"

> "So, ladies and gentlemen, <u>you are going to have to look with particular care at all of this</u>, you may think."

-'great.... This finishes civil and criminal this week... Bingo - I couldn't want for more than this.'

Hodson moved on to review the evidence of other witnesses:
[*transcript again*]
"Pamela Armstrong is a lady obviously with considerable experience with these drugs, well qualified of the effects of taking Dalmane, a Director of CITA. They are very addictive and affect our endorphins.

"People feel fear when there is no need or reason to fear. They become agoraphobic. They become submissive – they feel fear when there is no reason, but they do not know the cause of that fear. In 1988 the Committee for the Safety of Medicines said they must not be prescribed longer than 3-4 weeks. They then affect the way someone sees and perceives things

"She said – 'you can't counsel someone who is taking benzodiazepines because they are too confused – with short-term memory damaged. There is just chaos in their lives. <u>They cannot cope with rational thinking and they cannot take up offers of rational help</u>.'"

-'oh boy, are you listening you civil lawyers – do you understand any of this?.... if only!!

My eyes roamed sideways; the jury was listening and looked interested – they understood.

He continued:
"She told you that Dalmane is the most long-acting of all the benzodiazepines. Technically it is off the approved list of advised

drugs. It sedates the brain during the day following ingestion, and that causes confusion of thought process.

"She said – 'People want to get away from the fear at all costs and get away from people, and some will get their memories back. The person adversely affected by the drug may be alive to the fact that they can't do things as they did before, but wouldn't know why or be able to do anything about it. Memory may improve after the person stops taking the drug.' Then she told us of the effects if anyone had anything to drink, alcohol-wise that is – completely debilitating and so on – 'a person will nearly act as an automaton.' Repetitive mundane work can still be done, but anything which requires levels of thought processes is difficult.

"BUT AGAIN ladies and gentlemen, Miss Armstrong has no instruction about the facts of this case….. And this, of course, is the point Mr. Hatton makes - if his memory was affected, then how did he know where to make the payments?
 -*'oh god, here we go again - ruddy judge hasn't had the facts at all'*

Then he quickly reviewed the other witnesses:
(*Transcript continued*)
"You then heard from Petrina Rendall. She told you about her relationship with the defendant from 1986 to 1990 – obviously quite satisfactory; a good a caring man - a sincere person. Then he changed dramatically following a trip to the Far East at the end of 1988. Some bizarre behaviour followed. She told you he changed dramatically as a person. Once she told you she feigned an attack of hysterics, trying to get him to notice her. He refused to go out and mix. She told you of a later incident in a restaurant – removing a chair as she sat down, and how all fell apart between them – *'I couldn't get through to him. He changed his habits – getting up later and later. He was taking tablets every night and sweating at night and looked drugged up in the morning – stumbling into the bathroom'*
"She told you that he asked her to lend some money to Peter Harper, from her house sale; she said 'don't be so ridiculous' – she would never lend money or trust that man. She had been to Murgatroyds and saw the defendant working as a table clearer, which she found rather amusing. Then she saw him in early 1994 – he was frightened and told her not to open the door to anyone."

"Peter Ritson told you of the effects of another benzodiazepine on him – Flurazepam"
- *'I don't believe this... Aidan you should have put the evidence in as I asked'*
It wasn't my man Marron QC, but Hatton QC who came to the rescue: "My Lord – I hesitate to interrupt.... er, it is the same drug my Lord – Flurazepam is the generic name of Dalmane"

"Oh - I am much obliged Mr. Hatton - well there you are. Peter Ritson was also taking Dalmane. He told you of the effects on him. He could not function - he became agoraphobic and fearful of everyone. His family life fell apart and everything became chaos. He couldn't concentrate on anything. He wrote a book about it. But he could do instinctive things and could drive a car but his memory was severely affected - there are black holes in his memory. It induced paranoia, total confusion, although he could handle routine life, but this was over a four year period. He lived in fear and chaos and relied on his wife to run the business"
- *'if only all the evidence had gone in of what happened to me 1990-94: I went nowhere and did nothing - do they know?'*

"Finally, you heard from Richard Aston, a businessman from Leeds, who had been a client of the Defendant for a number of years in the 1980's. He told us some work had been sent to the defendant in error – 'I went to see him at his office to discuss it, but he was vacant - he wasn't the same man. I removed all my legal work from him.' Later, he came to see me and my wife at our house, and burst into tears, saying 'people were taking money from him.'"

"So, there we are - Dalmane," said the judge. He continued:
"And then you heard from the Defendant... of hitherto good character."
- *'Oi, since when is a man doped up and robbed no longer of good character because he's been set-up by lawyers'*

He then reviewed my limited evidence and it was my loss that there were so many holes in it all. Just before lunchtime he finished. Balanced? – could be worse and could have been so much better. Hodson reminded them to faithfully follow his guidance as to the law and those issues to be decided. They may have heard of majority verdicts, but they must all agree.

An hour on, just before 4 o'clock we were called back in. The judge wanted to draw stumps on the day.

In no time Louise and I were over the swing bridge and on the A1 South to Yorkshire. Passing Moulton, I asked her to call in at the famous Black Bull. A couple of drinks and I'd persuaded her to stay for dinner as well, then it was back to Leeds. Like a tight photo up the wide Sandown hill, I didn't know which way this would go; I should've won by a distance...
..but my jockey... er... questionable style!

Next morning Louise picked me up at 7.30 am, but I hadn't slept a wink - drained and feeling like death warmed up; imagine how you feel when your lungs have collapsed, scarcely able to function. We got to the side of the court for 10.00 am. Unspoken reality was I may never see her again in years.
Getting out I said: "OK...it's today. I'll tell you this. I have to win Beales... if I can't win that, I can't win anything"
"Thanks for telling me"
"See you later." I sped into court with the same direction to the jury who left us at 10.35.

It was time to pace again, even when in oblivion. Just before lunchtime we were called back to court. I took my place in the Dock and the barristers appeared, as did the two CPS girls. Judge and jury entered.
Associate: "Members of the jury – have you reached a verdict on any of the thirteen Counts you are considering?
They had selected a foreman, in his thirties, who sat nearest the judge at the end.
"Yes we have."
"And have you reached a verdict on all the Counts?"
"No"
Hodson wanted to hear what verdict they had reached this far. What a damned day to suffer one of those dreadful days, but they are at least once a week.
Associate to Foreman
"Count One" and she read it out in full.... "Have you reached a verdict?"

"No"

"Count two" same procedure

"No"

"Count three" - same again.

"No"

"Count Four"

"Yes"

 - *'Oh god ... which is this? – they look relaxed... don't flinch'*

"And what is your verdict – Guilty or Not Guilty"

"Not Guilty"

 That moment passed so fast

"Count Five" - same procedure and for the remaining thirteen

"No" - each time

Judge: "Thank you Mr. Foreman. I would like you to continue considering your verdicts after a break for lunch."

As I slowly walked the concourse Aidan Marron joined me.

"Beales" said I.

"Don't read anything into it…"

"Umm, Mr. Marron… can I have a word with you about mitigation if the rest don't follow suit"

"I've told you… There is no mitigation for what you've done." And he was away.

 -*'Ruddy hell... he just stopped for a coffee break on the road to Damascus…. There was no conversion…. '*

I looked down and smiled – well, what else do you do? Then it was back to pacing. After an hour, from the ledge I saw Louise's car return and take its place in exactly the same parking spot as yesterday: an omen? Well, we all look for them. I asked Kate to go tell he there was one verdict in only, so far – "Tell her it was Beales" – not that it meant anything to the team. I sat down in the middle then paced.

Just before four o'clock Kate Moyler appeared:

"There's no verdict, but the judge wants to know what's going on, so we're all going into court"

In we went and I took my place in the Dock, joined by a Security man this time. Counsel took their places as did the two CPS women, just in front of me, with Kate Moyler to my right, all with their backs to me.

In came the Judge, then the jury filed in:

"Mr. Foreman, have you reached verdicts on which you are all agreed?"

"Yes"

- 'Ruddy hell, can't Freethcartright ever get anything right....'

I remained seated, head slightly bowed, but my eyes raised so I missed nothing. My mind was spinning; my chest was hollow from fatigue and mentally I was half-dead.

"Count One" which she read out in full – theft of Building Society funds of £98,000 etc…

"How do you find the defendant – Guilty or not Guilty?"

"Not Guilty" came the firm powerful reply

I was unmoved, but reckoned if there was one NG to theft, they all had to follow suit.

-'pretend you're at the dentist SK... put the pain away; there isn't any... think of that sexy blonde in the gown'

"Count two" - in full again, then asked the same question.

"Not Guilty" came the same voice

"Count three" – *'another theft, I must win this'* – same long words, then the question

"Not Guilty"

-'this is it.... must be a false accounting... they may want to find me guilty of a lesser offence

"Count Five" (we'd already had count 4) – and she read out the charge

"Not Guilty" came the positive response

- 'Right, next problem is Kang... what number's that? – damn it, don't know'

"Count Six" - I watched the heads of the two CPS girls drop six inches as the truth rammed home – they wouldn't get away with it. Thank god for juries

"Not Guilty"

And so it continued for ages – counts six, seven, eight and nine passed

- 'Where's the Kang count? God, it must have been in one of those... I'm safe'

We were on to Count ten, and still it went on and still the firm reply

"Count Twelve" – she read it out in full, as with each…

"Not Guilty" – *'nearly there now'*

"Count thirteen" – again the delay of all the words…

"Not Guilty"

- 'well, that wasn't bad .... thirteen photo finishes up that famous hill... all went my way... jockeyless!'

The heads of the two CPS girls had now disappeared. I looked towards Hodson; he was ashen-faced. Would he vomit? Two days ago he had tried to send me to prison and the jury had just gone 'up-yours' to him, as I had to my legal team. But in fairness, he'd never been told what this was really about – and he presided!

- 'Stay calm SK... eyes will be on you...not a jot of anything...'

My man Marron was on his feet: "My Lord, I have two applications. First is that my client be released from custody, and second for his costs."

"Granted Mr. Marron" and the judge continued...

"Ladies and gentlemen of the jury, I must thank you for meeting your duties in this case and I now formally discharge you from the jury. You may now leave the court."

The nearest one got up to lead them out.

- 'Do something SK – you'd promised to shake their hands – they're too far away.'

I stood and bowed to them as they filed out, but I was on autopilot. This had happened so quickly, and I wasn't with it. Well, actually it had taken about ten minutes. The judge got up, bowed to counsel and walked out.

The Securicor man opened the door for me to leave the Dock. Away and out was to my right, and Kate beckoned me in that direction. But rules of life took over; I was going left. You know the rule. You've just been to the worst possible dinner party; the food was atrocious and the company worse, but you stay as long as possible in good grace, then thank the hostess for a smashing night and say you must do it again soon. Out left, to the front of the benches, where I approached my stunned QC. I had to do the decent and proper thing, without being pompous or a hypocrite:

"We've come a long way," said I, with out-stretched right hand, which he shook. No more words.

Without facial expression, I returned round the back of the court to the exit, leaving the silent six lawyers behind me with the two reporters; Pam Hudson's face was down. Oh to have been a fly on the wall. Out of the double swing doors and I walked straight into Jock Clark, again, head down, just in front of me. A quick punch to the stomach, a chop as he fell and a kick as he lay there, 'No - not even wishful thinking.' Clarkie had told the truth when he got into the box, and I admire him for that. He'd been set up by Williams and Isaacs as much as I had. I held out my right hand in an 'honours-even' gesture. He dithered, I withdrew, he offered and I accepted. We said not a word, and I was away.

For two years I had dreamed only of this moment, but mentally I wasn't up for it. Outside, I saw Louise walking to her car. She wanted me to call Petrina.

We went into the red BT phone box by the quayside and I reported events quietly. I can't do this emotion thing, but it was there, just beneath the skin. My eyes were so tired, albeit lifted by the events. I can't do the celebration bit either. We had more money left to spend on calls, but who do I ring? I'd lost everything and everyone from these events. How I love Geoffrey Williams! I didn't have Kit's work number to ring him.

Leaving the box, I espied my Friends from the North ten yards away walking towards Flynn's Bar. I had to say thank you - that must be right. Louise went to the car and I approached the jury.
I dithered in front of them, as they entered the bar.
- '*present yourself in orderly fashion SK*' -
"May I say thank you, but it can't have been easy with so much missing from the evidence…"
"Well, how are you now" offered a pleasant lady, halfway into the bar. I'd seen her wince when hearing I was bankrupt as well as all this; this was stiff upper lip time.
"Thank you - just a little shaken. Wish I could sleep!" was my version of a joke, and I turned away and to face the foreman as he crossed the road to join them. I held out my right hand:
"Thank you sir," stony-faced as ever, he accepted it and replied:
"We just hope you can rebuild your life and career and make something of what's left of it all."
That was it. You're not meant to fraternise with juries, but I think that was excusable.

I returned to the car where Louise was talking to Kate.
"Sorry, but I don't have any friends in there, and may as well be away. I want to see my dog now" was all I was going to offer a member of my successful team; shame on me.

Louise drove off, leaving Kate standing there: "She said you're like ice - she's never known anyone as cool - you haven't batted an eyelid for one moment from day one. Then said 'we've won' - so I told her, but '*you*' all told him to plead guilty"
"Nice one. Could we just get away, I really would like to see Holly if you would be so kind."

I'd be a fool to pretend this was over.
"What's really happened?" she asked as we reached the A1. I was frightened of any emotion coming out. I couldn't even thank her for all she had done. I related the events.
"It isn't over you know - they won't accept it"
"But they have to, it's a jury verdict."
"Yes, but there's so much to come' Mike Thurston will do me over with those two from CPS and there's the civil claim. I don't know…. More than anything I want to get Williams now."
"Oh Simon, can't you give it a rest – you won; it's over"
"Just you wait and see. Mike will block me doing Williams and we've got Thorold to come yet. Remember - not one of them was even at trial - they don't begin to understand. D'you know, my own counsel - *my own counsel* - summed up on the basis that I'd stolen all this money. But I'll get the bastards who did me"
"Leave it – you won, that should be enough"

She drove on in silence, and I'm afraid I wasn't good company on what should have been a very special time. But we both chuckled as she overtook the prison bus taking prisoners from Newcastle to Durham prison! In an hour and a half we were back in time for the Yorkshire TV Evening News
"Leeds Solicitor cleared of all charges" was headlines

My interview at home was heavily doctored. Split Ends followed it with an interview with the little old lady who'd sold me papers each morning since 1980. I did my pools there each week and had won over £10,000 in early 1993, then doubled my stakes and put them on four weekly at a time:
"Oh yes, he did his pools here all the time. I often wondered where all the money came from, but all his cheques cleared" said the little old lady
-' *the little skunks… why the hell did I bother'*

178

Petrina arrived with my beloved Holly-dog, who'd returned from Staffordshire as if this was inevitable. She wanted to go out for a celebration meal, (Petrina, not Holly) but that was the last thing on my mind. Until I knew what was happening on other things, I mustn't speak. A reporter from Yorkshire Post appeared down the drive, as Olwen had nothing from me at court; I had to talk to him or he could publish anything

"Will you be suing anyone about these drugs?"

"Oh no, I'll just put it down to a bad card in life." I said that the false stories about me were such that I'd probably have to move away to build another life. Louise went for fish and chips then left me alone. I slept and awoke – was it all a dream.

Was the nightmare over?

Next day it was front page, with my photo captioned 'fled the court in tears' (sourced from 'my solicitor' as Olwen couldn't find me). Early Friday morning Mike rang to remind me this was far from over. Until Calibre was done, he wouldn't help me expose Williams and Law Society - *what a surprise!*

At lunchtime the YEP was out - Front page:

"Cleared Kaberry – Now I fight to clear my name"
A fair report, **but** - 'see **Editor's Comment**.' I turned to them

> "*Simon Kaberry has been acquitted by an understanding jury.... but is a broken man, struck off by Law Society for gambling clients account.. bankrupt... would the jury have had similar sympathy for a heroin addict*"

The Editor would continue that theme for years, each time I tried to get back up, he would report I was struck-off for theft.

On Saturday morning seven letters fell on my doorstep. I opened them expecting the worst, and instead had seven tearjerkers from former clients, saying how glad they were. I wanted to plan to start again, but couldn't - so much unfinished business. The SDT 'Ruling' was like a ball and chain fastened to my ankle. Only when released could I move on. Same for you surely.

The next part of this story runs from the Lords Bingham and Phillips to High Court and Appeal Court judges to Law Lords, and incompetence of lawyers, as legal ranks were closed on me, in the name of 'the greater good' – that the truth never be told.

CHAPTER T W E L V E

The Second Sting
- 'what becomes of the acquitted?'

Always act honourably, and do the decent thing, even when all goes belly-up. Reach an '*honours even*" state in victory; never create a situation where your foe loses face. It's pointless and a maxim we try to keep. I now had to work with these duffers to build a new life.

With the limited reporting and failure to cross-examine, I remained a pariah - mysteriously acquitted after taking all that money. I needed my lawyers more than ever - to put the civil claim.

I was missing the last seven years of life, and all you take for granted - home, possessions, capital, inheritance, income for the past seven years, career and earning capacity, my reputation, was often unwell, and had lost my family, and realistically, chance of family. Cornerstones gone - I don't think I had any choice but to look for 'justice' - a helping hand to rebuild a new life. I was now forty-eight. Paul Balen and Oliver Thorold now surely had, in me, the best possible prescriber benzodiazepine claim, even supported by a jury finding of fact. What would you have done?

Walk away and rebuild a new life? – where and how? Borrow money to start a new life? - Bankrupt, I had no bank account and no borrowing ability. I needed a role in life; I wanted to work and live again - and this experience meant I had much to offer. Reputation - more than anything, I must have mine back.

Destitute, I was dependent on legal aid to bring any civil claim. I was only too mindful that they were frightened after wasting so much money in the group claim. As experts, they controlled whether funding would be extended to sue 'Z'; they advise LAB. On Monday morning 28 April - two years to the day since I first met Paul Balen, I rang him, with my bright and positive voice. He had heard, but his gut reaction was to 'drop' my civil claim.

In misuse, civil claims are the 'compensation culture', which seeks blame for accidents in everyday life. What had happened to me was more than an accident.

I went straight to my writing table.

Adel Willows
Leeds LS16 8AF
Monday 28 April 1997

Dear Paul,

"...may I say, frankly, I was terribly disappointed by your initial reaction that I should now 'drop everything'.

"... I strongly suggest that you should also sit down and take a proper proof..... In court I was left very much on my own to fight my own battles all the way – and I did.... Ian Hindmarch...two years ago....... said that my chances in a civil claim were always stronger than in the criminal court...."

"There are some strange consequences to my trial and verdict, none more so than your initial reaction.....you know I have reservations about the advice of Oliver Thorold, but I am willing to stick with him if you assure me he really knows the subject and is willing to learn my case.... <u>please no more delays.</u>

"Paragraphs 6, 7, 8 & 10 of Thorold's (February) Advice contain inaccuracies........you need to discuss all with me.
Yours sincerely,
Simon Kaberry

I took it to an agency to type and fax immediately. One day, a barrister would ask Balen why he took that attitude – '*drop it.*' How would he answer?... and why he had done zilch in 2 years.

Paul Balen and Oliver Thorold will have discussed what to do with me. But they had not even put the GP on notice of a claim, so he could have had a Watching Brief at trial. You see - I was meant to lose, wasn't I?

"... you wrote that acquittals would be good reason to proceed"

"Well... er... that can't be right can it... er... I can say Law Society found the allegations proved in civil law"

"Good line. Mike Thurston tells me he may yet be charged again as well"

"It gets better... just leave it to me - I'll sort him."

"Bye"

As badly damaged goods, no other solicitor would help me. To outsiders, I had clever, successful lawyers. Without car or cash and nothing left to sell, this was worse than prior to trial.
Paul Balen sent me a copy of his buck-passing letter to Ollie...

> *.... I require, for LAB purposes, a written Opinion in the light of the acquittal for an extension of funds to issue a writ... would you give this some priority"*

To me he wrote:
> *"Incidentally, is the Official Receiver your trustee in bankruptcy, and if not who is? Will you let me know the date of bankruptcy and the date of your discharge?"*

This innocuous line was critical on how to proceed, but passed by. Balen also wrote again that he *"would discuss trial with Mike Thurston and Nick Paul"*. I snapped back.... the thought of either Nick Paul or Mike Thurston advising on trial was *'ludicrous.'* ... *'you seem unable to understand anything... I nearly lost at trial because of them... but Hindmarch saved the day.'*

Acquittals were quickly an irrelevance; that I was again under the control of my hopeless lawyers was a living nightmare. I knew this time they could block me. Normally, I can absorb pressure like a sponge – but this was different. Without money for food, Roger gave me food on tick, to keep me going. They all trusted the system that soon I would be able to repay them.

Thursday 15 May was one of those glorious May days, as I looked over the smart green lined and trimmed lawn and tulips to the rhododendrons. Three weeks to the minute from leaving court in Newcastle, the phone rang:
"Simon" came Michael Thurston's ever laid-back voice. "And how are we today?"
"Go on....." My heart was pounding. I knew what was coming....
"Well I've just been talking to Pam Hudson at CPS"
"Will I ever forget her?"
"Well.... she has decided, after consultation with David Hatton and police, that they are to prosecute you again. They are going to

charge you with conspiracy with Calibre people to obtain mortgages by deception. Now I've got the name and number of someone called Sgt Bowles of Bradford Fraud squad. I've spoken with him, and he wants to arrest and interview you, but I'm afraid the charging won't be until the end of this year."

- 'I can't take this – he's shafting me again; Mike is doing me over a second time'.

I could see more years of hell. I ranted at him for over a minute; he'd not seen any witness, done nothing for me. I couldn't take two more years of this…. I was nothing to do with any mortgage applications as he should know by now.

I felt the blood drain from my cheeks as blind panic ran up through my body and my stomach churned - I'd lost it. If Mike Thurston, who knew me, was doing this to me, what did his partner Paul Balen have in mind? All I could see was disaster for the next years. I ran upstairs and the contents of my stomach ended up down a basin. The end of the year - seven months. Then another year to trial and all the uncertainties again, where would I live – another year, and Thorold will use this against me again. They're all in league? I saw it all clearly. I queried whether I was psychotic?

Over the following weeks, I sat daily, fuming - I couldn't move in any direction. On 22 May I received Thorold's 'Further Advice' to LAB on my civil claim. Just three months earlier he had written: - *'acquittals would be good reason to proceed'*,

It was 'all change' from Ollie now:
[I precis his written Advice]
"1. Acquittal does no more than establish that the offences alleged (theft of client account) were not proved beyond reasonable doubt. The prescriber can prove the same thing, but to a different standard of proof (i.e on balance of probabilities, my counsel said I had taken the money – despite the evidence.) Because of that, I must pay Law Society personally for the money stolen from me and recover that from the doctor

2. *"This would be an expensive claim and 'I owe a duty to the LAB' not to risk its funds.......*(on top of the wasted 35 million)

3. *'I need also to satisfy his Trustee in bankruptcy that it would be reasonable to proceed* (this is wrong in law, but the key)

4. I must consider the extent to which Mr. Kaberry contributed to this situation... he clearly has an alcohol problem.

4.   *Mr. Kaberry would have to establish that the effects of the drug .....led to his insurers paying out for his negligence(but they haven't) and resulted in his bankruptcy (caused by forgery!)*

5.   *The jury could not possibly have adjudged the effects of the drug* [you have read the judge's summing-up]

6.   *'There would be no escape from putting at least one medical expert to support him and Mr. Kaberry would be cross-examined at length.* (inferring to a lay reader there was no medical support). *The jury couldn't possibly have determined the effects of the drug*

8.   *"I want Mr. Kaberry to make admissions to me of his wrongdoing"* [He demanded that I admit I stole the money]

This was incompetent, divorced from the real facts, but LAB would accept it, from my lawyer. This man is (still) the self-proclaimed legal benzo expert telling LAB - and they would act on his advice. Same with the infamous Meadows and Southall.

Quite naturally Tony and Ann Turner needed their house - they wanted me to move on, but they were being very good about it. I had a brother a few miles away who now had a lot of money - but he wouldn't be helping me.

Louise, who is blessed with common sense, quietly read the Advice. About fifteen minutes later:

"I don't follow… this is a different Opinion from the first one… and what's all this about contributory negligence? – why are your own lawyers trying to put you down?"

"He's trying to say that I contributed to my condition, so that reduces my damages by a similar amount. Simple example is not wearing a seat belt when hit by another car; you start by losing 25% of damages for your 'contribution' to your own injuries. He's also twisting Law Society - who have paid out wrongly for my dishonesty, with SIF, who haven't paid out, and are my insurers for my negligence, but haven't paid out. So he's writing I was negligent and must recover for that. It's all wrong. I don't have to repay my insurers - so he's wrong again. That's why we have insurance. I don't have to repay for my negligence."

"... but how could you have contributed?

"He's calling me an alcoholic…. Because I was so quickly drunk by my own admission – remember I wrote *'one glass of wine sent me tipsy'*- He's inferring I'm an alcoholic."

"But I thought they were your lawyers… y'know … working *for* you, *putting your case*! You've no alcohol problem. Everyone knows that. You can't win…"

"Stop being such a defeatist… no, they won't win…"

"And the jury… they did judge the drugs…"

Panic wins nothing - I'd had many months' practice with these lawyers. I waited; they had to see me. Another disaster struck. Andrew cut the phone line. Petrina paid for a 'Receive only' phone-line a month later, but I was stuck unable to call out for help in the crucial weeks and months to follow. It was a bitter blow…. now incommunicado.

Mike Thurston came to Leeds on 20 June to take me for arrest and interview. There seemed to be just one policeman in charge of a million-pound plus mortgage and other fraud investigation, yet in over three years they'd achieved - nothing. And done - nothing? He claimed to have undertaken 'hours of painstaking research.'

The policeman offered me chance to view some of his papers, which seemed to be limited to an Interview of Graham, reading my letters to Sarah Wade and checks on status of all Calibre mortgage applicants. All seemed to be frauds. But no solicitor would know that. Graham, when confronted with cheques made out to him and Calibre, had said I had given him the money – 'to pay Kaberry's gambling debts.' I took copies of my letters to Sarah Wade. A solicitor would be struck off for breach of Undertaking by Law Society. Not that my letters admitted anything; they confirmed I had been set up by the Penson team.

The frauds by Calibre involved five firms of solicitors. The forgeries at my bank were shoved under the carpet. There was no evidence of any conspiracy with me. Next the officer said he and his partner each wanted their summer holidays and they'd arrest and interview me in 'a couple of months.' Mike could spin this out for more costs and another trial.

Law Society, Chancery lane refused to answer my letters for an inquiry into these events – cover-up by Jane Betts was in progress, along with Penson's boss Eileen Kirton. To kick, I filed <u>my</u> Application against Geoffrey Williams in the Law Society's Tribunal alleging 'unprofessional conduct' and 'unfitness to be a solicitor' due to his 'deceit' on the Tribunal, causing enormous loss and damage to the justice system and Law Society – he had misled SDT in July 1995 with catastrophic consequences. I knew they would protect him - but how.

- "*Freeze him out*" - was surely being whispered in top ranks. No organisation should be allowed to self-regulate.

Paul Balen palmed me off with a pretty young lawyer, Laura Smith. We laboured on in an hour-long meeting; her draft 'Witness Statement' for me was hopeless. If I didn't sign, or amended again, I would be accused of 'refusing to co-operate with my lawyers'. I knew their game. They refused my requests for a different barrister from Thorold and arranged a Conference with him, and Lader and Hindmarch – both experts – for 19 July. But I wasn't allowed to see Malcolm Lader first.

Louise took me to London. No sleep, on Elaine's floor, I approached Doughty Street Chambers, exhausted and drained, with exactly the same fear one must have when being wheeled into heart surgery – knowing all your surgeon's former patients have died on his slab… you don't want him to touch you. My batteries were close to empty; it was a Lost Day.

First sightings in the Waiting Room fuelled my fears further. Paul Balen had written, "*much will depend on your experts, especially Prof. Hindmarch.*" He was my ally, my longstop, spinner and batsman and trump card. He was cancelled as advisor. The highly competent but ill-briefed Prof. Malcolm Lader arrived. He had only seen me in the impossible May 1996 Consultation. This is no way to run a proper civil claim. Who else to help me*?*

- '*oh god – I don't believe it*' …. Nick Paul joined us as 'trial evidence expert.' And you, the taxpayer would pay these professionals handsomely. It's their system.

A Marx Brother beckoned us into a Conference Room:

-'*step right this way folks… walk right on in - and leave all hope behind….*'

Thorold swiftly moved into attack mode - that those acquittals have no impact, for the doctor can make the same allegations and prove them to a lesser standard of proof; on balance of probability I had stolen the money to gamble and was therefore liable to repay SIF as insurer to Law Society. As diligent insurer, they wouldn't have paid out without first checking that it was true, he said. But SIF are not insurers to Law Society and hadn't paid out. Thorold didn't want to know that – it didn't fit. We loathe one another, but he was in control of my access to justice.

The claim was for compensation for losses arising from being put in a mentally impaired condition, when working as a lawyer and in my family life, by the psychoactive drugs prescribed over four years. I had no idea I was taking daytime sedatives; had I known what they were, I wouldn't have taken them. Well – would you take drugs knowing they were injuring you? Thorold already held advice this was top end negligence.

Malcolm Lader said that he would have expected a series of witnesses to support my contentions; people who knew me. Of ten statements, he was given none. Nick's appraisal of trial, issues, evidence and argument was as incompetent as before. As I protested he said "Simon – the doctor will be able to call Peter Harper to give evidence against you."
But what would he say – 'that I became an easy touch for money.' That would be magical.

Accordingly, Thorold said I must first recover, for my *negligence*, all the funds acquired from me by the others, and paid out by my insurers SIF. He said that figure is 1.9 million. This was paid by Law Society for my dishonesty – but I hadn't been dishonest; I didn't have to repay unless Law Society would take me to court. They'd never do that – expose their own stupidity! Thorold said 'he would make the admissions for me'. I knew the drug was causing injury, but kept taking it. I schemed and stole with care, sending 'exactly the right amount each month' to Banks, so no one was suspicious (its not true) - covering-up my thefts. My books of account were accurate - but police claimed the reverse. I didn't live in confusion, as I had been skilful in what I had done. He said I didn't 'fall into a hole from which I could not escape.' Lader sat there quietly, knowing this was bunkum. You've read the Judges's

Summing-Up. But Thorold would find every possible reason to deny my claim.

Then he repeated that I was an alcoholic. "*When did I have <u>time</u> in that schedule for an alcohol problem*?" Thorold, backed by Nick Paul was determined - that I must have an alcohol problem.

Then the insults started again: "Mr. Kaberry seems not to be a man capable of accepting personal responsibility in life." Law Society wouldn't have published without checking first. Malcolm Lader seemed bemused, just as Ian Hindmarch had been earlier.

I sat tight refusing to accept this hopeless advice. Finally, after his third visit to refill his tea, he sighed:
"I am sorry but I owe duties to the Legal Aid Board.... And for the reasons we have discussed, I must advise them that you have no viable claim to pursue against the prescriber of Dalmane 1989-94. If you have a claim, and that is by no means certain, you are contributory to your mental condition by reason of your alcoholism and that defeats your claim."
"But I have never had any alcohol problem. Name one person who will agree with you!"
 '*Keep calm. .. keep your composure and dignity at all times SK.*'
I got up, put my chair under the table and walked from the room.

Outside I was dazed, angry with myself, for I had seen it coming and done nothing. I walked into the light rain as dead as the other patients who have been to Doughty Street for help on Benzos.

"Come on let's go" said I to Louise. What had happened was obvious; we were past Milton Keynes before I splurted out…
"He shafted me...... the bastard did me properly...... thoroughly......
I'm not a man capable of taking personal responsibility in life....
I'm a ruddy alcoholic who stole all that money.... The GP wasn't even negligent!! The bastard......"

[When medical experts Meadows and Southall got their advice so wrong about causation of injuries to children, they were castigated by lawyers. – careers over.
Has any lawyer, held out as an expert who got everything wrong, ever been brought to book?
 No. Why? It's a closed shop]

One thing was certain; I didn't have lawyers with those so oft-read about 'sharp legal minds.'

CHAPTER THIRTEEN

'They'll block you at each turn'
Accept your life is over -

Back home, I awoke next morning. Was it another bad dream? By 7.00am, on a warm July morning, batteries re-charged, I was at my desk, pen in hand. Thorold would write an Opinion for LAB. Funding would immediately be cancelled; without it, no lawyer would act for me, and no medics help me. But the insults clouded my judgment. I had to stop it.

The letter I composed over the next 48 hours reflected the atmosphere of frustration and anger. I traded insults – *'knowing you as I now do, you are not a man who will eat humble pie'* – and *'I won't be thrown onto the scrap heap of life by you.'* I wanted to shame him - *'I will issue a writ myself.'* But without him I couldn't get the essential medical reports, nor funds or credibility to see anything through; we both knew that - *'I don't owe my insurers SIF - it's Law Society, and they will settle any claim they may have, not that I admit any as I haven't been dishonest*
Petrina typed then faxed it to each lawyer on Tuesday 22nd July.

Honest, competent lawyers would have written a short Opinion, immediately after trial.... reading like this:
> "Mr. Kaberry seeks to bring a claim in clinical negligence against.... - virtually a total loss claim. The expert supporting evidence is overwhelming. He suffers ongoing ill-health in consequence of long-term exposure.....
>
> We have already advised the Trustee in bankruptcy of the pending situation, and now require extended funding to take an Assignment of the right to sue the negligent prescriber, and to issue a writ. The trustee has a duty to assign in cases such as this. I recommend funding be extended forthwith to advise the trustee and creditors of the true position and to take an Assignment. Once assigned, Mr.Kaberry will owe nothing to any former creditor (although it appears there may be none anyway)

unless they can prove he acted fraudulently.... and that issue has already been tried subjectively.

Further, we must apply to the High Court to set aside the Findings without trial of the SDT in July 1995. What happened in SDT was scandalous – the courts will be gravely concerned when they hear of the consequences"

From a call-box I rang Michael in some faint hope of help. All he would say was that 'he had heard, but it was nothing to do with him.'

I told him at least I could sack him now.

"Well I'm sorry that's how you feel, but don't go wasting your time fighting Law Society and us. "They simply won't let you..."

" *'They'* ...what do you mean Mike 'they'...?'"

" 'They'... they are the Legal Establishment. They couldn't give a toss what's happened to you. Now don't you go wasting your life fighting either us or what Law Society have done to you – 'they' won't let you. Doors which are open will be slammed as you approach; doors which should open will be locked. At each turn they will stop you and block you...

"Mike – who are 'they'...

" *'They'*... you'll never see them... they are **The Establishment** - you'll never see anyone, but... each turn you take... Simon, you're a nice chap, you've got lot's to offer - got a super garden, don't waste it. Go work as a gardener - just accept that life as you knew it can never be again."

Paul Balen wrote to me (30 July):

"....I am satisfied all the issues have been explored...... .the position in which you find yourself, whilst tragic and unfortunate, is no different from anyone else just acquitted at trial.......Oliver Thorold is an extremely experienced barrister and he has formed a view which we must accept. .Law Society is 'a separate matter', and we assume that the Trustee will pay all your damages over to it. ...

Concluding -

"I am sorry but your case is not viable....you must respect the views of....Oliver Thorold.... and, hopefully, me also. It would be entirely wrong of us to give you false expectations and allow your case to succeed in recovering any compensation.

'The smarmy git!' said I on putting his letter down. He even claimed Malcolm Lader didn't support me - a lie.

....

Events passed between 22 July and 26 July 1997 about which I knew nothing for another eight months. Thorold asked Laura Smith to *'find out the position of Law Society.'* Miss Smith didn't investigate the law - the answer lay there and with the trustee. She phoned Neil Rogerson, thinking she may find the truth there - as the young tend to, when speaking to their elders.

"*Law Society claims subrogated rights to recover for payments made by the Compensation Fund under sections 36 Solicitors Act. But if Kaberry brought a civil claim against the prescriber they 'would contemplate a commercial settlement with him'*

But Rogerson had blundered; to have that right, I had to be guilty of dishonesty. I wasn't, so they had no subrogated right. Miss Smith, being inexperienced, accepted what she had been told and sent this fax to Thorold (obviously after talking to him first):

> "... Have spoken with Neil Rogerson, Law
> Society Compensation Fund Manager to
> ascertain what rights Law Society have....
> Mr. R indicated that in the event that Mr. K
> did pursue a civil action; the Society 'would
> consider a commercial settlement' *although
> as counsel pointed out, Mr. K is in no position
> to discuss such an arrangement at this time* If
> counsel requires any further information... contact us."

i.e. - Law Society told Thorold and Balen that – *if it had a valid claim* - they were looking to 'talk terms' to mutual benefit. My lawyers and Thorold then buried the offer.
[doctors are struck-off for life for changing a patients records]

Two days after that offer, on 26 July 1997, Thorold signed his Opinion - I set it out later, but it is based on an assumption that the trustee in bankruptcy would 'take' my compensation to rebuild a life from me, and simply give it all – 'to SIF as insurers to Law Society.' Their offer to talk got no mention - and they knew I owe nil to insurers. On 2 August 1997 Balen wrote again that he was *'absolutely satisfied' that Advice was right* - before I had seen it.

They kept the Opinion from me for over 2 weeks, by which time it was filed with LAB and all funding removed. On 31 July I met with solicitor Joe Shammah in Manchester and completed a legal aid application to fund his work to set aside the SDT 'Findings' and get my career back. This would be lodged with LAB Manchester – the same office which, separately, had Thorold telling them I had no expert support and was a thief.

My Journal makes horrible reading of the anguish I lived in those days; but I never gave in, although knackered. There had to be a solution. I would find it. I wrote to new President of Law Society, setting out the facts and history. I wanted to see someone there.

Meanwhile my Disciplinary Proceedings against Geoffrey Williams sat in the Solicitors Disciplinary Tribunal - Mrs. Elston had to process my Application; this was a very serious matter – 'lying in and deceiving a court' – with terrible consequences. There must be zero tolerance of that. I guessed phone-lines were whispering… *'don't worry; we'll take care of it'*

On 13 August I received two letters in the same post from Freethcartright. The shorter letter, from Paul Balen, acknowledged my last letter, seeking his help and a meeting. He wrote:
> "....*I see no future in further correspondence*..."
> (i.e.'Get lost' - or another two words '.... ...')

Corderey – the Bible Guide on solicitor's conduct and duties, states clearly it is a solicitor's duty to discuss and explain counsel's Opinion with the client.

The fatter letter had the Opinion, dated 26 July. As we do, I turned quickly to the conclusion:
> *This case does not justify legal aid support....... for the reasons set out herein"*

This Opinion is an object lesson in everything that could be wrong – in one long document.

First, he wrote that he assumed the doctor would make the same allegations as made at trial and, on balance of probability… that was true; no trial allowed. (*my barrister - about me*) and…
Second, in consequence of that, I must seek to recover all those sums 'for my negligence' about 1.9 million – from the prescriber.

That would make a claim of 1.9 million plus, say a mere £500,000 for my life, capital, home and 20 years income (its far more than that – about four million are the actual losses) = total claim 2.5 million. But, he then said that due to my alcoholism, I would be 25% contributory to the situation, and after the litigation, I would have to 'give' the damages to the trustee who would pay 1.9 million to SIF, and after that, there would be nothing left for me – as I was 25% to blame = I had no viable claim (ie net damages would only be 1.9 million of which I would get nothing).

So – *after* a jury had unanimously acquitted me, *after* police had admitted there was no evidence I had stolen anything – MY OWN LAWYERS were telling authorities, I was guilty – to end my chance of rebuilding a life. And they'd never spoken to the trustee, and got the conclusion wrong in law. It's that sinister feeling again, isn't it. Why do Thorold and Balen want no benzo claim to proceed? What would our judiciary make of this advice when it was put to them – Lords Bingham, Phillips, Nicholls, Scott, Brown and Lords Justices Aldous and Chadwick? Read on.…

If a doctor gets his diagnosis and treatment wrong he pays. If he makes false allegations of his client to hurt him, he's struck-off. Here you enter the closed shop world of cover-up and corruption.

LAB, acting on that advice, refused funding for Joe Shammah to bring my appeal against the 1995 Sting, as well. Thorold had blocked funding for both my civil claim and to restore my career.

I went over my position – pretty bad. I could appeal the decision of LAB clerks to accept that Opinion. An LAB Appeal is before a committee made up of local solicitors – often not the best ones, as they're busy making proper money. And that appeal committee was being told I had cost them - personally - 1.9 million pounds, by taking client account to the races.

Exasperated, lost silence, Louise read it then said:

"I don't think you really see it... I mean where your problem really was all the time?"

"Go on..." She put it to me slowly - that one man was at the heart of everything... Mike Thurston...

"Oh yes I know that. God only knows what he's been saying to everyone. Just think of it - he's had the ears of Williams, SDT, Marron, Balen, Paul and CPS"

"Yes but surely you just go on and do it yourself"

I explained why I couldn't – but had until April next to get things right. I'd run straight into practical trouble. Instantly it'll be plain that I have (a) no solicitors to support me – *after a trial!* and (b) no expert's report. They'll say – show us your reports; I haven't got any. I need expert's reports just to issue. I'll ask for time and have to admit that I'm appealing to the LAB Area the expert lawyer's advice that I have no claim. It'll be a waste of £500 - and I don't have that either so can't afford it. So I'm buggered again, to put it crudely. I had eight months get my act together - the Limitation Date, being three years after learning of the negligence.

I wrote out pages of submission LAB, Louise paid for it all to be typed and off it went. No lawyer could see me until I won that battle. Heaven knows I tried; problems of being poor. No medical expert could write a Report unless instructed formally by lawyers.

About noon on sunny Friday 22 August a car slowly emerged down the gravel drive and pulled up at my front door. Holly, wearing her studded collar - our attempt to make a softy appear fearsome - circled the stationary car, with its occupiers in awe of a Ridgeback. They'd finished their summer holidays and now wanted me to attend for arrest and formal interview – we agreed Monday 1 September at Weetwood. Four months since I was cleared. How would you cope, for you can't complain?

As I've said, we're all quite good in adversity. We dig in. I lay in bed on the Saturday night at midnight before the Monday interview, with radio 4 droning on as ever in the background; there had been a car-crash in Paris. Dodi Fayed had died and Diana was injured. By three I dozed off. At seven the news was out and I was numbed like the rest of England.

Weetwood police station at 9.58 am on Monday 1 September 1997: At 10.00am Sgt Bowles arrested me again. I recorded that this was an unlawful arrest. It was farce for over three hours, when I said I'd had enough and was going – there was nothing for me to answer I hadn't already. They released me on bail, to March next - four years on bail. Forget all that nonsense about civil and human rights - this is England. That meant I couldn't discuss anything or plan anything - more uncertainty. In charge was Hudson at CPS

Back home, I lay on my bed in the September warmth and once again my powerless position knocked me for six. Downstairs at 6.00 pm, unaware of all this, my neighbour caught me
"Ah" said he kindly – "the very man.   We need our house for people to live in, when can you move out"
'Oh god please… is there to be no end'
"Er...well...   umm - I've still got a few problems Tony - a bit difficult right now"
"But Simon, you did promise - as soon as trial was over".
He was right. What the hell do I do - where do I go? How do I get there and what do I live on. Louise came from work and took me on a mystery trip out to unwind. The week following brought a letter from my brother Andrew to whom I had written for help. For three years he passed within five minutes of my drive, and not once called to see how I was coping. Not a word since trial, save cutting the phone. He'd run away when his brother needed help – things hadn't changed much since our youth! I'd been told he had made millions in cash by sitting on Peter Wilkinson's shirttails. Now he wrote I was lucky to be acquitted! I smiled.

Out-of-the blue came a ray of hope. By letter 11 September Law Society President replied that (1) there would be an inquiry into my complaints about the Penson gang, and (2) I could appeal the loss of career *unopposed.*

Separately, I received a letter from Mrs Elston. Tribunal had ruled 'secretly' that Geoffrey Williams, without asking me to attend, had ruled allegations of lying in court, deceiving media and ruining two police investigations (Criminal contempt) "were not 'prima facie' evidence of conduct unbefitting a lawyer and advocate in court – so he had 'nothing to answer'. You couldn't make it up!!
- the closed shop and Omerta in operation.
'What would you do there?' - Accept your impotence?

I demanded sight of the Order; I wanted 'the name' - *who was giving Judicial Protection to Williams?* It arrived. None other than 'Anthony H Isaacs' - the very solicitor who had a vested interest the truth should never be made public - covered it up with ease.

-*"we work in the interests of justice and public good"* – my bottom they do. This ceases to be so comical, when you grasp that this is how the system works today - and will until the Isaacs' of this world are removed, with self-regulation ended. Lord Phillips later read the events, joined the cover-up, and made Isaacs 'President.' It stinks.

October 1997: "Right" said A.J Wilson the chairman of six Manchester solicitors - they'd read the Opinion and my Submissions - "…have you seen this?" waving some other paper at me. Months later I discovered it was Thorold's secret 'side-note' to them only, that I'll try to fight on, but mustn't. So the Appeal Committee followed the Thorold – I couldn't have any funding for lawyers to sue Z or get the essential Reports. And this was an important claim to set precedent, and bring negligent doctors to account – at last. That's how the system works; exactly the same for you as for me. But they gave me funding to appeal the career loss - limited to another QC's opinion.

I had five months left to raise money, and issue my writ.

CHAPTER FOURTEEN

'Saving the Day - salvation'

Redemption, absolution and salvation come from the same village of life. If you need it, redemption is earned over time and you must seek out absolution, but salvation can hit you from nowhere. Mine came in a dark Sainsbury's car park at the end of November 1997 - seven months since this nightmare should have been over, yet it was worse. The solution arrived.

As I walked back to Louise's car that evening, I bumped straight into Geoff Martin. A little older than me, of similar height and affable personality, with an office diagonally opposite mine in Leeds city centre; he was one of those (unkindly?) referred to as one of life's vultures - an Insolvency Practitioner. A man I always acknowledged at functions or in the street and eminently open and likeable:

"Now then" he started cheerfully - "what're you doing with yourself these days"

"Oh don't start me - I'll never stop."

- don't moan... no one wants to know another's problems...

"Well we read all about it and I saw the boys in blue in your office that day..."

I started. He stopped me; this was neither the time nor place.

"Simon - just stop there: I'm in all week - this isn't right. I'll explain"

"But I haven't any money..."

"Don't be silly, give my secretary a bell and come to the office; we'll have a coffee", said he walking away... "I'll explain......"

Louise continued to fund me as did Roger; I was trying to get by on Benefit. Still - soon I'd have my career back. The investigation into Penson and the Law Society staff hit the unaccountable walls of self-regulation – *'freeze him out'* was the simple answer. I finally received a reply from OSS about the inquiry. They wanted to know if I had *'anything of interest to add'* - the letter was signed Robin Penson - in charge of an investigation into himself. I smiled. *The home of Independence!*

I'd chosen solr. Howard Cohen for my career appeal, but he passed me down to junior partner McDonnell. I met a young boy-like solicitor with a mop of near black hair falling across his forehead, wearing an off-the-peg three piece pinstripe suit; the 1950's look. Fine, if that makes him feel like a lawyer. I explained what had happened. He said he would select a barrister who would put my case and take on the powers of Law Society. I said he must be 'non-Establishment.'

He selected and briefed a man called Guy (not Michael) Mansfield Q.C.; and we would meet on 4 December in his Leeds office when Mansfield was visiting Yorkshire. I looked him up – know as much as you can of those with whom you meet if only to try to understand them. *'Oh my god – what have you done to me, - oh holy boy-solicitor'.* Guy Mansfield, on my reading of him, would never expose dishonesty within the legal establishment; he was very much trying to get further into it. A year younger than me, Harrow educated, the son and heir of a hereditary peer, married to a French girl at just 22 and recently made a QC and part-time Recorder. So far as I could see, he was still wet behind the ears to real life. He was very much a part of the Establishment which had destroyed me – my foes.

I presented myself at Geoff Martin's smart Leeds offices and joined him in the Conference Room.
We passed pleasantries, then….
"Right then, what's all this about you lost a personal injury claim because you're bankrupt... or what d'you say... Trustee will give Law Society all your damages?"

I related the events and the history. It took sometime and he looked surprised – 'oh yes', he'd heard I owned Murgatroyds, but now knew it was all a big scam; I never had. It took me about fifteen minutes to finish… with Thorold's advice and reasoning to cancel my claim - that I needed trustee's consent and then he would take my compensation and give it all to SIF. Law Society is author of its own losses, and public losses by Penson's and Williams' deceit and stupidity.

"No....no....no, this is all wrong. It's quite simple really... First and foremost is that they've got the law wrong. It's not about the Trustee's 'consent' at all - it's much more than that. You have no right to issue any writ... on your bankruptcy, your legal rights become vested in the trustee in simple terms – there are some exceptions, but let's talk this case - the practice - the way it works. Second is our first duty as a trustee - is to take steps 'to realise assets,' and if they exceed the value of the estate debts, that is *your* money – so we must take you into account. We are y<u>our</u> trustee as well to that extent. Now from what you say, you don't owe anything to Law Society or SIF anyway. I can't judge that here and now, but it's the practicalities that matter. If you're right Law Society has much to answer for.

But that's not our problem - leave that one to your lawyers... anyway, as I say, we have enormous real power. Now there's an asset here worth a million pounds or more - your life - but you had legal aid to sue - you were in a very powerful position. We can do any number of things including simply giving you the entire claim - depends... er, to an extent, on what the creditors think - lots of things. We can make anyone *prove* their claim if it's dubious - we don't accept a claim simply because it was made - Law Society or not - and if we accept.... and you say we shouldn't, and are taking your money – then y<u>ou</u> can apply to court; we aren't judges"

"Hang on... you say I can't issue; well that makes sense, but you can't either... there's no money, so nothing ever happens"

"No 'course not, that's why *you* are, or I suppose I should say '*were*', in such a strong practical position. We have to work with you to realise the asset, or you with us - our first duty is to the creditors – and you, for we are your trustee of your share, and you were due over a million pounds – more maybe. Your losses exceed the losses of the estate, so we will do what we always do... we assign the right in law back to you, sometimes on terms and sometimes the whole lot. It depends from case to case...

We can't run a clinical negligence litigation case – we're insolvency people. And once assigned in law to you... the creditors can't touch any award to you... well again there are some exceptions if you've been fraudulent.

...Now in your case, it may be that once they know the truth, the creditors will let you keep the lot - if there really are any creditors. Sounds rather immoral all this... should you even be bankrupt - did you sign any guarantee" He paused. We talked the ramifications. This made logical sense. We went over the process and options for some while.

"So, as I say... that's your first port of call – the O.R. He's a civil servant, so don't expect decisions from him. He'll appoint one of us as Trustee – but this work should have been done years ago. The trustee can simply dismiss the Law Society or make them prove it and you can take us to court if we accept a debt and you say 'no - that's my money.'"

"Right - I can't go and issue any writ... you've got my rights"

"Yup - there's lots of authority. The present lead case is Heath v Tang - Court of Appeal job. Let's face it - it's in everyone's interest for you to bring this claim – the solution is that we will assign the right back to you to bring the action – first though, you need lawyers."

"There are other complications like no medical expert's reports, but I know they support me, and the barrister tried to say I'm an alcoholic – so just watch yourself Geoff, 2-3 glasses of wine and you're an alci!"

"What... beg your pardon?" he expleated... "you're not an alcoholic as well are you!"

"Yeah - I'm the first alcoholic never to drink much."

"Look this should have been sorted two years ago – finishing it now won't be as simple without lawyers, but see how you go. Come back and see me anytime... there's a simple solution really."

I had absolutely no money – and without that, I had no access to lawyers. My family didn't want to know me and I couldn't look to friends for thousands, which is what this would cost. I wrote immediately to the OR's office. Next was my meeting on 4 December with Guy Mansfield QC. As expected I met a charming man; it's the way most lawyers of standing – confident, articulate and relaxed. But, as I was learning - never assume competence in any lawyer. I was on top form, kept my calm, and chatted politely, as one must in these matters, until my hoped-for counsel and saviour said:

"You see... It's a matter of *'the greater good'* – righting the wrong done to you, or exposing the Law Society. Of the two, the judiciary will always... well, you see, on your own admission, you weren't fit to be a solicitor."

- *'shit - 'the greater good!'... don't let public know what law Society did - protect Williams and the mob.... stay calm, don't alienate him'*

202

But he agreed that he would do nothing until McDonnell had got a Report on the effects of the drug. The courteous meeting ended with nothing achieved. The cost to you? McDonnell and Mansfield did no more work and charged LAB about £5,000 for their 'Advice' – but gave none. Some would call it theft – but not lawyers. I was back in limbo, reliant on the boy-solicitor to do some work. I doubted everything about him.

Days later, there it was – R v Min. Of Defence *ex parte Murray (8 December 1997)*. Murray was a soldier of twenty years. He had reacted to the anti-malaria drug larium administered to him by the Army, and became violent to an officer. Causation of that aberrant conduct was the effect of the drug. The Army Court Martialled him, and dishonourably discharged him; with that he lost his pension as well. It's an absolute offence to strike an officer – just like it's an absolute offence to make a mess of a lawyer's accounts. A solicitor took Murray's case to Divisional Court and Lord Bingham, the Lord Chief Justice, ruled that this was unfair and overturned the Army ruling. He supported the ruling, - 'a man shouldn't lose his professional career.. "if there was medical explanation for out-of-character conduct." I took the decision to McDonnell who agreed - "looks to me like this is on all four with your case. I'll pass this to Mr.Mansfield".

Now there were solutions to everything. I had to make it happen. The fourth Christmas in this solitude and impecuniosity was upon me again. Those words – 'don't fight us, they'll stop you at each turn' repeated. By 'they' he meant types like Lord Bingham - now in my sights. I would get there - soon. I had faith in honest judges. If I fell asleep by midnight, I awoke within two hours, often less, with my mind going over and over the events of 1995 and trial itself. Perhaps now I know what Post Traumatic Stress Disorder (PTSD) is – the consequences of an event live with your mind forever – destroying your real life. I relived every moment time over and again. It can destroy you.

I must have gone a little barmy by then – reporting Hudson to the DPP – who sent my complaint about her, to her! Aidan Marron agreed to see me again on 9 January 1998 in his York Chambers: "Mr. Kaberry - people are talking." He said sternly - "You're making a nuisance of yourself ... and 'these are powerful people'"

- *'No they're ruddy civil servants! Who's he been talking to?'*
"Now, take it from me... back off, or they will find something to charge you with."
- *'Who the hell have you been talking to? What's going on behind the scenes - this stinks of corruption'*
I would walk away if I could, but they'd got me by the balls at the moment.

Finally I met with the OR on 14 January 1998; he confirmed the advice from Geoff Martin, and that there had been no approach at all from Freethcartright at all. What's more, there was no claim lodged by SIF. Penson, refusing to recover the funds and assets for Law Society, had lodged a claim in 1996 before the truth was out. It had not been accepted. (nor ever was).
-*'Wow, practicing solicitors would have Penson, Williams, and solicitors KD Yeaman and A.H.Isaacs by the goolies if only they knew what SDT had done with their money.. little wonder the cover- up. This had cost each one of them about £1,500! - needlessly'*

I knew where I wanted to go, but how do I get there? Now I had to wait for a trustee and then get an Assignment in law, quite apart from the medical reports. Thorold, Balen and Thurston had put me in an impossible position. I needed funding back

I needed my Freethcartright files, and hatched a plan to get them before they were doctored. It was late January - Paul Balen was away, so wrote him a letter, backdated, demanding the files by return. Then I rang Mike Thurston to bemoan my situation, and dropped in a complaint they were sitting on my files, and I was about to report them. Next day they arrived from Laura Smith. Two lever-arch files with very little in them.

I sat in the very cold Sitting Room (Holly was so cold she stayed on her settee covered up) that morning 29 January 1998, wrapped in my Crombie overcoat, scarf and flat cap ahead, and started to read.

Balen's notes confirmed: "if acquitted - *it would be good reason to continue.*" Thorold was adamant that the claim was *already* time-barred in May 1996 - so any further delay would aggravate the situation. I made a note - my own lawyers had motive to block my claim in July 1997 - because they delayed a further year. There was Thorold's fax to Paul - I should expect a lengthy sentence. *'He never expected to see me again'* - so did nought.

Eight months on, Balen asked Thorold to issue urgently to be in time. The moment passed and no writ was issued. What the letter tells anyone is that my solicitor Paul Balen thought in February and March 1997, I had a case to pursue. But on 28 April he asked me to 'drop it' - a massive claim to restore me to life. Explain that?

Next Thorold cancelled Hindmarch i.e. he got rid of my supporter. My blood curdled as I read a Note from Kevin Beaumont, Aidan Marron's clerk in York Chambers. The message read -

> "Mr. Marron found Mr. Kaberry to be a very difficult client and not at all appreciative of all the hard work done for him and the acquittals secured... he is not prepared to assist in the civil claim"

- *'oh Aidan – you pompous little .... - after I made you a star...'*

My hard-hitting letter to Thorold of 22 July followed next was Laura's Note dated 24 July 1997. He knew it wasn't SIF (Solicitors Indemnity Fund – my insurers) as he wrote in the Opinion. She told him Law Society offered to talk - he buried it.
- *'the absolute bastards.... you actually knew your advice was wrong.'*

That wasn't the end. Thorold added a short secret 1½ sides 'side-note' to LAB. It warned them I would try to fight his Advice, but assured them that he had investigated everything very closely. This is what they had waived at me at LAB Appeals.
Want to scream out – *"the utter bastards... I've got you now"*.

The evidence of deceit and incompetence by my own lawyers was certainly 'compelling.' My lifetimes' training struck in – do nothing in haste. I was alone. I had no money and no friends - no phone to call for help.

Up and down the Beechwalk to absorb the peace you get from tall trees, Holly getting as far as the paddock each time, then sitting down to await my return; but then she was now an old lady - going on eleven - but so gorgeous. Her once black smutty nose was grey. We had been through much together over the last years - day after day.

Crushed between Roger's mincing and sausage machines and with large beasts being cut up around me, I rang some Leeds lawyers looking for help. Not one would even talk to me:
"Simon" said a man younger then me from my original firm - "take it from me, you don't want Leeds solicitors. You've got to get yourself away from here - be honest... no one here will help you..." I was 'untouchable'. *Thanks Geoff!* said I of the protected one.

Finally solicitor Joe Shammah called me. I accepted his guidance that in law I must give Balen and Thorold '*the chance to right what they had done*' - and re-open legal aid to fund lawyers to do the work they hadn't done. A call to Domakin at the LAB told me he could not re-issue any funding to sue Z unless Thorold would back me (as it was cancelled on his advice).

On 10 February 1998 I sent critical letters to both lawyers headed:-

"Professional Negligence"....
asking them each:
(a) to explain why they had failed to approach the trustee to take the available assignment so I could issue a writ;
(b) to explain why they advised wrongly on all aspects, including that there was no medical support and
(c) To help me re-open Legal Aid, who would only re-issue on their advice;
Balen replied that my letter had been passed to 'SIF' *his insurers.* Thorold did as barristers do: he refused to even acknowledge any letter. Cold February passed, and I waited for everyone. I rang McDonnell each third day - it was now six months since he first saw me. He was either in hiding or 'just waiting for Mr.Mansfield' – hopeless.

I desperately needed money for everything - but all was sold by then. Uncertainty drives you wild along with the knowledge that we are taking on real unaccountable power. Holly had re-started creeping onto my bed every night at about 1.00 am; she felt the pressure once again, and took advantage of her old softie daddy. Yes, I had gone a little potty; wouldn't you? How naïve I'd been in

August 1995 to say it could only get better from thereon; unanimously acquitted - the lies exposed, life was getting worse.

I chased McDonnell. After an incident we had angry words. I didn't trust him. He didn't like me. Good grace paid a visit to stop my throwing him out of the window. In six months, he'd done nothing.

It was April and I had to try to do something – to later give evidence - '*I did all I could to mitigate and sue Z*'. Richard Aston loaned me the writ money by cheque to Richard Jackson. His secretary Lynne typed a writ against 'Z'. I needed to issue within three years from the date of knowledge that I had a claim.
"But I thought you said you couldn't issue as a bankrupt... and what about the missing medical reports?" said Richard Jackson –
"They'll ask you to give an undertaking to file one, and god knows what you're going to do at that? You can't give it"
"Yes… but I have to try, then show I was thwarted by Thorold"

At the court counter, I explained I wanted to issue a clinical negligence writ, without legal aid. "Have you a medical report?" – No. "Well, we need one; can you give an undertaking to file one?" (She thought I was a solicitor). Then I asked if bankrupts can issue writs; they checked then confirmed 'no' - it would be struck out. But I could now give evidence I'd tried to get out of the mess Thorold and Balen had put me in.

I sacked McDonnell and asked that all papers be sent to Lincoln solicitor Gilbert Blades, who I (wrongly) thought had run the Murray case. To block me, McDonnell wrote to LAB cancelling funds for my career appeal. I kid you not – that is what happened, with an application to pay him £5,000 for his time and advice. Lawyers at work; it's their system.

My neighbours needed me away - I was in their house and you, the taxpayer, were paying minimal rent for me. On 7 May 1998, on one of my better days - feeling well and at ease, a letter fell on my doormat. I walked into the sitting room, opening and reading as one does. From a Police Inspector, it told me a decision had been made that I was not to be prosecuted in Calibre. I smelt complete cover-up. As I read it I was ranting and pacing the sitting room..... Holly cowered - but she'd done no wrong

– "*the complete bastards – strung me out for another year - the little incompetent shits – the buggers*"..... I screamed
They won't get away with this. First, I needed proof positive.

4 June: Eviction Order was made for 4 July 1998. Domakin cancelled funding for any Appeal to Divisional Court. McDonnell told him he held 'an Opinion' from Mansfield QC. – there isn't one. There are lawyers like this!

I had submitted the full history to LAB Complaints office.
By letter dated 24 June 1998 LAB replied ….
"*I can well understand your concern at the way you have been treated by your former lawyers. But a decision was made by Area Committee to refuse you legal aid to sue the doctor, on the advice of those lawyers, so you cannot have funding....*
However funding to sue the lawyers (for negligence) is an entirely different thing....
"*Further, with regard to the manner and conduct of your lawyer, you may wish to consider reporting him to the OSS at Victoria Court, Dormer Place, Leamington Spa....*

I reported Thorold to the Bar Council, but couldn't report Balen as that is to the Law Society, where I am frozen out.

For the past two months I'd been trying to raise cash - for new lawyers, and to live. I had just one asset left; my 1/3 share in our joint inheritance from father, which he had once told me was his real inheritance** for us – due to mature in 15-20 years; I had assured him I would not part with it. At 65 it would be very handy - a lot of money. Right then, it was worth comparative pennies. Roger the butcher offered to lend me, secured by a transfer of my share to him; I trusted him to hand it back later, when I paid him. My brothers, as trustees, could block that deal. They had me over a barrel. They demanded it in toto - millions of pounds because I had no bargaining position. I hoped my situation would shame them into helping me. But far from it - they took the lot for coppers; each of us knew that in a few years it would be worth millions, but right then, my situation was desperate. Kit couldn't do it, and put his share in his son's names, but it was no problem for Andrew, who had distanced himself from me since The Sting. Weak men kick those who are down - to make themselves feel strong. Strong men don't - makes them feel weak. But without cash (a) I couldn't reach lawyers (b) I would have nothing to live on - and (c) Thorold would get away with it. Within weeks I would have nowhere to live at all. As I say - it takes all to make a world. I smiled at them. [**this isn't true - his real gifts to us were life, reputation, way of life and standards, good spirit and generosity, health and education - wonderful gifts. Use of them would be each individual's choice]

Little wonder that ever since, I am invited to no family function, wedding, anniversary etc. They got my inheritance for pennies and would make millions from my situation. You grin and bare it. It was surely a 'no choice situation' for me, and plenty of choices for them.

Just as I prepared to leave my home - end of sunny June 1998 Lynne Houghton wrote she had been appointed my Trustee in bankruptcy. No one had told her it was urgent.

I packed up and the remnants of possessions went to storage. Then I met Lynne Houghton, a spinster with mousy hair in her thirties who looked as though she could play bridge in a golf club lounge, at her solicitors in town - double costs from day one. I set out the history – I shouldn't even be bankrupt and had no debts. There was an asset to sue the negligent doctor or lawyers.

Question – '*will you assign my legal rights back to me?*'

The answer – '*when you have lawyers to verify what you have just told us*'. You need:
(i)   a medical report to confirm you have a claim, and
(ii)   funding or legal aid for lawyers to bring it.
When I had those, then she could make an Assignment. Balen and Thorold had throttled me well and true.

Petrina took my beloved Holly-dog to live with her parents in Staffordshire. That Lip was always stiff. Never – *ever* – let anyone know the pain, the sorrow, the hurt.... I assure you... you keep smiling and buggering on...

'*Right SK.... What's life in store for me next? ... I will return*'

Simon Kaberry

CHAPTER FIFTEEN

Discoveries – what really happened...
Seeking Justice in English Courts

I really loved my home - and all its warts. On 4 July 1998 I drove away up the tree-lined drive and green leaves of the beeches, limes and chestnuts - for the last time after 41 years. We try not to look back; we never feel sorry for ourselves - does no good. It's got to be "here 'n now." I was singing from Oklahoma as I swerved the potholes and the loose gravel snapped to the sides.... *'Oh what a beautiful morning, oh what a beautiful day, I gotta wonderful feelin' evrythin's goin' ma way...'* and it had to. Then *"he who would valiant be..."* to Balen's words of advice. The girls would sing Gloria Gaynor's song. This had to be the last punch, for I held the evidence to bring an unbeatable civil claim to regain my life. It wouldn't take that long. But by god, that day... umm.

With cash, I'd got an old banger; my worldly possessions were in three suitcases on the back seat. And at 49 years of age I had nowhere to live. Life was never meant to be this way - honest! First night I tried to stay with Petrina, but she - no way - wanted an ex-man hanging about as she tried to rebuild her life. I charged off and begged a bed from my oldest friend since schooldays in 1954 - but no one wanted to know me. Saturday night, Louise met up with me and we stayed in a small hotel. This was a pretend world - pretend you're on holiday, and keep laughing. The cash I had for lawyers would soon be gone: I had to preserve it.

This winner and survivor was now a loser. I ate humble pie and asked for a room with Petrina again - how roles had changed. The joy was that my best mate returned from staying with her parents, although truth was Holly may have been happier there. The house was tiny, and Holly couldn't go off rambling as she had all her life. An old woman shook her fist at Holly when she rambled into her garden and threw stones at her. Louise resented it; not allowed in.

Now - which lawyer? In Leeds, with the truth press-gagged, I am blackballed - to this day. Nor would anyone interview me for any job - my CV ends 'struck-off for stealing two million to go gambling.' The humbling experience of signing on each fortnight continued. No bank would even open me an account. An old family friend now living in Dorset offered – "Come and stay and bring the dog - you must come" - far removed from the prejudices of Yorkshire.

First I stayed in London, but no one would help; that cost me. So I made an appointment with a firm of Bristol solicitors who claim to specialise in suing other solicitors, and left food for Holly (big stew to warm up for each of the next five days), with Petrina's neighbour, who would feed her and let her out each lunchtime. What a horrible life for wonderful old Holly; Petrina returned at 6. Holly was too old for such a long trip. Anyway my 'bedroom' was the outside potting shed on a spring hospital bed. Holly - sleeping outside in a hut? - no way. Me - I can take anything. I stayed five days, drove around the Dorset towns. A very tall man at the lawyers saw me for some time. He needed a lot of money, far more than I had raised, so applied for legal aid. Patience… I would get there. Money was going fast and the car broke down; cost £600 to repair - a fortune - it had to go. The cash on transfer of my future to my family had gone in no time. But the seed was sown.

Discovering what really happened
It was August 1998. One Friday early evening I walked down the Ring Road and up into leafy Horsforth. I rang the front door:
"Now then" said Tony Heatherington, beaming, but with a sheepish guilty grin - "Simon... Good to see ya... come on in; how've you bin doin'? Read all about yu'"

We went into his front room - life looked good with two Mercedes in the drive. Tony was all grins.
"It were great." He was spluttering, not certain how to cope with me; but not embarrassed. "Simon…. 'ow can I tell ya'; we was all round TV here when you got off… but I said you would."

I calmed it: "Tony, now - I'm after information. I haven't seen Graham yet, so can you fill me in? Now - I got a letter last May that I'm not to be charged for conspiring with you, as I didn't - but what about you two?"
"Ah…. er… well, how can I put this? Well, Graham'll tell you anyway when you see 'im. We 'ad a bit of a fall out, shall I say. 'aven't seen 'im in two year. Go see him – ee'll tell ya"
I wasn't there to pick a fight or take sides – information only.

"No, I want to know about police and you. I know Peter Harper was let off with a Caution for theft, receiving and forgery..." he guffawed at that – "but what about you... and Graham. Have you been arrested or charged yet?"

"Nor wey… they came, they arrested mi, but it got 'em nowhere. Actually, they didn't know what they was doin'....."

"Go on… You see after July 1995... I don't know anything..."

"Yea we saw that… there were a few good laffs.... well, you know what ammin – dorn't get upset, but you was always going to get off weren't you?

"If only!" I smiled – "I can tell you it was a tight thing at times"

"Yeh well.. er.. Graham and I .... well you've gotta understand, we 'ad to look after usselves, we agreed the line - anything we got was used for your gambling debts. But I can tell you now; I never expected to see that letter you wrote fer us in Yarmouth, published by the Law Society - as a confession found in your office!"

"Yes, my friend Geoffrey Williams…."

"Well I'm sorry as I seh, but important thing is you was acquitted.... I'm sorry - all I can say. Where you living?"

"Don't go there - I've nowhere to live…. that aside, there was no evidence I had ever conspired with you, was there?"

"Well you was our solicitor, but then so were three other solicitors......"

"Quite - that's my point. So when were you arrested and what did you say?"

"They came 'ere at 7.30 in morning trying to be clever… Then I just sat there and never said a word. Without you, they couldn't touch us… they said you was going down - but you beat 'em"

We talked on. Then he sheepishly asked:

"Tell me this Simon… didn't anyone ever want to know where the money was… an' those cheques?

"Well I know someone went to my Lloyds account and emptied it, but he took too much and was caught on film, but it wasn't you - was it? Well, Jenny agreed with me – it wasn't you"

"No... it weren't mi, but I told 'im ee got greedy." He continued – "but what about them company cheques? Didn't anyone bother chasing them?

I played dim - "*Oh those* - no - you're safe. Once Williams said I had taken it all to gamble, all lawyers rowed along with him – refused to trace any cheque. All I knew was that I had scores of blank cheque stubs.... I was asked where the money was, and had to answer I didn't know.... I tried to get copies, but had no money and my lawyers... er... dead losses – refused to trace anything"

"...I don't believe it ..." he was shaking his head in disbelief - "you're telling me no one even tried to follow them..."

" So it was you?... all those blank cheque stubs" - I wore a forced grin to put him at ease. No one was going to prosecute any of them now

"Or naw, they didn't come to mi, but I knows where they was goin'. Some went to Calibre, others went elsewhere....... er, 'other people' shall we say. We 'ad it all planned what to sey if anyone asked – but no one did! .." he was grinning in his way. We were two crooks together in his eyes.

I'd stood trial for what he had taken from me, and their joint frauds, been re-arrested, and he saw me as his mate

"Look, Simon, if there's anything you want, just give us a ring or come round." Well, I'd rather like my money back, but touch him and I'd be tainted.

This was all needed for my action against police. These people should have been charged – for what I was charged. I could reach a jury - publish the truth and hold my head high again one day. That would open everything else about Law Society and CPS.

18 August 1998 was a big day in all these years. I travelled to Manchester for yet another appearance LAB Appeals Committee.

"Right Mr. Kaberry" opened the chairman "You had legal aid limited to counsel's Opinion on merit. There is no Opinion, so we will re-issue the legal aid limited for just that"

"But I scarcely need an Opinion - the appeal is unopposed" I retorted.

"No - limited to counsels Opinion" said the man who plainly was my junior, but he hadn't been doped up and set-up.

Another counsels Opinion - and funding transferred to Gilbert Blades. I'd lost a year with the useless MacDonnell. Back in Leeds, there was a voicemail message on Petrina's phone from the tall man in Bristol. Funding was also issued to 'investigate Oliver Thorold and Paul Balen at Freethcartright for professional negligence' – limited to counsel's Opinion on merit.

It was eight years since Petrina and I had parted, and so much water had passed under the bridge, there was nothing capable of rebuilding. Louise wasn't allowed up the small garden path to visit me. I had to find somewhere else, but until I set the 1995 'Findings' aside I couldn't even work for any lawyer. That is a terrible penalty to carry. And I was too ill at least one day a week to work – couldn't sleep.

More Discoveries

One Saturday shortly after, with PDs car, I presented myself at Graham's house on the outskirts of Bradford. He appeared from the side of the house - didn't seem happy to see me:

"What's this then - first visit…. out of the blue in years… you may have been in touch - haven't known what's bin goin on". He explained the front door was still triggered to the nearest police station, and gave me the history after the Sting. He hadn't seen Tony since returning from Spain.

With our meeting defrosting, he explained that after my arrest they had kept trading and made good money. As they traded on, he had gone to London to meet his Tony's 'partners'.

He continued, head down and shaking in disbelief - "I could write a book about it; but no one would believe what I saw. He had some funny friends, to say the least, and owed them – I mean these aren't people you play with. I met people you thought were just in films. Talk about crooks. And when they met me - no kiddin' - they kissed me, and again when we left…. he was in with some very dodgy types." Then it was The Sting on me, his departure, and a Sting on him as well. They've got the money.

"I can tell you - they're not people you argue with. Guns! - they've all got guns. Everyone who's anyone knows Frank as well - still dines out on the Kray connection. That's why police set alarms on this house. It's still triggered to them, haven't used front door since."

If only Freethcartright found this out for my trial or the civil claim. "I don't get this... do I take it police never arrested you... in over a year since I was arrested. Then they actually give you protection........!

215

"Yeah - that was August 1995. Tony made off with the lot. Fortunately, I'd got about forty grand stuffed away to get us by – I had no income."

-Where the hell did he get forty grand from; he was bust just two years earlier and in arrears with his mortgage.

He continued as I listened stoney-faced:

"Fraud squad came much later - late 1995, no, were it 1996.....? Came early one morning. One force was protecting me from Tony and another was arresting me. No kid - I saw them pick up your files in the attic and put 'em back! They hadn't even got the Calibre bank accounts. As far as they were concerned they'd got you, so weren't really bothered. They showed me what you'd said – you know, about me. You were fair. They said you were going down, and then they'd think what else to do after."

"Help me with this... you continued to pay the mortgages after I was arrested. Then it stopped...... and prats at Law Society paid them off. So, question is who's got all that money. There must have been over £500,000 on that aspect alone... *and* you got to keep the properties. There must be twenty flats there worth a lot of money... what, about forty grand each – that's £800,000.... on Howgate alone - then Harrogate. Who's got that and the cash?"

"Well, after you were arrested, we continued as before. We kept going... we paid the interest on the mortgages, but then... it came clear everyone was being told by the Law Society, that it were all you. So we stopped... none of the mortgages was registered as you hadn't even done the registration to Calibre..."

He grinned - "We had the deeds - so we sat on it, rented them out and Building Societies were fucked. Law Society repaid all the money to the Building Societies and banks..... Law Society held your trial, said you'd paid the mortgages and stolen the money - we were in the clear. Then I went away - came back, and had been stuffed as well. It didn't go into Tony's name, but he and his mates are in control of Calibre."

My turn to shake my head. He agreed there was no evidence of conspiracy between us.

I continued - "Did you know Tony had been helping himself to client account - forging cheques? And someone was caught on film taking cash from my personal Lloyds account

"I wondered where all his money was coming from. You see he was skint when he came out of prison early 1992, but by late 1993 he seemed to be loaded… I knew about Lloyds… it weren't him though – was one of his mates – but don't go near them. I mean it, they're dangerous… got guns, and they use 'em" - more looking down, and shaking of his head

I was there a good hour and we left on reasonable terms. I would set this before Judges who would listen. They couldn't all protect Williams. Media would be listening to the truth this time.

My Bristol lawyer was going to use 'agents' when instructing a London barrister. That would be hopeless. I rang round – hitting the closed shop world of lawyers. Finally I tried a cold call to Kingsley Napley. A young man in their clinical negligence department told me they had a very similar case ongoing right then. A client (its been in the public domain, so I can name it - man called Davis to whom I refer later) had been a successful businessman, prescribed a drug for a nasal problem. He changed dramatically, becoming a reckless fiend. He went wild, chasing skirts, having been a reticent type. He was sent to prison, bankrupt and lost everything. The causes of all these problems were the side-effects of nasal drug prescribed to him. The trustee in bankruptcy then assigned the right to sue the prescriber and the LAB funded the claim. Sounded on all fours with my claim – save I hadn't done any wrong. Kingsleys were bringing *exactly* the same claim that Thorold and Balen said couldn't be brought. And it succeeded for very substantial compensation for him.

McDonnell and Guy Mansfield had taken all the £5,000 issued with the certificate. More delays, as Blades sought more money. On 14 December 1998 I would be fifty; ten years of life 'missing.' I was eligible under the Homeless Persons Act to force Leeds City Council to offer me a flat and filled in more forms. We found a bed-sitter within walking distance from Petrina's house, so I could visit my beloved big dog that she left alone from 8.00 am each day, at lunchtime. She had been a real friend to me, so I must visit her each morning and afternoon; horrible life for her.

Into December and Kingsleys would see me. Blades chose Lord Thomas of Gresford QC, as my counsel. When ennobled, you have to say "of 'somewhere'" to avoid confusion with other lords of a similar name. *Another ruddy Welshman* I thought, followed by – *bury your own prejudices SK!*

Fortieth birthday, I stood dinner for forty. On my fiftieth birthday I moved into a smokey, smelly bed-sitter with hard concrete floors, on which I had to sleep until my bed could be retrieved, and a table and chair from storage. The chipwood walls needed stripping of all the accumulated smoke stains. There was no bath but a shower. Kitchen has room for one person, but not a washing machine. This was to be home - and I had to adapt. I had to apply for free rent, paid by the council and council tax relief. I should be working and contributing to life generally - instead I was now a statistic, dependant on the state, and must fit into the new mentality. A state emergency loan met set-up costs - £250 came, but that would be deducted from my fortnightly GIRO. Also deducted would be my water rates and electric supply costs. That left a GIRO of £22 per week to live on. But soon, I was bound to meet honest judges who would put an end to all this – career back, reputation restored and compensation for some of my losses. I smiled a lot; it's what we all do. I reckoned it would take about 6-8 months.

But if I got a job, I'd lose legal aid and my lawyers wouldn't act for me. I had a new weapon for the first time in four years. Yusuf Nurgat loaned me a WP system and printer with Word on it. Now I could draft my pleadings against police. I even started this book.

20 December: I presented myself at Kingsleys Napley and met Richard Foss aged about thirty. He was to be my solicitor in a 'professional negligence' against the lawyers. They had the two small files of Balen from the tall man in Bristol.

I offered the full set -"No; we only have legal aid to cover our time reading these two civil files. That is the extent of funding."

"But – you can't follow the facts without these other files..."

"No – take them away. When we need further from you we'll be in touch"

- '*I've been here before… read and grasp the files…*'

I was ushered away by Richard's chatty secretary, who I befriended as my point of contact. Only when lawyers said I had a claim would Lynne Houghton assign the right to sue - '*Just give them a month and by February, they'll have grasped it – don't be a nuisance SK......* ' All I needed was a medical report from Malcolm Lader or Ian Hindmarch.

Next day I attended Lord Thomas's Chambers at 5.00 pm. Dr. Johnson's Buildings (he didn't live there) are just through the archway opposite the Courts in the Strand, via a ginnel leading to Middle Temple. I had looked Thomas up - a Liberal politician from Wrexham way. The Liberal voice in the House of Lords on Legal Affairs, people would listen to him for sure – but would he shout the odds – against the legal establishment! What I didn't know until too late - he sits with Lady Bonham-Carter, the Liberal who had set me up. I met Gilbert Blades - an awfully nice man aged late 60's or even maybe seventy. We chatted politely, as you do. But he made it plain - you don't expose Law Society... "'they' won't like it."
 - 'Oh dear – stay quiet SK ignore them, and just do it!'

Lord Thomas was also an approachable man, about six foot and with full crop of hair, polite manner, and a listening ear. Would he expose *'that ruddy Welshman'*, or Lady B-C!
"Right Mr. Kaberry. This letter is the one - this letter from the President of the Law Society; this one dated 11 September 1997..."
But now it was 20 December 1998; MacDonnell had delayed me over fourteen months - cost me a year of earnings.
"Well yes, but we have to expose what they did – the consequences"
"No - your legal aid funding is limited to advice on 'the merit' of an appeal. Now according to this, you're unopposed... so..."
And Gilbert joined in: "So Lord Thomas can do a simple Advice to extend funding to apply to appeal itself."
I had no money and was alone in all this – an outsider.

Christmas in a council flat was yet another new experience. I now had no car to get about. 'Soon' - I assured Holly - 'soon this nightmare would all be over' and we could have a home again. I had to walk everywhere each day. Hours spent being splashed as I walked 30 minutes to get Holly her lunch, then thirty minutes to take it to her. It does breed resentment. These were the worst months, but I could see the end – soon; reality was the entire year of 1999 was the lowest times. Still I was 'losing' at least one day a week through sleep deprivation. But I knew I would win through - what would you have done? Give in?

Richard Foss's ever chatty secretary told me he was "reading the files" - in January... then in February... and still in March.
"Is Richard a particularly slow reader?" asked I. In fairness, I knew Richard was working 24/7 on another big case. Gilbert was never in his office. "We're just waiting for LAB to come through" - "And what about the Advice from Lord Thomas?" – "Oh yes, that as well." Lawyers at work.

April wakes people up. Thomas finally did his Advice (3 months to write one side of paper and be paid £2,000 for it, for you are a clever QC) and LAB extended funding to pay for my appeal, which was lodged in the Divisional Court. They deleted all my accusations from my affidavit in support. It was served on Mrs. Betts at Law Society, who sent it to the man who had cost them and the public so dearly – Geoffrey Williams. It was a simple 'unopposed' Application for permission to have a full appeal – Williams opposed and it was adjourned.

Richard Foss chose Hugh Evans of 4 New Square as my counsel; it's a large set of Chambers in Lincolns Inn which deals with professional negligence. I kept saying – "all we need is a medical report, then the right to sue is assigned and I've won."
"No - I don't have funding for that - just to get a barrister's Opinion on the merit of proceeding." Lawyers churning papers; that's litigation.

Kingsleys made it plain – if anyone was so bold as to employ me I would lose legal aid, and they wouldn't act, unless I could miracle a large amount of money. It wasn't such a dilemma, walking about with a Finding of dishonesty!... and ill-health at least one day a week. Pride had long since been replaced by realities of life - living hand-to-mouth. I wore second-hand shirts, and relied on Louise and credit from Roger. They say sleeplessness causes depression, but I don't understand that concept – it never broke me. I was going to win and rebuild my life. There was no defence to the civil claim and no reason why the SDT Finding shouldn't be set aside. It was inevitable.

I drafted my actions against Law Society and police. What's more, research told me I had the right under section 303 Insolvency Act to make application to a Judge against a trustee to force her to act if she won't. My claim against West Yorkshire Police was, (1) unlawful arrest and false imprisonment after trial and (2) hiding evidence at my trial in the hope of securing my conviction, and (3) incompetence: letting three men walk away from justice, whilst putting me on trial.

All court fees were met by Fee Exemption (equality of access to justice) for the poor; I issued writs against Law Society, alleging 'Misfeasance in Public Office' - the unlawful abuse of the power.

West Yorkshire police applied to the Court to strike out my claims before the evidence was ever heard - get a Judge to block me. But there was never any evidence of my conspiracy - that was clear since August. They disclosed their Accountants Report which concluded that 'Kaberry could draw comfort from the fact money hadn't gone to him.' Trial had been told there was no such report. This was scandalous – the concealment of evidence to try to pervert justice. Remember Stefan Kiszko? It still goes on and judges, as you will read, to the Court of Appeal - cover it up to 'maintain public confidence.' But if it happened to you?

Meanwhile, each creditor, now aware of the truth offered assistance.. .Graham Sykes, for Courage, now wrote:

8 October 1998

Dear Miss Houghton,

Re: Simon Kaberry

We gave instructions in 1995......etc to make him bankrupt...I am aware that the bankruptcy severely prejudiced his civil compensation claim arising from the negligence....... Acting fairly and responsibly, Courage say:

(1) *We do not wish to take any part of damages properly due to Mr. Kaberry intended to compensate him and to rebuild his life.*

(2) ....

It seems to us that the claim lodged by Law Society is invalid. As petitioning creditor we call upon you to reject it...... They appear to have caused much of this situation and have wrongly defamed a man who has been shown to be innocent.

Had we known the true position in 1995 it is unlikely that we would have proceeded with a bankruptcy petition.

So - I immediately had full support of 'creditors.' The law then was that you lose your personal pension if bankrupt. Miss Houghton and her lawyer were after mine now I was 50; she could cash it in, then divide it between them for their costs of getting it. I'd only paid in for a few years – a fund of about £70-80,000, so they wouldn't get much.

Courage and Black Arrow (another guarantee) also supported (letters) my Application that the bankruptcy should be annulled. In other words, had Freethcartright worked for me, 'creditors' wanted none of my compensation - *it was going to be so simple. .*

I was well and alert for the first day's police hearing at Bradford County Court before Judge John Altman. As I arrived, dressed as the lawyer I once was, I was stopped at Security Checkpoint:
"Are you sitting today sir," said the guard, diverting me where Judges go; the same thing had happened at Newcastle. I smiled at him: "Well, I'd like to be for sure, but I fear there'd be too much proper and real justice administered if I were sitting.."
Obviously I'd make a good judge and look the part.

We argued our respective cases for two full days - long enough for a trial which was reason alone why this shouldn't be struck-out. The jury should hear all this and try the case, I said. Altman said he wanted to 'think about it' and would give judgment later - *two months later*! The issue was simple – could I put these matters to a jury to decide.

I was actually my own full-time lawyer now. Next came my Hearing in Leeds County Court on my 303 Application – to order Miss Houghton to reject Law Society claim. It was put before Judge John Behrens in Leeds. I knew Behrens from 1977 as a gawky, gangling young man; a sort of Bernard Levin look-a-like with fuzzy hair and full of his own pomp with much inherited family wealth. Now he was a Judge. One of my 'Lost Days' struck on our Hearing day - 8 December.

In court, I was a walking zombie; mentally I was drained -fumbled my papers. Behrens walked into court and had filled out into a big man, more pompous than ever before. I was in no position to put my case; I told him I shouldn't even be bankrupt – he mocked me:

"Mr. Kaberry - you couldn't pay your debts when they fell due... of course you should be bankrupt."

-' prat – so would you be if someone stole all your inherited wealth and income then forged your signature to a guarantee'

He didn't want to know… "Mr. Kaberry, the trustee has neither rejected nor accepted the Law Society claim. She may well assign the right to sue whoever it is you want to sue, but only when you have shown her that you have a case. As I understand it, you have not done that. Now, a time may come when you have that evidence and then you see her again. It's terribly simple. You will find I decided this point in Ord v Upton which the Court of Appeal has upheld. Until you have the information and medical reports, you cannot make her do anything... then she will assign."

And he continued: "Costs...you - Mr. Kaberry will pay the costs of this Application, and as you haven't got any money, Miss Houghton can take the costs for her and her lawyer from your estate" (that means my pension fund).

Duly humiliated, I left court. But Behrens confirmed that Thorold had left me in an impossible position in law in July 1997, unable to mitigate that position. And I had *Ord v Upton.* So there was much good in that losing application. I went to read the Appeal Court decision – the trustee has 'a duty' to the bankrupt to assign. 'Oh yes' - there was much good in this bad.

Back into Court next day for the delayed Altman ruling. Police had done no wrong - nothing for a jury to hear ! *"You can't sue police"* - the usher mumbled to me under his breath. I asked for Permission to appeal that strike-out - "Very well Mr. Kaberry – put your grounds in writing and remit them to me to consider."

Let me explain the 'appeal process' in law. In civil cases, if a judge refuses you Permission to appeal his decision, you have to go to the Appeal Court (London) and persuade a 'Lord Justice of Appeal' that there is something to argue in law. Usually, the first judge will tell you to get lost, but can grant Permission; then you have a full hearing later before a full Appeal Court (usually three judges). Louise came to visit for dinner and couldn't understand my delight: "You don't follow... it's so fantastic – just to feel so well, that's far more important than all this crap... even living in this doss-house!" Our health is far more important. Altman refused my Application, so I had, by the Rules, 30 days to file "Application for Permission to Appeal", in the Royal Courts in the Strand. I lodged my Application.

Each day I visited Holly at lunchtime and again late afternoon. Petrina left her car for me to take Holly to her doctors. As a poor person, I qualified to take her to PDSA. Holly and I had to wait an hour and a half for each appointment in a crowded surgery, with a variety of council house dogs growling at one another, and Holly looking aloof to it all. We'd lost not just our home but a little dignity. She was getting to be an old lady and was slightly leaking urine; they told me her heart wasn't good – in fact they said it explained why she sat down and just looked at me when I tried to make her go for a walk. It was awful, but needs must – they do a wonderful job there helping the poor and infirm (owners and dogs).

My career appeal had been re-listed for November 1999, and then taken from the List without reason. 'Someone' was delaying each move I tried. It took Fossie from July to December 1999 to arrange for me to meet my counsel Hugh Evans. The entire year, so high in expectation, was gone; it was a horrible year - worst out of all of them. I sought help from the Leeds Law Society solicitor on Law Society Council - a man called Roger Ibbotson, who I knew from my training days. I sent him chapter and verse of The Sting, the consequences for all lawyers, me and public, and the cover-up. He refused to see me, or do anything. What happens to men who won't expose Establishment wrongdoing? Correct – they become judges (as Roger has).

Funded by Kit and PD, I travelled to stay with Elaine in her Mayfair flat. Put on my now ten year old smart suit, but that matters not – wear a good overcoat and walk along Jermyn Street and up though Burlington Arcade into Bond Street and anyone can soon forget how poor they really are. One day I will return!?
I presented myself at the offices of Kingsley Napley at 9.10 am. I watched Richard read the Lader Report and notes of the July 1997 meeting. Fossie could do nil until counsel said we had a claim. But why do we need a barrister to tell us that! We should have been ready to issue proceedings six months ago.

We took a taxi to New Square via Lincolns Inn. Anyone visiting this place can only be impressed. Picture Jamie Lee-Curtis visiting counsel's chambers in 'A Fish Called Wanda'; its lovelier and more sedate, secure and privileged than it looks on film – and this was a grey winter day. New Square is at the back of the Royal Courts in the Strand, in between the Courts and Lincolns Inn. We were shown up to the room of Hugh Evans which overlooked the Square.

A very tall man, 6' 5'' at least, slightly gawky, in his late thirties came to welcome us. First impressions were good; this was no pompous Aidan Marron or devious Oliver Throttled. I could talk to this one. On his desk were my files, labelled with yellow markers all over. He'd been working. I was calm, very well and self assured that day - had to make a good impression.
It got better:
"Well Mr. Kaberry…I'm going to give you a kind of inverted compliment, if I may" he said with a slight guffaw – "Assuming you are a clever man, which I do, you must have been mad to even try to do what they said you were doing"
Silence. The raised eyebrow look. He continued….
"Because anyone with an ounce of sense would have known you hadn't the slightest chance of getting away with it… So you, being logical, you wouldn't have even tried"
   - *'glory be…   glory, glory be….after five years….. A bright barrister - he got it straight away'*
"Yes, but there's also 'the fact' that I didn't do as they alleged – the facts don't support the allegation."
"I'm sure you're right, but that doesn't mean we don't have a number of obstacles to cross….. and it won't be easy, for example… those amazing confessions of yours. Now you want to allege that Oliver Thorold deliberately delivered a bad Opinion to put you down. That's a very dangerous thing to allege and not at all easy to prove. One question is whether it even should be made. Judges won't like an attack on a barrister"
I explained why he had no answer, and had lied. It did me no good – he wouldn't accuse another barrister of dishonesty.

But he agreed we needed a medical report. Proper Instructions to Lader and Hindmarch followed by informed reports as should have been drawn in 1996 would determine whether I had any case

-*'but that's what I said a year ago... we've wasted an entire year... don't despair, we're getting there'*

"Right then, I'll draw an Advice for LAB to issue funding for two medical reports then we look again. OK".

Within six - eight weeks the reports would be in place and what could my former lawyers say then? Houghton would then assign - what defence could Balen and Throttled have... would *they* take personal responsibility for the position they'd put me in? Within this next year 2000 - this would be over. It was inevitable...

.... thank god I'd persevered.

C H A P T E R   S I X T E E N

"First Sightings of Men of Honour and Integrity"

You know the feeling - "*I've come too far to turn back now.*" My perseverance would be rewarded this year for sure - five years on and ten years missing. But what else ? - sanity?

Only too conscious that so many years were missing, I gave Richard Foss to 30 June to get the medical reports. In default I would walk away. I still had to win just one of those three target cases; just having the truth published was a complete win.

My Appeal to set aside the SDT Kangaroo court was listed before the Lord Chief Justice of England Lord Bingham for 10 April 2000 - four months on. Before that, my first taste of the Appeal Court beckoned - to appeal Altman, now listed in the Court of Appeal. Precedent supports me; I was bound to be allowed a trial.

I must persuade a 'Lord Justice of Appeal' that there are 'triable issues' to put to people like you. Rules require you file the 'Grounds of Appeal,' and a skeleton argument, setting out a resume of your arguments. The Judge is meant to have read those before coming into court. What's more, this concerned the concealment of evidence by police at my first trial, that three men had made off with fortunes, that the jury had already decided I was confused, and there <u>never</u> was any evidence that I had conspired with anyone – quite the contrary. The police case was that they were told to re-arrest me by Hatton QC - a barrister.

Access to justice and a fair trial is '*a fundamental civil right'*. But 'Claims' can be struck out before any evidence is heard and tested to prove it, if a judge deems the claim are 'frivolous' or 'vexatious' or an 'abuse of the court process' (as stated in numerous cases including Ashmore v British Coal Corp 1990 2 ALL ER 981 – per Stuart-Smith LJ) <u>or</u> 'bound to fail.' However – how can they judge if a complex matter is bound to fail, without hearing the evidence first! I had bundles of it. Police can lawfully arrest one of us as "*part of the continuing police inquiries*" and that is a full defence to such a civil claim.

This was a serious case of abuse by police - they charged a man who couldn't have done as alleged - then hid evidence from trial, which confirmed that - then, after acquittals re-arrested him, for 'conspiring' with those who had deceived him - and never charged the wrongdoers. But the problem was there for me - any trial would inevitably expose the Judge's friends - Law Society.

Litigants in person stand in the front row to address a Judge. Into a completely empty court came Lord Justice Kennedy - like all of them - public school and Oxbridge. This one was Ampleforth in Yorkshire first. A big gruff man, his attitude was - 'who's this ruddy nuisance.' He handed down some case law - that arrest is 'just part of the investigative judicial process'. I'd read them; mine was readily distinguished. He heard me without listening, then swiftly delivered a pre-drafted Judgment, that it was quite right that I be arrested, detained and bailed - even without evidence to answer - "Mr. Kaberry should have known better" said Kennedy -known better than what? - to expose wrongdoing in Establishment. Sorry - but Kennedy stinks. Those words echoed … '*they'll block you at each turn.*'

This was my first meeting with these Men of Honour and Integrity. They can't all be like that - *can they?* - *One down.*

A couple of years later the case of a friend of Michael Lawrence came before Kennedy. The friend had been arrested and detained after that murder – 'as part of the ongoing inquiry.' But there was no evidence he had anything to answer. His case for wrongful arrest and imprisonment was struck out before trial in a lower court; Lord Justice Kennedy re-instated it, saying police '*should have known there was no good reason to suspect the friend.*' Exactly the same as my case. The friend was later offered substantial damages by police to settle. What would a jury have made of my case? Hidden evidence, no one charged – cover-up. No way did I conspire with them.

Likewise, the Hamiltons sued the police for 'unlawfully being arrested, detained and questioned' on the silly allegations made by Nadine Sloan. The High Court followed Kennedy's ruling that police can't have the protection of 'part of the ongoing inquiry' if they know the allegations are silly. Think again of the Kiszko case

- sixteen years in prison after police hid evidence. A judge blocked the prosecution of police for 'perverting the course of justice' on the grounds of public interest. The policeman's lawyer? - Kerry Macgill;[Kerry had told me they got the judge to 'stay' the prosecution of Supt Holland on the grounds that Kiszko really was guilty - hence not in the public interest. Years later DNA evidence showed this to be false and the crook is in jail]. This is our honest and open legal world – 'the best in the world!' so god help the world. But it's your world too. Until they are made accountable to an independent committee, this abuse of trust will continue. And it gets far worse....

I was living hand to mouth as a very poor man, scraping by from day to day. I walked for miles each day to visit my beloved dog, left alone in Petrina's home; that hurt more than all the insults. I was so sad for the life she lived in her later years – no more plodding off around the gardens at Adel Willows as she had all her life. I continued to sign on each fortnight and go over job applications and make calls for jobs as clerks, - all to be rejected as "he's too qualified". Another time I applied as a PA to a man like me – "I fear your skills would be wasted on me." Untouchable.

And through it all, I still had my lifetime hobby, but I didn't have any funds to do as I used to. Worse still, I had lost the will, risk and eagerness (and ignorance) of the younger man. The years when nothing mattered have taken a big toll - what had been a highly profitable hobby no longer was possible. I'm not that interested.

Now the big one – to set aside that awful 'Finding'. Gilbert Blades and Lord Thomas made it clear - "no way (putting my real case), for 'Bingham wouldn't like it' - an attack on Law Society". All my allegations about Williams - out. But I had the bundle of exhibits, so put it al back in - my own "CHRONOLOGY."

I read up on Bingham. His father sent him to Sedbergh (not top-notch), in the Dales between Yorkshire and the Lakes, then Oxbridge etc. A contemporary of his at College told me the reason they wouldn't have him as Chancellor was his pomposity as an Undergraduate. So, he doesn't like elections and accountability. I remembered an article suggesting, on his transfer from Master of the Rolls to LCJ he was a weak man, not up to the job. And my old man, despite being of limited words about home, had said something disparaging of him; just what I couldn't remember. His son Harry had given up work to write and care for his wife when she was knocked for six by ME. So, he should understand mental issues. Was such a man up to punishing dishonesty and public deceit by closed-shop lawyers? I reckoned it was touch and go, because he has made so many speeches about "the importance of independence" of lawyers and been a dinner guest of my foes so often, where he was lauded and praised - pay-back time? I'd learned the words of impartiality, honour and integrity are meaningless. But I kept faith - no choice.

Staying with Elaine, I arrived at the Royal Courts at 9.30 am and waited outside Court Four - "The Court of the Lord Chief Justice of England and Wales" states the ancient plaque. Not that ancient for this building only went up in the late 1890's. A rather insignificant man was also waiting; this had to be Geoffrey Williams - buggered my life. I wasn't allowed to hit him. Williams and Law Society were represented by Timothy Dutton QC, who had been at my school Repton some years after me.

10.30. Enter the Lord Justice Chief Justice Lord Bingham. On his one side The Honourable Mr. Justice Jackson and on his other side The Honourable Mr. Justice Astill. Divisional Court is a hybrid. Not the High Court and not the Appeal Court – something in between which deals with administrative processes and reviews of such decisions. The sole issue was whether I could have a trial before being judged a dishonest thief and struck-off; Law Society argued I shouldn't have one - work that one out. I was supported by Bingham's own decision in *re Murray* – 'a man should not lose his professional career when there is medical explanation… ect'

My noble lord stood to address them. '*Bingo*' – he took them straight to my <u>Chronology.</u> They opened it. That set out the entire history - the negligence, the thefts and frauds on me, The Sting and consequences - my trial and acquittals and that I was suing my former lawyers who had blocked this Application, let me down so badly; included was my SDT Application about Williams and the cover-up by Abraham. Bingham and Messrs Jackson and Astill had all this to read then and later.

For over an hour and longer, my noble lord spoke with force, but they weren't my words. He took them to a letter from Mike Thurston, advising that if I didn't get the 'Finding' of SDT set aside, I could apply for a Judicial Review:

"A Judicial Review – *of me??!!*" smarmed Lord Bingham, as if to prove absolute power does corrupt absolutely.

Bingham read my letter to SDT that "*to act judicially, you must allow me to defend*" and "*what happened to me could happen to anyone... even someone reading this...*"

Bingham:"I don't understand what Mr.Kaberry was trying to say!"

On behalf of the Society Dutton argued I must <u>not</u> be allowed any trial before losing my career on a Finding of gross dishonesty. The irony of the situation should not be lost.   Dutton QC was paid by every practicing solicitor – to argue that solicitors should <u>not</u> be allowed a fair trial before SDT. Further Dutton later became chairman of the Bar Council, an organization which allegedly seeks honesty. Is it true all men have their price, be it as contract killer, or rogue in court, dressed as honourable? Bingham referred to the jury verdict as 'colloquial' – that's 'common' to you.

Dutton: "My Lords" he said - "insofar as this appellant alleges misconduct by Mr. Williams, I must remind you that Mr. Williams is a respected and experienced solicitor. It shames us that this man (me) - 'convicted as he stands by the Tribunal of dishonesty' - should allege anything. Wherever there is dispute between them as to what was or was not said about an adjournment, you must accept the word of Mr. Williams rather than of the convicted man."

- *'Oh you little toad... how standards have dropped at Repton...'*

But I observed the three honourable men in wigs nod quietly in agreement. I had attacked a lawyer representing Law Society. Law Society made accountable - Heaven forbid; next it would be Judiciary being accountable! – "the importance of independence"

My counsel responded in the afternoon. More words, all joined up, but together they amounted to little of any moment save:

> "My Lords by the very rules of natural justice by which we all live, this man must be entitled to a trial before losing his career and being adjudged dishonest".

Simon Kaberry

My Journal entry that I could 'trust Williams' was exhibited. Bingham said it was *'evidence of nothing.'* (no evidence allowed) "Could you return Lord Thomas - tomorrow at 9.30 am?" Bingham and I eyeballed one another, sitting directly opposite, me being on a raised bench; I nodded - "Well Mr. Kaberry is indicating he will be here anyway," but I would never be allowed the courtesy of any Witness Box or to address him.

Next morning, court was packed with students there to hear justice administered in England, unaware of the truth behind the charade. A Judgment by a Lord Chief Justice. Bingham knew the consequences for me if he refused my application - I awake each day, and live out my days proclaimed a dishonest thief, without trial - in defiance of a jury. It would blight anyone. He started...

"This is an Application by Mr. Kaberry for permission to appeal the Findings of the Solicitors Disciplinary Tribunal on 26 July 1995"... he then recited limited facts and his Judgment proceeded with these rulings:

(i)   I was guilty of delay - "he wrote to everyone complaining and saying he would appeal, but didn't" (*ignoring the chronology which explains how I was blocked by Freethcartright then Guy Mansfield*) ;

(ii)   Hence no factual or medical evidence - to enable a court to fairly judge anything - could be presented; (*this was an Application for permission to appeal*)

(iii)   Law Society's Tribunal made "a strong decision, but not a wrong decision" to deny me the right to a trial in July 1995 (*strangely no one sniggered – how on earth can a ruling to deny a trial be anything but wrong!*);

(iv)   Williams and Law Society "deceived no one" in Tribunal and 'met a public duty' (*it is commonly agreed, they published a pack of lies to media, committed a criminal contempt of court and ruined two police investigations, saving three men from facing justice*);
        [if Bingham were a politician, he'd surely be run out of office for such a complete cover-up]

(v)   The Jury verdict was irrelevant, for I admitted that under the influence of the drug I was not fit to be a lawyer (*likewise Bingham would be unfit to be a judge if doped up – so he should lose his career, home, reputation, income and pension if unable to think-straight?*);

232

(vi)   There had been 'no injustice' to me in 1995 or since. To justify this, he 'invented and found proved', a new charge - that I had written to a client saying I had done something when I hadn't. It's not true. He extracted my confessions again.

One of those special - *'Establishment 6 Justice 0'* moments.
We get them whenever a Judge is asked to investigate wrongdoing by Establishment or his colleges. He'd repaid those dinners; only when there is independent accountability will things change.

I watched Tom Bingham closely - he would shame any second-hand car dealer in the 'fibbing without flinching' stakes, knowing he was selling a pup. I assumed my ever-stoic solemn face; it's pointless huffing and puffing. Time to smile – at last some sound advice from Freeths – *'yes, we do have bent judges who would block me at each turn.'*

But at the very end, Bingham, realising his breach of oath, said that *'nothing that I have said should stop Mr.Kaberry applying to be restored to the Roll,'* and on such *Application "he can deploy the medical and other evidence"* which I had wanted to give in SDT and before him then, but that was *'completely at the will of Law Society to decide if he can have his career back.'*
-'i.e. "go be judged by the very men who set you up, caused such damage and deception, and who have a vested interest that the truth must never be told....' Sounded fair to outsiders.
Reality - I hadn't a chance in hell.

All vows to expose Williams lay in tatters; he'd buggered me a second time. How would you cope, knowing at any time people can openly say there's a finding of dishonesty against you, as they do, to this day. How would Bingham cope?
'That's two down - one to go'.

Don't think that just because a man is a Lord Chief Justice, you'll get a 'logical and honest' verdict. Lord Hutton was an LCJ (in N.Ireland). He heard that David Kelly was likely to expose serious 'wrongdoing' (deceptions) by UK and USA governments. Kelly was 'exposed,' taking the storm well, but was concerned about his wife. He went for a walk at 2.30, chatted to people, seemed well and not subdued, but didn't return; he died sometime between

10.00pm and morning when he was found in a field. He had a few painkillers in his blood, but not enough to cause injury, and his wrist was cut, but he appeared to have lost little blood. The knife used to inflict the injury, had no fingerprints on it. He followed a religion where it is a sin to commit suicide. This man had much to live for. Lord Hutton ruled - he committed suicide, because he was unable to take the pressure of his honourable act and public duty, for which we would all applaud him.   Let's say - 'a curious verdict.'   So - what of Lord Bingham's?   You tell me. Do you want him to judge you? He'd just shafted the rest of my life to protect his perceived friends and Legal Establishment, hadn't he?

Walking up Chancery lane, I looked for positives, but there was no good in any of this - *bastards*. Worse - the big fear was that all Judges would now follow the Bingham line
- *'block him... don't let him expose our system.'*
... *'doors which are open will be slammed, doors which should open will be locked....the greater good to protect Williams/Isaacs'*
- or am I wrong?
Between April 2000 and April 2008 I petitioned Tom Bingham twelve times, setting out the history and consequences. So that I could have some peace of mind before I died – could he hear my Petition, as senior law lord, and set aside that dreadful 'Finding' without trial, that I am a dishonest thief; it blights all I try to do and leaves me open to attack each time I try to get up. To each petition he refused to answer. He could have, but that would mean allowing the truth to out. 'Man of honour' - you tell me.

As in 1999, Richard Foss had done little constructive January, February, and March; 3 months waiting for the funding. Now in April 2000 he was instructing the medical experts.   Prof. Hindmarch claimed 'conflicts of interests' which I took to mean his current research was Roche funded.   Conversely Malcolm Lader was willing to receive Instructions and see me. I wasn't sure of him - he was on first name terms with my defendants.

Richard Jackson 'loaned' me his old 5-series BMW, and offered to employ me as a part-time clerk for those days when well enough to work. That required permission from those who had set me up - the consequence of Bingham's Order. But with a car, for the first time in two years I was mobile – with fuel from him too.. Old friends never have to be asked to assist in troubled times -

confirms life's old adage, does it not. Brother Kit, only too willing to help, was down in Kent.

Lader is a man who excels in 'Star Rating' in the medico-legal world with a C.V. to die for. Author, research unit, expert in countless cases in courts and with an entry in International Who's Who, and a former member of the drugs licencing committee. No getting lost this time, funded by Kit and PD, I presented myself at 10.58 am for my 11.00am Consultation. It was one of those bright sunny June days which was reflected in my appearance and demeanour - at my convivial and naughty best, able to joke and self-mock my position. He quickly allayed my fears:

"Now, Mr. Kaberry, we meet again. And this time I have all this information" said the smiling professor, surely not far from retiring, but very fit and active. I sat in front of him....
"Oh dear, how can I put this - er - without offending... umm... I thought you wouldn't want to help me... you see, you know Oliver Thorold and Paul Balen so well from the group claim... forgive me for being a little blunt... but er... you're on first name terms with them.... been to bed with them, so to speak." I dithered in apology - "so, suing them.... you can't help me?"
"No, that's no problem. Now - they live by these rules, they make livings - very good livings - suing medical men, and must live by those same rules... and they got it wrong in this case"
 - '... and I'd doubted this strong man.... shame on you SK.'

We all know when we've had a top meeting and carried the day. This was one such. We discussed matters for well over an hour to 12.30. I complimented him on his office with its super view from the south across London to St. Pauls.

He actually still had pretty crap instructions, so I'd sent him my statement this time. I explained I still couldn't sleep beyond 2 hours and often was unwell, at least one day lost each week. Now it was June 2000 and this work should have been done in June 1996. If only - I'd have had my home and career back.

I returned to walk the West End - those shops I could no longer afford to visit - one day my life would return. I'd love a new shirt and, more than anything, a pair of shoes! But did I really want that life again. I was happiest mowing a lawn and walking in the

Dales. One thing was certain – I'd be a damned good lawyer. I sat scheming. If Fossie wanted another year, I would take over myself. The Assignment would now fall into place from Houghton, as soon as I had this report.

Back in Leeds I had another Hearing before Judge John Behrens - GuffawQC. Backed by Courage and Black Arrow, I asked to annul the bankruptcy - something good lawyers could have done for me in 1996/7. It never should have been. Penson's unaccepted claim gave him a vote; having destroyed me once, he opposed annulment - before his claim was even judged valid or not. In we went before the guffawing John Behrens. He wasn't interested. Instead they were after the surrender of my pension:

"Well, if Mr.Kaberry won't comply with surrender of the pension fund, we can send him to prison"

"But I always comply with the law, My Lord."

"Well" said Houghton's solicitor -" there is another way Milord... you can order that a District Judge sign the surrender document if Mr. Kaberry refuses to co operate"

Back at the place where I must live, Houghton's lawyer rang me:

"We're having your pension Mr. Kaberry… and there's nothing you can do."

I sat in my horrible flatlet in silence for five minutes. I'd lost my home, career, income and possessions. My family have my inheritance - my real pension as planned. I'd only paid into this for a few years - pretty tiny, and I was to lose this as well. I had to win the civil claim that would restore a pension. What do we all do when life is as rotten as that? I went to see my beautiful dog at Petrina's; her smiling face and waggy tale – so pleased to see me always makes me glad to be alive. My best mate over these years was unable to walk far. We had a good long chat; she understood.

Fossie rang. After remonstrating for my delivering my own statement to Lader ("do that again, and we won't act for you"), he told me he held the Report.

"Right - what's he say?"

"Well, it's a very powerful and supportive Report. It concludes that all your problems with the Law Society, your inability to work properly and your problems with police and in your social life are

all *direct* consequences of the maladministration of Dalmane. He actually goes further and says Dalmane is not a suitable drug in these days and the prescribing was negligent, so.........
"Richard - I just want this over…
"Well, I've already spoken with Prof.Lader – and we've arranged an all-day Conference for Tuesday 27 June at 4 New Square"

The Lader Report is lengthy and detailed – as good a report as anyone could want in such a situation… (extracts)
"…at interview Mr. Kaberry came exactly on time with a case containing a volume of papers. He was very much as when I saw him 4 years ago - affable, avuncular, and well-dressed. His vicissitudes do not seem to have affected him. He was cheerful without any interludes of overt depression or anxiety. He was articulate but not talkative, humorous but not fatuous, and was much more focussed and less prolix than 4 years ago. In short he is completely psychiatrically normal
(*All who need such words from a top psychiatrist – raise your hand now!*)
Then he related the effects of dalmane.: "the effects of Dalmane are typical of benzodiazepines. Dalmane… is very long acting and its effects persist the following day after use. Taken regularly it will accumulate in the brain. Its effects during the daytime are manifold and quite adverse. Some people, such as Mr. Kaberry become profoundly impaired.… Dalmane can have major effects on mental functioning ranging from total amnesic to mild drowsiness, diminished awareness of surroundings, impaired intellectual function, and an inability to organize personal life, poor memory and clumsiness. <u>Awareness of these impairments and deficiencies may itself be impaired</u> so that the user becomes increasingly befuddled (confused to you and me)..…. Recklessness in daily life and professional activities may follow. '<u>Suggestibility will increase</u> and the <u>user becomes a pawn in the hands of others.</u>

He went on to say the doctor was negligent and dalmane probably wouldn't even get a licence today.

He said I was adversely affected by the drug in my professional and social life… 'his relationship disintegrated, his day to day life became disorganised, he became listless and lackadaisical, then reckless and careless of the consequences of his actions.' And 'The effects of the drug are so insidious that the individual does not maintain insight into his own impaired performances. <u>Thus Mr. Kaberry would not have been aware that he was behaving even erratically or ineffectively</u>. Only after the discontinuance of Dalmane for several days would any clearing of the mind occur.

"IN CONCLUSION I am of the Opinion *that his professional, personal and social problems 1989-94* and subsequently are <u>***direct consequences***</u> of his regular and sometimes excessive use of Dalmane. Such unsupervised use by a prescriber is unacceptable practice"

Malcolm Lader OBE   June 2000

Balen and Thorold had told LAB this expert - leader in the world, did not support me. I'd soon see them squirm in a Witness Box. I'd gone to them for help and they lied to and about me. Well…?

27 June: It started as a convivial meeting, but soon it dawned on me - Hugh, nice chap though he is, hadn't grasped the facts. He didn't grasp how the drugs work, nor what had actually happened. We continued from 11.00 am to 4.00 pm when I was left with just my lawyers. Could we now get on with this?
  "Look I've got some thinking to do," said my counsel.

Three days later I rang Richard Foss.
"Simon, I'm sorry. Counsel thinks Thorold was wrong - that all his reasoning was wrong, but the fact is you were struck-off for dishonesty… any court will want to follow that….."
I said 'fine' I would proceed alone. Immediately, I arranged to see Lynne Houghton. Next day Fossie rang to say that Hugh wanted a Second Opinion from a silk on the dishonesty aspect. You, as a non lawyer, wouldn't have known what to do, but I did.

I met Miss Houghton and lawyer on 7 July 2000. I had the Reports and funding – all I'd needed since that first meeting. Her lawyer accepted that if they didn't assign I could sue her in breach of trust. Houghton wrote to all creditors – <u>all agreed to the Assignment with all compensation to me - even Penson agreed to the Assignment</u>. It took just *four weeks* to do the work Thorold and Balen should have done.

The Assignment reads: -

This Assignment is made the 15th day of August 2000 between Lynne Margaret Houghton of....... and Simon Edmund John Kaberry of..........

RECITING – the bankruptcy

NOW IT IS AGREED AND DECLARED as follows:

1.The Assignor <u>hereby assigns</u>...... all the assignor's legal and beneficial interest in potential rights of action in civil law against (i) law Society (ii) Freethcartright and Anthony Oliver Thorold and (iii) the former medical practitioner 'Z' in consideration of payment of the sum of £1

2. The Assignee covenants..... to keep the assignor indemnified from and against all claims, proceedings, expenses arising out of this assignment and potential rights of action.

6.   <u>It is agreed and declared</u>:

  (a) that the assignor shall have <u>no right or interest</u> in the said actions and claims, nor <u>in any award of compensation</u> or settlement arising from such, personally nor as Trustee to the Estate of the assignee;

  (b)   That the Assignor shall not incur any personal liability directly or indirectly (nor to the estate) arising from the conduct of the said claims being pursued by the assignor.

7.   If at anytime any provision hereof is or becomes illegal, invalid or unenforceable in any regard under any jurisdiction, neither legal liability, validity or enforceability of the remaining provisions hereof...... etc shall in any way be affected

Signed as a deed etc......

'Golly....... by Christmas this will all be over..... I'll soon have some money and be able to plan a new life and home.

Simon Kaberry

CHAPTER SEVENTEEN

Meet - The Lord Phillips of Worth Matravers,
and The Hon Mr. Justice Douglas Brown
 – *"we look after our own first?"*-

I sent the Deed of Assignment to Richard Foss smugly - it took me a handful of weeks to do what they hadn't done in two years; that's all I ever needed. I liked the only people to have helped me, but needed them to do it my way. Instead, Hugh wanted an 'Opinion' from another barrister on this point -'can a unanimously acquitted man sue his negligent doctor for being doped up, rendered confused and suicidal and then deceived and defrauded, with his career taken without trial?'– you pay for some expert to give that advice! I wanted to scream.

I returned to the place where I have to lay my head one sunny August day, to find a note from a YEP Journalist.
"Mr. Kaberry – would you like to comment on your damages claim in the High Court against the Law Society – please ring..."
Writs are public records - mine had been found. I had no comment - ten days later - big Headlines -
[Up-to-date photo of me and my address disclosed]

Swindling solicitor sues Law Society
"Simon Kaberry a struck-off solicitor who was cleared of swindling more than £500,000 from clients is suing the profession's controlling body the Law Society... the Writ filed in the High Court alleges breach of duty of care.... Mr. Kaberry was struck off five years ago after the Law Society found him guilty of a catalogue of improper conduct. It was alleged he had lost as much as £3.5 million from clients accounts through... gambling on horse races. Mr. Kaberry, who is also a bankrupt.... was cleared by a Newcastle Crown Court jury... after claiming that at the time the money had gone 'missing' he was addicted to a powerful prescribed sleeping pill, which 'had clouded his judgment'... He declined to speak about his action against the law Society. But **Geoffrey Negus, spokesman for the Law Society**... said: '... this is not the first writ he has made'. He said that an Application to the High Court in April last rejected Mr. Kaberry's application to have his certificate to practice restored....

241

"The scale of his wrongdoing was colossal and for him to be restored to the profession would be a massive blow to public confidence in solicitors. We could not allow it*"***

Like the local spiv who got away with his deception, Geoffrey Negus was repeating the Law Society's untruthful allegations. *"Lord Bingham - did you learn nothing at school of these consequences of appeasement."*

Put very loosely, 'Defamation' is either libel (in writing) or slander (by word alone) of words which will 'reduce a man's standing in the eyes of right-thinking members of society' - thus damaging his reputation. Defences are truth, fair comment or 'privilege.' Now I had this wretch Negus to deal with as well - he actually *intended* to injure me and deceive you - this gave me access to a jury.

I know defamation law in theory, but I don't know how to plead a libel claim. A visit to Law library gave me a recent Court of Appeal case of Safeway Supermarkets PLC v Taylor:
The facts and law stated were:

> Mr. Taylor lived adjacent to the entrance to a Safeway store. He resented all the noise and inconvenience. So, being a sprightly sort, he battled them and put up banners with 'plainly' defamatory words about Safeway and anyone foolish enough to shop there - I chuckled as I read it. Safeway sued him in defamation and asked the court for "summary Judgment" saying 'plainly the words were defamatory' and wanted an injunction. It went to the Court of Appeal which ruled that only a jury can determine whether or not the words are defamatory – there is no summary procedure for that issue. It is whether ordinary people using ordinary tests, standards and common sense will judge the words to be defamatory.

So – no judge could block me on that issue; a Claim would even expose the cover-up Bingham had endorsed. *But how do I do it?* If I got the pleading or procedure wrong, our judges would use that as reason to get rid of me. No lawyer would help me - complain about the incompetence of Law Society - yea, but suing it – nay.

I wrote to 'Bar Pro Bono' for help. It's a 'charity' of barristers who are allowed to give free assistance to litigants if certain criteria are met. After a few months they decided I had a case and passed the papers to a specialist barrister. I wrote that I did NOT want any "Counsel's Opinion" – *just* simple drafting a claim. I waited... and waited... and waited. Then I chased. Just before the Limitation period (a year in defamation claims) was up, I received a "Counsels Opinion". A young lady barrister advised that Lord Bingham's ruling in April is 'a complete defence to Law Society', who can defame me at will, for the rest of my life. So I had to let Isaacs, Bingham, Williams and Negus go multiply together. My big claim was now ready.

OSS had held Richard Jackson's request to employ me for five months. They sent me a copy letter from Leeds solicitor Anthony Sugare - "*.. due to the press coverage... it is not in the interest of Leeds solicitors that Mr.Kaberry be allowed to work*" wrote Sugare - a man of such strength of character; or not, as the case may be. But then I've always questioned any man who needs 25% of an A4 page to sign his name to a letter - wanting to be someone he can never be. So I couldn't work as a clerk either.

As expected, Law Society also applied for 'Summary strike-out' (no evidence allowed) of my two writs against them. In the Misfeasance claim, I would have to establish at trial that as regulator they '*knowingly or recklessly acted dishonestly*' in the exercise of its powers in 1995. Dishonestly for these purposes includes "*closing your eyes to the truth and not asking obvious questions, indifferent to the consequences.*" There are eight tests to meet set out in a Judgment of Lord Steyn in a House of Lords BCCI decision. My other claim was a Declaration that I owe them nothing. Their London solicitor refused to take any call from me; her instructions from Penson – '*freeze him out*'

The Listing Staff decided I should be given a High Court Judge - in Chambers. 'Chambers' means in private - no media. That's how they keep the truth hidden. I stayed the night before with Elaine so as not to be drained - still often very ill. PD paid.

High Court Judges automatically are made knights (non-hereditary titles); I got a new boy judge Sir Stanley Burnton, or The

Honourable Mr.Justice Stanley Burnton. We were put in a room just off the Bear Garden on the first floor.

Then I saw him - a mummy's boy face, grown up to be a High Court Judge. And that look - the sneak from the Lower Remove; it said 'I know all about you from head prefect - you're dead'. Nice counsel told Burnton, I couldn't have the Declaration as there was no claim against me, and my claim in Misfeasance was "a collateral attack on the judgment of Lord Bingham, who had ruled Law Society 'had met a public duty' in 1995." i.e. young judge, dare you take on the boss? Good point.

This High Court Judge had read my 'Skeleton' argument setting out my powerful claim - it met the eight tests set by Lord Steyn; he knew I was after the Law Society for deceiving the public etc., (public breach of duty of care) and a criminal offence under Contempt of Court Act. Mr. Justice Stanley Burnton then struck both claims out from proceeding to any trial of any evidence and ordered me to pay full costs of the Law Society fixed at £6,000. I asked for permission to appeal, which he duly refused.

I lodged another appeal to the Court of Appeal, and asked the Listing Office to have both heard together – against Bingham and Burnton.
Within three months I was back in the Royal Courts, - we all have hope!! I was listed before Lord Justice Tuckey (aka Sir Simon Tuckey); he'd read the history of all this in my 'skeleton.' I smiled at him and got one back. I put my submissions - no man should be left with a finding of dishonesty without any trial, and what about the jury - look at the Judge's Summing-Up (which I put before him). I'm sure he'd had a little chat about it the night before, with Bingham. And as for striking out the Misfeasance claim – there were three men still 'laughing like extras from a *S*mash advert with £100,000's.' He heard me for fifteen minutes, then quietly, as they do, Tuckey read out the judgment he had already drafted. It's all charade, this justice game you know.

He opened - "Mr. Kaberry has courteously put his case." I made notes as he delivered Judgment. I bowed and smiled and he did likewise - forget this integrity crap.

A simple comparison illustrates the double-standards operating within our Judiciary today, and which will continue until judges are made independently accountable. Algerian pilot Lofti Raissi was wrongly accused by Home office of being part of the terror campaign on Twin Towers. Careful examination showed this to be false, but the mere allegations and holding him, ruined his life and career. Our Appeal Court ruled he can sue for substantial compensation – *"the public labelling of him as a terrorist by the authorities, particularly CPS, over a period of months, has had and continues to have a devastating effect on his health and life… and police and CPS were guilty of serious breaches."* Compare that to this – Law Society by Williams, Isaacs and the clerks led by Penson hijacked the system, saved wrongdoers from ever answering and ruined my life, by publicly labelling me a dishonest thief to gamble – even after I had been acquitted unanimously. But our Judges led by Bingham and Phillips won't allow lawyers and their systems to be accountable – at all. And you have yet to encounter the scoundrels Chadwick and Aldous and the 'three disgraces' - Lords Nicholls, Scott and Brown.

It was now a staggering seven years since arrest and end of life as you know it. I had absolutely nothing, from a good life, save a determined, if deluded, view of my duty to see this through; if I didn't, I would never forgive myself. Is that right? Would you?

As earlier, I was still often very poorly. The big joy I had each day was visiting my beautiful dog in late morning – 'boo-boo-bear', although with age she didn't want to do a lot. I was so sad for all those hours she spent alone – in that tiny house for a big beautiful dog. For nine months I had been borrowing Petrina's car to take Holly to PDSA. Humiliation of my poverty was long past. Holly often struggled to get up and couldn't walk far; she would simply sit down. At PDSA she looked with disdain at her fellow patients.

12th September brought the worst day of the last ten years. Louise and I had taken Holly special presents at lunchtime and I had visited again at nine o'clock, when she has asked to sit outside; I knew she wasn't well. The phone rang at 5.15am.
"Simon - quick... she's dying... she's foaming at the mouth outside." She was the most important person in my shallow life – my daughter substitute. I sped round there in a flash in Richard's car to find Holly lying on the grass at the front, gasping for breath,

but looking up at me, her eyes glazed in fear. My best friend was asking for help.

"I've called the emergency vet" said Petrina.

I knelt beside my loyal mate, assuring her it was 'all right' and stroking her neck and back gently, but it was no good. I knew what had happened because it had threatened before, but I'd averted it. She'd been asking me to sit outside when I left – she knew. Now she was gasping for breath through fearful cloudy eyes, looking up like a seal. The lady vet who had given her a hysterectomy eight years earlier arrived. It would have frightened Holly more to carry her to the Range Rover for oxygen. We explained her recent problems. The vet inspected Holly:

"It looks like her organs are simply fading" she said – "I'll put her to sleep"

"No" we both retorted as one.

"Right then, she needs oxygen, help carry her to my truck"

"But we can't move her... she's too heavy and it'll hurt her more... she's frightened"

"What shall we do Simon......... shall we let her...?" asked Petrina in fearful quiet voice.

I looked at Holly, lying there, glazed eyes, and fighting for breath – my best friend through all these horrible times. She had never growled or hurt anyone in her life – a friend to all. She'd kept me going for years, now looking up at me for help. Our brains can sort issues quickly. Holly was thirteen – a very good age for a ridgeback. Even if she recovered with oxygen, it would happen again. She could walk, but slowly and had difficulty getting up and was leaking badly which embarrassed even her. She was frightened, lying there. That next day could be tomorrow, when she couldn't get up and we called the vet when she wasn't fearful. That would be far far worse.

I heard myself saying quietly - "O.K. then" and the vet went to her vehicle and returned with a needle. I looked away but continued to assure my frightened friend all was well, whispering... "Just wait boo, its all right... just wait". It was important she didn't know – or do they know? Whilst I'm sure I had no real choice, the events then and which followed have lived with me ever since. Petrina held her left paw and leg as the vet injected her. I stroked her gently, assuring her it was all right – 'just wait boo…'. I watched as slowly her head went down to rest, and all the fear was gone from her face which no longer looked like an old lady, but a young puppy. I heard the vet say those terrible words – "She's gone." As her head went down, so I felt my heart sink – my best friend and I'd let her down.

We're Brits – we don't show it; our lips are naturally stiff. Petrina grasped Holly – "I love you Boo". I said nothing. I'd just killed my best friend, after two awful years. I adored her, lived for seeing her each day; she really had kept me going through those awful years. We can take all the shit life throws at us, but not our friends. I broke the silence in the way we do: "Right, who's for a cup of tea." Life goes on; think about something else, acknowledge its happened, but move on.

Petrina fetched a large picnic rug; we placed Holly onto it and carried her to the back of the house. She was human you know. On went the kettle then the vet went, and I left Petrina alone – just how she felt, alone with our best friend's body outside, I don't know. I needed to get out fast and be alone. Someone else must have got into the car with me, for the moment the doors were locked and no one could hear, he let out the most agonising wail of grief and sorrow, and he was still there as I returned to my the place where I must lie my head. This was far worse than the risk of being done over by my own lawyers and sent to prison.

Mid-morning I rang Ann at Adel Willows, who said it was fine to bury her in the top wood. One of those lovely warm September sunny days and I returned to my old home for the first and only time. It was better than I remembered. I dug deep all day, down to four feet in the deep clay subsoil in the top wood as the sun glinted through the tall beeches. We waited to 6.00pm for Louise to finish work, before driving with Holly in the boot back to her first home, and buried her beneath those shimmering trees, on that lovely summers evening. I filled the sides and top with large flat stones so she should be safe – no foxes to dig at her. At 2.30 am, I drove back to sit in the black darkness of the wood by her grave, and promised her a headstone as soon as I had money - "here lies a real friend in troubled times and good." Those with children who die young or in an accident, or suffer tragic death within the family will rightly say 'you're pathetic;' - but it takes all to make a world.

September ended with a simple, succinct Opinion from Roger Henderson QC - common sense turned into legal words – 'don't be so bloody silly, of course he could have sued the prescriber in 1997 - there is no issue of public policy.' (as Hugh asked)

Permit me to explain. Sometimes it is 'public policy' that a claim cannot be brought. The lead 'public policy case' is Clunis v Camden Health Authority – a tragic story you may remember. Michael Zito, a young married man, was murdered by a schizophrenic called Clunis, who had been released 'into the community' from a secure hospital. Clunis sued the Health Authority, arguing that, had they treated him properly, he either would have had the correct drugs to control his conduct, or he should not have been let out early. Because of breach of either duty to him, he had been able to commit this horrible crime, and would never now be free again - ever. Leaving the tragedy aside, you can see that, in law, he had a point – the Health Authority had breached its duty of care to him as well as Michael Zito and his family. If it hadn't, he wouldn't have committed the crime and could enjoy freedom later when well and safe to others. The Courts, rightly you may think, ruled that he could not even bring any compensation claim on the grounds of 'public policy' - he had committed a criminal act, and a horrendous one at that. Clunis 'naturally' had the propensity to cause injury due to his condition – that propensity wasn't caused by the defendant; that was the public policy issue. But what if intrinsically a man isn't a danger to anyone, but is injured so that he then becomes such – e.g. from negligent medical treatment? Think on it – if your life was turned inside out like that. There is another case on just that; a man was electrocuted at work, and the mental injury so caused made him start to beat up prostitutes; he was sent to prison. Should he be allowed compensation for the ruination of his life? think on that. It wasn't decided, because the barrister failed to plead the case properly!***

[*** in June 2008 Clarke M.R ruled a victim of Paddington Rail disaster can sue for extra damages for suffering personality change caused by PTSD suffered then, which later caused him to kill someone, eventhough convicted of manslaughter, and sentenced to be detained. Not surpisingly the dead man's family are livid. This raises difficult or impossible issues. If he is so ill, and liable to injure – does he get paid more each time!]

248

However, my case had nothing to do with public policy – quite the reverse, it was public policy to have it heard, to set precedent that GPs will be brought to account Rather than get on with it, my two lawyers wanted *another* 'second Opinion' on insolvency law and practice – would the Assignment have been made, and if so, on what terms? I could give a lecture on that for free - I'd already given him (i) Heath v Tang 1993 then (ii) the practical remedy to the problem, confirmed in Ord v Upton (assign is duty), and (iii) the Assignment from the trustee 2000 <u>and</u> a statement from her that she would have assigned in 1996-7 had lawyers done the work, and (iv) letters from the creditors in 1998/9/00 that they wanted no part of my compensation, and I shouldn't even be bankrupt - they wanted the claim assigning.   It really was "Job Done and Case Proved." It was up to Thorold and Balen to prove that what did happen, wouldn't have. Tall order.

But no - a Consultation was arranged with a silk Mrs. Jane Gusset QC. Off we went to her lovely chambers - they had charicatures of themselves on the walls in the Waiting Room – sort of the '*ho-ho, aren't we wonderful*' spirit. The cost to you, the taxpayer would be about £5,000. Far worse to me.

"Well…" started the forthright and pleasant Gusset QC:
"I understand, Mr. Kaberry, that Hugh feels - and I must accept his views for this purpose - that you will be liable to the Law Society for the compensation they have paid out to the Banks."
"No - I won't," said I with a big grin, as we do in these circumstances of crass legal stupidity. I explained why. Law Society could have recovered it all and put the rest to insurance - they are authors of their own losses - will never go to court.

They ignored me. The Gusset 'Advice' was that I would have sought from Z, all my own compensation of, say, over a million, plus 2 million for Law Society, making a 3.5 million plus pound claim. The Trustee would have assigned the claim on the basis of dividing the total award as to half to me, and half to her, so I would get 1.75 million rather than one million. What utter rubbish. (no one *ever* valued my claim anyway)

The year 2000 was gone like 1995-6-7-8-9, waiting for lawyers. Hugh and Richard now agreed to bring a claim; first they had to

(i) get 'extended funding' from the LAB, and (ii) write a formal 'letter before action' setting out the claim, to give the defendant the chance to settle, and only then could we issue any writ.

Richard drafted 'a costs claim' for the LAB to approve all funding to be incurred, concluding - I kid-u-not - £685,000 for my lawyer's costs! Now you can swiftly understand why you read of such vast 'court costs' in civil cases. It could have been done long since for £20,000. We all knew Thorold and Balen would throw in the towel rather than enter any witness box. They'd lose their careers if the truth ever came out.

Finally in March 2001 a long five page 'letter before action' was sent to Balen in Nottingham and Thorold at his Doughty Street Chambers. I was assured this was 'Court Protocol.'
"But" said I "we already know what Throttled will do... Barristers don't answer complaints - they think they're above the law." He hadn't answered in November 1997, or February 1998, nor had Balen. True to form, Freeths answered they had passed the claim to their insurers SIF (my insurers), who refused to answer, and Thorold refused to acknowledge - must have been shit-scared.

Meanwhile I proceeded with Bingham's suggestion of 'deploying the factual and medical evidence' to SDT on my Application to be restored to the Roll. If I didn't, I'd be accused of not trying to mitigate my losses and get my career back. Law Society appointed Liverpool solicitor Jon Goodwin, who wrote that I was not to phone 'for he would take no call' nor discuss anything.

I filed a detailed statement (8 pages) for the Tribunal to read prior to the Hearing, setting out the full history – I asked for a full day hearing. I admitted that when sedated, my brain was no different from theirs; I couldn't see I was being deceived.

Hugh finished the Particulars of Claim. I didn't like it. He refused to allege deceit; he refused to claim exemplary damages for lying to me. He ignored the Assignment and concurrence of all creditors that all damages be retained by me, and instead pleaded I would have recovered all payments made by Law Society and the Trustee would have split the award. I saw disaster - my lawyers were admitting I had been dishonest. But - as he left for his summer hols, Thorold was served; *'give him something to think on.'* It had taken a staggering *three years* to get this far, since his advice.

Same day, 8 August 2001 I attended SDT at 9.30am. Mrs.Elston - acting 'in the interest of justice' - had placed me last in a full day's Listing - no chance of a proper hearing. The Chairman was a solicitor from Carlisle called AHBoyd Holmes - very much my junior in every respect. In this man I found the nastiest piece of work in all dealings with lawyers; this one did not even pretend. First, he rejected my morning application to adjourn until there was time to hear my case, and the medical evidence which couldn't be called (Pam was away in USA). At lunchtime he repeated it. At 4.05pm I was finally called in to the room. Just one reporter remained; he stank of Bell's or Johnny Walkers. Holmes had chapter and verse from me. First, he retired to consider my application to adjourn until I could deploy all the evidence, as Bingham said I should; he refused that.

We started. As I approached exhibits which would show I was set-up, he interrupted me - didn't want to hear anything about the history (which he knew) or drugs. After thirty minutes, and as I approached 'Exhibit B', he stopped me.
"That's enough Mr. Kaberry. I want to hear what the Law Society position is," - it's his duty to protect their 'good name.'
Jon Goodwin, on behalf of the Penson gang, told him their position was simple. I had been 'convicted' of gross dishonesty - theft. Lord Bingham left that Finding untouched. Accordingly, I could not be restored to the Roll and allowed to work until I had shown acceptance of that Finding and 'Rehabilitation' for that conduct.
Solicitor AHBoyd Holmes snappily agreed. Did I have any evidence I had 'rehabilitated' for my dishonesty? Far from showing rehabilitation for being doped up and deceived then set-up by this court, I had tried to battle their "independence." (*folly*)

"Application Refused" and costs award to Law Society - that's the fifth time - no 'trial' ever allowed. His written decision followed later. He ruled I had shown "no rehabilitation" and, "he hasn't even repaid any of the money" (he stole). This man is a practising solicitor; would you trust him? And Holmes is a welsh surname. *What became of the good spirit of Men of Harlech?*

Neil Hodgkinson, editor of YEP reported his chosen version of this charade. He told people of Yorkshire my Application was 'thrown out' - I had taken all that money because of 'anti-depressants taken after the death of my father' - that had caused my problems. I complained to another self-regulatory body – the Press Complaints Commission sending them a Transcript of the Hearing - it was a fictitious report. PCC ruled his report 'did not breach their Code of Conduct.' *Vive self-regulation*!

I decided to appeal Holmes on a principle of law to the man who appoints Tribunal Members - the Master of the Rolls, Lord Phillips (now your Lord Chief Justice, and soon senior law lord), who had read what Isaacs had done to protect Williams, and *promoted him* to 'President' of SDT. The legal issue was the re-Murray principle.

The Master of the Rolls is the second in command to Lord Chief Justice. Its part of the 'waiting for dead men's shoes' that controls our legal system. Nicholas Phillips is a deluded but pleasant man, steeped in privilege. His father had sent him to that particularly attractive Dorset school just outside Blandford - top notch public school. After Bryanston and Oxbridge, then to the Bar. Like me, claims to be a keen walker, and he takes to swimming early morning as often as he can, to maintain clear mind and good body. He never really left the comfort and safety of his alma mater, returning to Bryanston as Head of the Board of Governors (in youth, we used to call such people overgrown schoolboys – unable to cope with the realities of life without the safety net of school).

With this background, I could be certain that no way would he let me rock any boat of his closed shop legal establishment. Like all of us, he can't help what his past has made him – but his shallow understanding of life became more apparent later when made Lord Chief Justice, suggesting that painting an underpass was good deterrent/punishment for wrongdoers, people shouldn't go to prison, and wants aspects of sharia law in our system; why!! He had appointed the SDT members who had set me up, and protected one another and Williams. Oaths to do right aren't enough to protect justice. I filed the full facts and history for him and the Lader Report - could I have a new life back?

I was listed for 9.30am in the Court of the Master of the Rolls (Court 73) used for the Hutton Inquiry. Law Society clerks instructed young Goodwin. In he came at 9.30 sharp and we bowed and I stood and gave him a pleasant smile:

"My Lord - good morning. And may I first say how sorry I am to trouble you with this matter at all and especially at this hour."

"Mr.Kaberry, that's quite all right, I generally deal with matters of this kind at this time" said the utterly normal man in an equally pleasant manner. He's the sort you could readily sit down with to share afternoon tea in a smart Cotswold hotel, and pass pleasantries without trouble. He continued:

"Mr. Kaberry: I have read your summary of the facts and events. You've gone into detail of how you were unable to work and what happened. So you need not go into that detail again thank you. And I have read the Report from Professor Lader"

I spoke well for over fifteen minutes, but could soon see that, whilst he courteously listened, I was scoring 'nul point' - didn't want to know; he'd appointed these men, Isaacs, Holmes etc…. what public confidence would there be if he exposed what they had done? Goodwin repeated his position. Had Nicholas Phillips wanted to do justice, it was so easy:

> *'SDT refused to hear argument first time round. Lord Bingham then directed they should hear the evidence and argument. They refused again. Mr.Kaberry was given drugs that ruined his life and mental abilities. I have the Report from a leading expert. Other than that there is no evidence he is anything but a good and honest lawyer. A jury heard and judged him… that has been the only trial'.*

You don't need balls of steel to say that. But no – Phillips extracted that the drugs made me reckless and a pawn in the hands of others. If I had been reckless, then I must be stood down for life. He made no reference to the facts or issue I put, concluding:

> "*Law Society must be free to decide who is and is not fit to be a solicitor*" (the closed shop/cover-up lives on)

On the basis of this ruling, if Phillips was given laughing gas before entering court, he must be struck-off from all legal work, vilified, and lose everything - because he found it all so funny.

Why do we bother? It's that hope thing we all have. The hope that we have strong men as judges. But that doesn't allow for human frailties. What good any judge without the integrity and balls to expose Establishment wrongdoing when under his nose. Or do you say he's right? I was within the Omerta – the silent code of protection which will remain strong until accountability is in place.

Onwards: Thorold and Balen were confronted by what they had done. They couldn't hide or refuse to answer any longer. Waiting in the wings was an Inquiry by Bar Council for lying to me and giving such hopeless advice. Balen's insurers SIF chose a Leeds firm Beechcroft Wansbrough, to act for them. Thorold's insurers Bar Mutual chose London firm BLG

Beechcrofts had acted for me in 1994-7/8 on all negligence claims made - they knew the Thorold advice, endorsed as right by Balen, that I must pay SIF was balls. They had dealt with a Harper claim against me; I hadn't known that. He alleged I had stolen £30,000, loaned by Courage to Murgatroyds (I knew nothing of this) which I had 'apparently' guaranteed, with Harper. Harper alleged I, as solicitor/partner, had stolen it, to avoid his liability on guarantee. Told by Harper I had stolen it, Courage had then made me bankrupt. When Courage later turned their attention on Harper, he sought indemnity from my insurers. So Beechcrofts asked for 'proof' of the loan. A trace showed the cash had gone straight to Harper's bank account - I knew nothing of the event. So lawyers acting for Balen actually knew I shouldn't even be bankrupt.

Fossie gave both defendants extra time to end December to file defences. That's three years four months to get that far. The six months I had given him or I would walk away – was two years. But the Claim realistically was indefensible.

Balen and Thorold each defended on the basis that my angry letter dated 22 July gave them a 'complete defence' – that they could not have 'foreseen' any loss from their advice, as I had written I would issue my own writ. Each lawyer argued an undischarged bankrupt, without medical reports, <u>can</u> issue a writ in clinical negligence – i.e. *they repeated their incompetence in pleadings!* As expected, Thorold also played dirty - he annexed my 'confessions,' suggesting they were true to any judge.

I asked Richard to apply for summary Judgment for me; i.e. strike out the defences as no chance of succeeding in law. All we need do is set the law and the Defences both collapse:
"No Simon – they must have chance to defend."

Instead the inevitable happened. Balen and Thorold took their *only* chance of success and applied for summary dismissal of my claim – i.e. strike-out my claim before any evidence is heard

Their Application was listed for two days before a High Court Judge in chambers at Royal Courts on 16-17 May.

Now another lesson in law. It's largely common sense. This was only an Application under Rules of Court (CPRs) that there should be no trial of any evidence, no hearing of the facts, because, even if the evidence and facts were heard, the claim was 'bound to fail.' I've mentioned some of the mountains of case law before such as Ashmore. A more recent Appeal Court decision is Swain v Hillman in 1999. There, Lord Woolf said:

> "these rules were not meant to dispense with the need for a trial where there are issues which should be investigated in a trial"; he said - "the judge must not conduct a 'mini-trial' of his own." (guess evidence)

Lord Justice Judge said in the same case:-

> "To give summary judgment against a litigant without permitting him to advance his case before the trial is a serious step. The interests of justice sometimes so require; hence the court has a discretion to give summary judgment against a claimant, but it is limited to those cases where, on the evidence, the claimant has no real prospect of succeeding.
> "This is simple language, not susceptible to elaboration. If there is a prospect of success, the discretion to give summary judgment does not arise merely because the court thinks the chances may be improbable. If that were the court's conclusion, then it has another discretion, which is to allow the claim to proceed but subject to certain conditions. I agree with Lord Woolf"

That is established law – there must be a trial if there is evidence to hear and the Judge mustn't 'guess.' All judges are bound by those rules – er, well, should be.

It was one of those fantastic mid-spring mornings as I walked down from Holborn tube, through the delights of Lincolns Inn, to New Square; that smell of new-cut grass - makes you glad to be alive. I was on top form. Richard joined me for our 9.45 Conference before Court at 10.30.

"Right" said Hugh "some good news. The Judge's clerk has phoned to say we don't start until 2.00pm. Apparently one of the defendants has only just filed his skeleton arguments – so that won't please the judge!"
- *'oh Hugh, can't you see the real effect: it will be the last thing the judge has read.... greater impact.'*
"Umm, Mr. Justice Douglas Brown.....does anyone know him?"
"No" responded one lawyer "I've never had anything before him and know nothing of him. But he's been there a long time.... senior chap"
"But obviously not very good, if no-one's even heard of him after eight years as a High Court Judge"
Smiles. "You could say that..."
- *'oh my god - an incompetent judge... all I needed now... !'*

Only I could see what was coming. By the time my man spoke a thick judge could be had down the garden path. Balen and Thorold would never have to attend or explain anything that they had done. In walked Sir Douglas Brown. Full crop of thick grey hair deeply parted and brushed aside; a sort of General Pinochet look-a-like, but not as alert. Already gone aged seventy, and never having quite made the grade, he had my future in his hands. This is our system. Quietly and deliberately spoken, he told counsel they had two days, so he hoped we could get done.

A man just younger than me called Martin Spencer from Paper Buildings stood to address the Judge on behalf of Freethcartright. Spencer set his case and took the judge to my letter of 22 July 1997, but omitted Balen's reply that he was 'absolutely satisfied' all had been investigated. Nothing either of my September letter, nor of my requests in November 1997 and February 1998 for help to get funding back. The 'chain of causation of lost chance,' said

Spencer, was broken by my failure to issue a writ as I said. Had I done so, there could have been no loss - he said. I was the cause of the lost chance, he said. But I'd tried and couldn't – wait for my evidence. Martin Spencer doesn't know the law (or is he a man who misleads?). This Judge nodded – he didn't either

As day one was ending counsel for Thorold stood. A woman again of similar age, but this time from Hugh's own Chambers at 4 New Square, Susan Carr was there to get Thorold off both the negligence claim and the deceit allegation, which naturally would end if this was struck out. He would otherwise probably be struck-off from practice. Her piercing voice filled the room
-'*Good god - it's the original shrieking blond...*'
And on and on she shrieked - scoring points all the way with this nodding judge. Her client could not possibly 'have foreseen' the loss which is alleged by the Claimant when he gave his advice (on 19 July) because of my letter (dated 22 July) [effectively, she was saying he is also a clairvoyant, if anyone would follow that sequence, as his Opinion merely repeated his advice, given before the letter] To succeed in a civil claim, the losses arising must be 'foreseeable.' And as for writing 'SIF' for Law Society, he simply erred, but no one was misled, and it made no difference.
-'*Then ducky – why does he call them 'diligent insurers' in the Opinion? Law Society are not insurers...This is utter farce... ?*'

The end came when Brown commented

> "It seems to me, Mr. Kaberry was just 'a fraudster at work.'... Now - whatever the jury may have made of him, the civil law may take an entirely different view"
> (ie. - on balance of probability I was guilty of stealing two million quid in twelve months – no trial allowed). Brown is a High Court Judge and they make 'em like that still. Then you praise their wisdom.

In the moment's silence which followed those words, the lawyers knew they had won - before Hugh had even spoken. Brown had walked into the elephant trap set by Throttled and his lawyers. And Brown said he 'took into account' that Law Society had found me guilty, appeased by Tom Bingham.

This Judge, surely not the brightest card in the pack - was firmly intent on saving these two lawyers from ever having to account..

Day two was half-gone when Hugh finally stood. All he had to do was show there are 'triable issues.' In mid-afternoon, he submitted that I couldn't issue any writ as they claimed – quite apart from the missing funding and reports. "Any writ he may have issued would have been struck out, as he was still an undischarged bankrupt - he had no legal right."

Immediately both opposing barristers were on their feet.
"My Lord," protested The Shrieking Blond - "Mr. Evans is making a new point not raised in either the Particulars of Claim or in the affidavit filed for this hearing... I object: he cannot do this...
"I agree," said Spencer - "we have had no alert as to this claim and contention" – but it's in my letter 28 February.

Two senior barristers were arguing that as they didn't know the law, so my counsel shouldn't be allowed to argue it - *lawyers at work.* Taken aback at their incompetence, Hugh Evans asked for permission to amend (**page 26 of the Court Transcript**); the Judge responded that an amendment at this stage may mean an adjournment – if requested by the defendants. In such an event, I would have to pick up the wasted costs for this Hearing; but I had warned them.

Here lay a mighty problem. If there was an adjournment, I would insist my own lawyers pick up the tab of these costs. Next morning we took our places again. Was there a way out for Hugh? Maybe he found one...

It's important that I set out in detail what happened next. This is **page29** the **official Court Transcript** of exactly what happened, which I obtained only far too late.
Friday 17 May 2002
Hugh Evans; "My Lord, may **I hand in the amendments, please**"
Brown J: "**Thank you**"
Evans: "And can I hand in two cases that I have prepared for you to consider
Brown: "Thank you very much.

Evans: "My Lord the (two) amendments are in identical terms. I confine the amendments to the limited point (the right of a bankrupt to issue and pursue a claim in the courts). I have sought at this stage to make the point, and if we see fit and this case continues, obviously we will have to seek leave later. You can see it, for instance, in the amended Reply to Defence of the first defendant at paragraph 12(d)

Spencer (seeing the judge was lost): "Does your Lordship have it?

Brown: "12 (d)?

Evans: "yes my Lord '(d)' – it reads -

> *"The claimant's claim against Z vested in the trustee in bankruptcy. Any writ issued by the claimant against Z will therefore have been struck out or probably struck out"*

Brown: "Yes

Evans: "**And I think I have to ask formally for leave to make that amendment in those terms…?"**

Brown; "<u>Is there any objection</u>?

Spencer (for Freethcartright): <u>No</u>, **my Lord**

Carr (for Thorold): **"My Lord <u>no</u>.** I will be making submissions as to the forms in which the amendment has been made, but I have no objection

Brown: *<u>"Very well then, I give you leave"</u>*

So, the appropriate amendment was made - unopposed by Spencer and Carr - that the defences are wrong in law. <u>It is on **pages 29-33**</u> of the official court transcript. What Hugh did was simple. He amended his 'Reply' to the Defence, that in law I couldn't issue. Problem over? Well one would have thought so.

Hugh then took Brown to the legal authorities to prove this proposition - based on the Insolvency Act 1986, and case law.

Discussing how to proceed, when a bankrupt has a claim, at the very end of **Ord v Upton, Lord Justice <u>Aldous</u> says:**

> "In such a case, the trustee, of the cause of action vested in him, would have to consider very carefully **his duty <u>to the bankrupt</u>** and would probably, *if requested*, **assign the cause of action to him**" (to avoid the injustice otherwise caused by the rulings)

Having consented to the amendment both Carr and Spencer then argued that wasn't the law! Courts in action - you can't make stuff like this up. Highly paid professionals at work. Sir Douglas Brown said he would 'consider the various submissions' and deliver his judgment at the end of the month.

I went for a Pizza lunch with Richard Foss:
"Simon - what're you going to do with life now…
"You mean, I've lost…?"
"Come on, you were there. Let's not delude ourselves… he's going to find every reason possible to strike you out. He didn't like you, so will carefully write a judgment which you can't appeal."
"But he's never heard me… they know they've won do they"
"Yes, of course. I'm sorry Simon, but it's as you told me… The Judiciary aren't going to allow you any claim. It's wrong, but we're stuck with it."

Logically, I had to try to stop the inevitable again. I returned to the place where I must live, and wrote directly to Sir Douglas Brown Kt. I referred him to the first rule of fraud - 'trace the money to find the fraudsters' - so it was not easy to see how he could refer to me as a fraudster! Next, I explained the history, facts and evidence – and set the law. … I offered Balen and Thorold the chance in November 1997 and February 1998 to help me get legal aid back. *'Look at the letter dated 24 June 1998 – that they are reported for professional misconduct'.*

Brown could order a mini-trial of an issue – e.g. my position in July1997 - April 1998 and hear in evidence what I had tried to do to proceed without legal aid and without lawyers. If he had not grasped it before - he knew all the relevant facts from my letter.

Judgment day was set for 30 May 2002 in Royal Courts. Lawyers get the written Judgment two days before, but cannot tell the client. I was told not to attend. I flipped. On 29 May I asked Louise to take me out for the next day for one of my favourite drives around Yorkshire, across to Arncliffe and then to walk the vales and fells of Littondale, over to Upper Wharfedale. I needed to feel free – beautiful May weather. My mind was a mess, as I tried to pretend this wasn't happening. Next day I listened messages from Richard that he was instructing another counsel to seek to persuade Brown to grant permission to appeal his own decision

Brown's Judgment is not all that long...

1. My GP 'Z' was negligent and I alleged that the drugs administered had ruined my life. I sued the two defendant lawyers in 'Lost Opportunity' for negligently not putting my case and pursuing it when I was their client in 'lost chance,' and advising LAB wrongly to cancel the essential funding

2. The lawyers applied to the court to strike-out that claim, on the basis (i) that the loss of chance to sue 'Z' was not foreseeable as a consequence of their advice, and (ii) I had written on 22 July 1997 that I would do the work they hadn't done and issue a writ – so I was the cause of any lost chance.

3. Brown ruled "Mr.Kaberry's decision not to issue a writ was a most unwise one," as the claim 'was worth a considerable sum of money'. The lawyers could 'not have foreseen' that their powerful advice, and side-note in July 1997 to LAB to withdraw funding would cause such a loss of chance, taking that letter into account. (he said not a word of their refusals to help re-issue funding twice) that he would issue a writ himself.

4. He ruled I could have issued the writ without medical reports. As to legal aid, needed to pay for lawyers to get them, and fund the action, he ruled I 'would have been able to persuade the LAB to re-issue funding later to sue Z.'
   [ignoring that fact that LAB wrote I could only have it to sue the lawyers, as they acted on the bad advice]

5. The submission of Hugh Evans that the advice left me unable to mitigate my position, and issue, as a bankrupt has no right in law to issue and pursue such a claim, until assigned, *was 'unsustainable.'* Brown J ruled - that that was not the law!!!
   [But its been the law since 1986 and earlier]

6. Accordingly the claim had 'no realistic chance of success', so there could be no trial of any evidence – strike-out the claim and order me to pay costs for trying to sue the lawyers.

A very dark hour for me – after ten years at this; no trial allowed. It's a nonsense judgment, designed to protect the lawyers; isn't it?

But Fossie was wrong; that judgment was most certainly very appealable. It was hopelessly wrong in law - I had a right of appeal.

CHAPTER   EIGHTEEN

The 'Men of Honour' in Court of Appeal and the Law lords....
... The legal Omerta in action - No Judge may find another guilty of dishonesty

Whilst Richard and Hugh were 'thinking,' what to do about that ridiculous Brown ruling, I filed my own Application to the Court of Appeal for Permission to appeal. Once more I was a confident and competent lawyer.

Hugh 'Advised' LAB the Brown Judgment should be appealed, but there wasn't any point. From Bingham down, the Judiciary would never allow any claim by me - exposing Law Society and bad lawyers - to hell with justice and public good, regarding these drugs. I lodged an appeal to LAB Area, to be adjourned 'sine die.' Judges have taken an oath to do justice 'without fear or favour' - surely I'd find one honest and strong judge there.

I filed (1) my Grounds of Appeal – why he was wrong; he had conducted a mini-trial, and causation of loss was the lawyers cancelling funding and putting me in an impossible position and (2) a detailed skeleton argument setting out the facts and law. (3) Authorities of Das v Ganju/Corbin v Penfold (Limitation is no problem), Heath v Tang, Ord v Upton (trustees have a duty to assign), Heini v Jenke Bank (dishonesty tests are subjective) and Swain v Hillman etc (right to a trial).

My Application was listed for 30 July – the last day before the judicial holidays. As ever I stayed with Elaine in Mayfair, funded by Kit and PD – so I could even pay my share for dinner at Langans (I still hadn't learned to accept I'm poor, and they do real English food - but I prefer upstairs, away from the flashy types). End of term meant one thing; whoever I got would be in a good mood. Soon he'd be mowing his smart lawn at his country house and trimming the edges with pride, then throwing the ball for his black Labradors, or planning weekend breaks with his mistress.

I presented myself at court again. I'd got Lord Justice Potter (Sir Mark Potter) – '*sounds a good enough name to me*'; he entered in sprightly fashion – empty court as ever;

- 'no grumpy old Kennedy, twisted Bingham or Phillips or weak Tuckey here - seems a decent guy this one': (he's not public school)
"My Lord" I opened with my best version of a gushing smile – "I am so sorry to be such a ruddy nuisance, but I know I'm right"
A winning line. He guffawed brightly:
"No-no Mr. Kaberry you're not a nuisance.   Now this won't take long. I've read all you have to say and your cited cases and it seems to me I must give you permission to appeal"
-'Yes! ... I knew I'd find a strong honest and competent judge'

He then delivered a very short Judgment giving me permission to appeal to a full sitting of the Court of Appeal, before three Judges who would hear detailed argument from me and my foes.
There were two simple reasons to grant Permission:
(1) First Brown had conducted 'a mini-trial.' It is well-established they mustn't do that. (*'guess the evidence'*), and
(2) Second, "you seem to have 'an arguable case' on causation of loss" - that the lawyers left me in an impossible position - ie. Thorold/Balen had put me in the shit.

It was one of those glorious summer days as I walked with a special spring in my step along the Strand and Charing Cross, to Trafalgar Square, visit Elaine in her Trafalgar Square office – but retreat on hearing her picking an argument with her well-known boffin boss. Then up the Mall with its banners fluttering in the bright green leaves and hot sunshine with the Palace in view at the end, up Clive of India steps into St. James' and back to the flat, my path to Amarillo OK.... and a future and restored reputation. All those doubting Thomases – of course I'd get justice in the end. Victory was a chance to pay my debts, open a bank account, build a new business, find peace of mind again, a home ! - some clothes, shoes and a life
- 'please Jesus stay with me!'

Serving Notice of my success on Thorold and Balen was special –
"*game back on*" - it said.... "*You won't get away with it*"

I'd wasted 2½ years with my last lawyers, and it was a staggering five years since the truth was out yet still I sought 'justice.'
-'Yea gods... over seven years since The Williams Sting'

The Appeal was listed for 19 December 2002. How do I get out of Hugh's pleading that I recover Law Society payments? Dunno.

I reached court for my 10.30 Listing in Court 66. Lord Justice Aldous and Lord Justice Chadwick – just two, not three as is the norm, what does that tell me? They had a full history of this debacle, and the essential evidence; I put in Witness Statements from Geoff Martin and Houghton, that I couldn't do anything until I had new lawyers and funding back, to get the missing reports – only then could the right to sue be assigned back to me, as it was. I added the File Note which showed Thorold buried the offer to talk, and letter from LAB 24 June that he be reported, and Bar Council would investigate later. LAB was willing only to fund a claim against the lawyers – the reverse of what Brown had ruled.

I sat alone on those benches. About me sat seven other lawyers – all there to oppose me. Barristers TSB and Spencer, and two solicitors plus some clerks - all those people.

In stalked Sir William Aldous and Sir John Chadwick. I'd heard of Aldous twice. He had ruled in Ord v Upton on appeal - saying a trustee must consider his *duty* to assign a right of action. He had to be with me. However, on 13 December 1996 Aldous had also been one of the three judges who had struck out the group benzo litigants after they had tried to continue their claim after it had been throttled by their own counsel (a certain Mr. Thorold). I'd looked him up, an old man who must be near retirement. Another Old Harrovian, followed by Oxbridge, so bound to be pompous and pleasant. But all was not gloom, for one reason for dismissing it, was that cancellation of legal aid (on lawyer's advice) left the litigants 'dead in the water'. So Aldous had to accept that Thorold's Opinion to LAB left me 'dead in the water' as well. Now I was suing him, as that advice was so very wrong.

Aldous sat in the centre to preside. Not short, but a scrawny man with a ruddy complexion on a roundish, brittle face; not the sort to have been put in any scrum at school. Sir John Chadwick was the opposite, seated to his right, my left. A big sturdy man, and as I later would learn, spoke with a rather peculiar voice, as if permanently sitting on a delicate part of his anatomy, or controlling escaping air. He'd make a marvellous pious monk, chanting as he walked the corridors, head down and hands clasped together to the front. He slunk back in his chair, stony-faced and double-jowled at least. This one was, as they all are, another public schoolboy; Rugby followed by Cambridge - all peas from the same blended crop. Once Judges, it's easy and endemic to programme them. Born in 1941 he was the junior by five years, and came from Chancery Division, far removed from the real world, before the Court of Appeal. All I was asking was for a fair trial; no more than that – an inalienable right, we are taught.

Aldous nodded. I stood. It's my appeal:
"Good morning my Lords, I appear in person, and this is my appeal against a ruling of the Hon Mr. Justice Brown…. etc..
And with that I set my case, taking them to the parties and history, my Grounds of Appeal and other papers.

I've never been trained for this, and hadn't conducted a moot for thirty years, nor a trial for twenty. But the blight of Bingham lived on - I am a struck-off lawyer. I took the two judges to the evidence and showed it to them - I needed to ram the evidence at them. The ruling of Brown that I 'could have persuaded LAB to re-issue' was bizarre, denied by the LAB letter dated 24 June 1998 – it had been to Area Committee who acted on the Thorold advice. Lynne Houghton could only assign when new lawyers had done the work. I'd been left in an impossible position.

As the morning closed, I then argued that I couldn't issue, and mitigate - 'Look at Martin's and Houghton's Statements' – the legal right was vested in the Trustee (Heath v Tang). I needed an Assignment - for that I needed funding, Reports and lawyers.
At that TSB and Spencer were on their feet:
"My Lords" they protested in near harmony - "this was raised before Mr. Justice Brown, and he refused permission to amend. It was not pleaded that he couldn't mitigate (and we chose not to know the law)… Further Mr. Kaberry has not sought to appeal that refusal."

I didn't know barristers lied in court and accepted that what they were saying was true. So did the judges.
"Where" said Aldous, "is the Order refusing him Permission to amend the pleaded Claim?"
"Well My Lord - there isn't one"

"Then how can Mr. Kaberry appeal an Order that wasn't made?" said the smug Judge

"But his counsel, Mr. Evans decided not to proceed with that argument. He accepted the situation"

"Mr. Kaberry..." said Chadwick, speaking in high-pitched clipped tones, controlling a large amount of non-oral hot air wanting to escape - "...is arguing that he 'lost his chance' to sue the doctor because of the position in which he was left in July 1997.... Now he must have the chance to advance his arguments fully".

-'golly... don't get carried away SK, but you seem to have found two competent judges'

I have transcripted for you verbatim what happened on 18 May. Spencer and Carr consented to the amendment; now they denied it happened. That they didn't know the law is excusable, but to lie? You or I would be sent to prison for misleading a court. Aldous invited me to draft an amendment over lunchtime.

But I am not a trained litigator and those were not my pleadings; I didn't know where to start. Back in court at 2.00 o'clock; Aldous delivered a Judgment that Brown J was absolutely right about everything. They knew they were doing the reverse of justice and the law, so, before finishing his Judgment, Aldous said I was now orally arguing '*something new*' in my representations. I should be allowed to plead that properly after taking legal advice from experienced litigation lawyers.

"But My Lords" protested my opposers - "you can't do that! You have dismissed the appeal, and the case is over...

"Oh but we can" said Aldous... "Our first duty and the first rule of the CPR's is that we must 'do justice' and that is what we are doing. There is strength in Mr. Kaberry's argument, and he must have the chance to plead it fully."

The Judges told me to seek help of Bar Pro Bono Unit ('*oh god – them again!*'). I told them that I could ask for my appeal to LAB appeals to be listed (for funding restored to Evans/Foss). I was given to 28 February 2003 at 4.00pm to file an amended claim. As I left I heard TSB saying – 'are you coming for drinks at Ollie's? – well we've won haven't we...' obviously the revered Doughty Street intended to celebrate Mr. Thorold's protection.

But I was still standing – *just.*

I spent the entire day following drafting papers for Bar Pro Bono, and asking LAB (now called LSC) to list my Appeal to Area Committee. It was listed for 16 January 2003 in Aberdare in the Welsh valleys. Louise paid the £15 postage for each bundle.

Richard Jackson filled his car with fuel to enable me to get to ruddy Wales. I needed to be up and away by 5.00am - very risky for a man who can't sleep and needs rest. I didn't sleep and felt like death warmed up - could hardly open my squinting eyes. But if I didn't go, I would be accused of not trying. My lungs felt as if collapsed and, truly exhausted, I was peering through the window in light rain as I drove on in darkness. But we all bugger on in life and I arrived lunchtime. The Appeal committee was three local solicitors; they understood less of bankruptcy and litigation law than you. On behalf of Thorold, BLG had written opposing the re-issue of funding on the basis that Brown J had correctly adjudged the law (ie, they flouted an Aldous's order to be represented at the next hearing). As I say, I was in no fit state to argue what day it even was. I was told the decision would follow 'tomorrow'.

Next day Fossie rang to say I had no funding. I'd been blocked for funding a third time by the wretched Thorold.

Five weeks left, I rang and faxed Bar Pro Bono again, waited, but last time had taken seven months. So as to be filed on time, I posted my version on 24 February. On 25 February BPB phoned. Leeds barrister Gordon Exall was willing to help me. I saw him in Park Square Chambers at 4.00 pm. It was one of my Lost Days – unable to follow what he was saying or explain myself well. BUT he had already done masses of work
"You see" said I "I don't like this pleading at all... so what I've done's a bit messy"
"Well, I shouldn't say this, but I agree. So I've redrawn it, but included large parts of the original so they can't say it's an entirely different being."

As I had filed something, we agreed I was not in breach and would have to ask for 'an amendment to an amendment.' Next morning, recovered as ever, I was buzzing in mental strength and adapted his draft – which was excellent and clear – to plead the full case as I wanted it, save for Law Society – that I recover their self-inflicted losses was still there. We could get round that later.

I saw Gordon Exall again next day - then filed my 're-amended' Particulars of Claim which arrived at Court on Monday 3 March 2003 - three working days late. On 20 March 2003 Aldous gave Permission for 'The March Particulars' to stand as the new Particulars of Claim, then adjourned again for a two-day hearing to decide whether to let those proceed to a trial. This time they 'recommended' that I appear by a Bar Pro Bono counsel.

I needn't set out the entire re-Pleaded Claim.   All I need say here is it pleaded that had my former lawyers advised correctly then:
(a)   I had all the medical support needed to successfully sue 'Z' (they said I had none); and
(b)   LAB would have extended legal aid to sue, (not withdrawn it on their advice that the trustee would take it all); and
(c)   The trustee would have assigned the right to sue with the consent of all 'creditors' (as I shouldn't even be bankrupt and had no debts) with all compensation to me.
- and I would have sued 'Z' successfully. Each contention by me was supported by the evidence in statements and letters, which would be given orally at trial. The Claim further pleaded that the lawyers left me in an impossible position, unable to mitigate as I needed funding for lawyers and medics, to get the Assignment from Miss Houghton, who filed a statement so confirming. She assigned after consulting all 'creditors,' who agreed this was the right course of action. Consequently, I sued the lawyers in 'Lost Opportunity' for the damages that would have been ordered against the doctor.

We all needed to know 'the position of Law Society.' So I wrote to Law Society's new Chief Executive Janet Paraskeva. Proving they are avante garde and inclusive of all genres of society, the Society appointed a modern lady as Chief Executive; one of those who prefers to snuggle up each night with another lady rather than a gentleman. But it doesn't change the attitude. Three letters to Miss Paraskeva and not one acknowledgement.

Ignoring me as ever, Penson did respond to my defendants. He now claimed the Law Society would agree nothing with me - *until after the claim against Z.'* (that gets Thorold and Balen off misconduct charges for hiding their offer made on 24 June).

'*Bingo*' - I was home and hosed, for this confirmed I didn't have to recover their 'losses.'

To ask Exall to take two days plus travelling for free, was not on. Kit sent me cash and PD funded a £50 room at Strand Palace, so I couldn't be distracted by Elaine. It was hot that July; my room was at the top and had no air-conditioning. It was stifling.

Since March a new round of QCs had been appointed - top notch competent types like Aidan Marron QC, Derek Hatton QC, Guy Mansfield QC, Lord Thomas QC, Gusset QC and Tim Dutton QC. Now it was Martin Spencer QC and Susan Carr QC for Oliver Thorold. Unusually one solicitor had been made a QC - on the recommendation of the Law Society. It was now Geoffrey Williams QC - man of integrity. *You couldn't make it up.*

I engineered a situation that I had a shocking Lost Day prior to the Hearing. That triggered some deep sleep which re-charged my batteries. I would bat first. I stood in the middle of the benches, with the two QC's on the front benches and their lawyers and representative from the insurers (who would pick up the tab of compensation) around me. It's quite nice being alone you know.
-'*Come on SK.... life is about to take a spin my way'*.

The simple issue was whether the two judges allow my 'March Particulars' to stand as the pleaded case for a trial of the evidence. You know the law – it's a fundamental right.

Aldous and Chadwick listened in blatant disinterest.
- '*Something's happened since last time... someone's said something - don't let him proceed'*.
It wouldn't be brown paper envelopes, but someone had got to these two....*"We're doing him... Tom Bingham and Martin Phillips say he's trying to expose Law Society and the two lawyers who wasted 30 million in that group claim... block him.... find reason.... or there'll be no public confidence in our closed shop"*

What else explains what happened over these two days? I held the evidence which made for an indefensible claim at trial. After lunch Spencer QC addressed them. He followed the same arguments as before - that I should have issued my own writ, so was bound to lose on those old arguments.

After about 30 minutes, and as he was getting nowhere, he returned to type, and bowled a daisy-cutter:

"My Lords... if you forgive me... you must have no sympathy for this Claimant.... My Lords you directed in December and again last time, that he should appear by counsel.... he accused his former lawyers of deceit and letting him down, he flouts all you advise and appears in person, he has no respect for the law..... My Lords, he has no respect for this court... you must not allow sympathy to play any part in your decision, and must decide this in accordance with the law."

-*'I've no counsel because your lot misled some welsh lawyers'*

"I've been accused of many things in my time" said Chadwick in his high-pitched clipped tones – "but sympathy for a litigant in person, is not one of them."

"Mr.Spencer - you do yourself no good" said Aldous, who then delivered a tirade of abuse at me – struck-off for what I did. I stopped writing and looked up. "Oh, I'm glad he's listening... I'm glad he's listening" he barked at me

-*'You horrible little man – I don't deserve this... Why?'*

Earlier the same Aldous had ridiculed the group benzo claimants - refusing them a trial of the evidence. It's a return to that sinister feeling isn't it. Spencer continued his argument that there had been no amendment before Brown - so I mustn't be allowed to argue the law now. He took the two Judges to page 26 of the Transcript, showing their objections on the Thursday. I assumed he was telling the truth - this was a QC. Aldous and Chadwick made notes - 'page 26'.

Spencer was ending with a very weak point - one which actually contradicted all his earlier arguments and the Brown ruling (that I could have got LAB to re-issue funding). He had dug out a fairly obscure amended Legal Aid Rule - Rule 33A. It states that '*generally*' legal aid may *not* be granted to anyone who has had the right to sue assigned to him from a liquidator or trustee in bankruptcy. That rule had been introduced to stop abuses when Liquidators of a bankrupt business, without funds, had assigned rights to sue to recover debts, to former directors/owners, who could have legal aid – thus funding the litigation; then they would share the proceeds. The amended rule 33A gives LSC an 'option' of refusing funding for those cases, but it isn't intended for clinical negligence claims - nor does it stop them, where the creditors want nothing. Its only a discretion to stop abuse of the system. For example in the Davis case, it was LSC funded after assignment.

"Why Mr. Spencer" said Chadwick "are you leaving you best argument to the 11th hour?"

"Well... My Lord - I'm just coming to it..." duly buoyed by such remark he made if forcefully

"By the LAB amended Rules My Lord, Mr. Kaberry was not entitled to legal aid, as the right to sue was assigned to him (earlier he argued I could have got legal aid re-issued to sue 'Z'). His pleaded case is flawed – for he was not entitled to legal aid and could not therefore have sued Z at all – ever!"

"Quite" said the Judge.

- 'Oi, what the hell's going on here – I've got bent judges.... he knows this is nonsense'

I sat still as the obvious, horrible, awful truth hit home.

We finished the day just before 4.00 o'clock and they left with tails high. It was scorching hot. Without air-conditioning, my room was so hot I couldn't even get to sleep. I lay there dripping. Usually I get two or three hours and can cope. Maybe I got the one. I felt terrible - spinning head and tight chest, but my eyes were OK. Mentally I was drained - no way to fight my corner.

Into court and TSB continued the Spencer lines. The Judges nodded. She concentrated that my counsel Hugh Evans had 'abandoned' any amendment of the Particulars - so I couldn't argue the law. I was bound by that decision, she said. Both Judges nodded. Page 26 of the Transcript, she said, covers it. All desires expressed before of doing justice had long gone.

As I stood to reply, my mind was clouded by fatigue and what I had heard and seen from these two judges. I answered the points they had made, until Aldous interrupted:

"But Mr. Kaberry - you weren't fit to be a solicitor... you were struck-off - you can't seek compensation for your losses" (this was the Bingham ruling that I couldn't set aside the Law Society 'Finding'). That's the reverse of all law and all morality.

It was a crass remark from Aldous, which no first year law student would make. It's like saying to a classical pianist whose fingers are damaged in a road accident – 'you can't seek damages for being unable to play the piano against the man who broke your fingers... because with broken fingers, you weren't fit to play!' That's the very purpose of our law - that he can. But Aldous is the judge; and they both knew other judges would protect them if they 'closed their eyes to the truth.'

Aldous's cheeks were flushed - he was enjoying himself at my expense. -
"But my Lord... that *is* the pleaded case - of course I wasn't fit in that condition to be a lawyer" was all my exhausted mind could muster. Silence; I was alone:
-'*Sit down and take it like a man... they're writing your life off here and now... stand and fall with honour.*'
My working mind was numbed as I heard myself retain dignity:
"My Lords, I don't think there's anything further I can say to assist you."

Aldous looked at the clock
"Right... Judgment at 2.00 o'clock" and off they went.

I packed all my papers away, ready for early exit. Unable to eat or drink, I sat in Savoy Gardens across the road – '*had it been such a wrong dream – to find honest judges*'. July 2003 was very hot. An elderly man was walking two aged Rhodesian Ridgebacks and sat by a bench - that superiority they have, but not as lovely as Holly; I had a chat with them. A statue to Michael Faraday: Remind yourself, famous for what....? And why there? - did he like the Savoy? I reflected on my position - I didn't have one. These two weren't into doing justice any more. As Lord Justice Brooke had said in the Davis case in the very same court:
"*it would be the very reverse of justice to deny a trial to a man who's life had been destroyed by drugs wrongly administered.*"
But these two had another agenda, not called justice.

Back in at 2.00 to face the inevitable of two dishonest men of integrity protecting their chums.

Aldous; "I invite Lord Justice Chadwick to deliver first Judgment"

-'*oh yes, Old Harrovian trick; get the fag to do the dirty work*'
Chadwick started. Its too long for here - Paras 36 – 42 are the
deceitful 'closing of eyes to all truth and justice'....

He began with misleading comments, then addressed the issue –
"Should we allow this Claim to proceed to trial of the evidence?
Does it have 'a real chance of success, however improbable?'"
- that's 'the test' referred to earlier.

First he ruled I could not have issued due to the bankruptcy, until
assigned in law by the trustee. (so I won – the very principle to the
Brown judgment is overruled)

"The question is whether this court is satisfied that the claimant
has 'any real prospect of succeeding' on the argument and
pleading...(at trial) that an Assignment was available with legal
aid. If not, then he must not be allowed to proceed to trial...>
"In my view, he does not meet that test....
Chadwick then 'closes his eyes' to all the evidence, ruling:
(a) there wasn't enough time to do the work (this is ridiculous -
    they had 3 years and Das/Ganju and Corbin/Penfold that time
    shall not be an issue if the Claimant has not delayed); and
(b) the trustee would not have assigned the cause of action – even
    if asked, (all evidence, law and justice deny this);
(c) the creditors would not have permitted her to assign (they all
    agreed to Assignment completely - as he well knew); and
(d) The LAB would not have granted legal aid after the
    assignment because Rule 33A gives them a discretion not to
    (he knows the truth is opposite – they issued twice).
- so I could have no trial of the evidence. Balen and Thorold
would never have to explain anything.
Further, he continued -
"In the Transcript of proceedings before Brown J which we have
been provided (by Carr QC)... Evans asked for permission to
amend (page 26)... the Judge said he would be sympathetic to an
application by the defendants for an adjournment... (there was no
such Application) if he did, so it must therefore be seen as a
decision taken 'after reflection and in the knowledge of the
consequences (not to amend and argue the law. In those
circumstances there is force in the submission made by Carr QC
that to attempt to introduce the same argument, or the same point,

on this hearing, - 'when the decision had been made not to pursue it before the other judge – would be a misuse of process'.
[But Chadwick had earlier given me permission as well! – "in the interprets of justice" last December - I never took my Transcript to court]

Para 47: "For those reasons, I refuse the Application to amend the Particulars of Claim. It follows I dismiss the appeal".
 "I agree," said Lord Justice Aldous
Remember Court Appeal's definition of dishonesty in the exercise of public office -
– *"closing ones eyes to the truth, not asking he questions honest men would ask, then proceeding indifferent to the injustice caused, are tell-tale signs of dishonesty in the exercise of public office...."*
Auld LJ. A corrupt judgment from rogue judges? Am I wrong?

'Ask for Permission to appeal SK' - I quickly discounted that. If I said this was a dishonest judgment these two would lock me up for contempt here and now. Aldous ordered that I personally pay all costs of the other lawyers for the past three Hearings. That means that if I <u>ever</u> was able to build a life, I must pay about £40-55,000 to these people.
Effectively Aldous and Chadwick said:
 " *'Up Yours Kaberry'* – *don't you try to bring bad lawyers and legal establishment to account again."* They bowed and stalked away, well-pleased with themselves; job done.

My notebook was in my case in seconds and I was out. I stopped and sat on a bench in the Strand. *'What a right chump I was... thirteen years of life like this, seven in litigation post trial and they'd done as Mike warned.* Had I been so wrong to expect to find honest judges? Still we bugger on; that's the rule of life. Well, I'd been buggered - n'est ce pas?.

Back in Leeds, I saw Gordon Exall, who'd got the Judgment from the Internet.
"Well... we'd have lost on that bit about the amendment. I didn't realise... I was shot down by my own counsel"
Gordon Exall looked at me, as if to say 'what do you mean?'
"Mr. Kaberry... you left me with the full Transcript of the Hearing before Brown here - look", he said - "page 29 onwards, it was amended... next day Hugh Evans amended and argued the law

correctly. It's a judgment - well, what I can say... it was amended before Brown, with their consent, and Chadwick ruled Brown was wrong to deny your counsel's submissions on law that you couldn't mitigate, then dismissed your appeal!"

"And the bit about legal aid...?"

"Well, evidentially it just isn't true is it... just like the rest of it"

"Can I appeal?"

"Well yes. First you ask them, set out grounds - and they'll refuse you. Then you can Petition the House of Lords, but only on a point of law of general public importance."

I filed my request, exhibiting the evidence which they ruled could not be allowed. I sent them a copy the amendment in pages 29-33 of the Transcript. Three weeks and a sealed Order arrived:

Before Lord Justices Aldous and Chadwick...

'Permission to appeal to House of Lords is refused'

'By Order of the Court;

A highly respected police officer warned a friend that police were due to raid his business premises. He was found out and charged with 'perverting the course of justice' – in trying to protect his chum from answering to justice. The Judge at St.Albans court said that he had much sympathy, but a nine month immediate custodial sentence was the least he could impose, *'for the public must have complete trust and confidence in all officers of the law'*

On that basis, Chadwick and Aldous as officers of the law, should be sent to prison; simple as that. They perverted the course of justice, simply by denying access to it. In the light of that strike-out Bar Council refused to look at evidence of Thorold's conduct.

I drafted my Petition to the law lords, exhibiting the evidence which refuted each 'assumption.'of Chadwick. Two QC's had knowingly misled the court - important issues of law and trust. But Bingham was now senior law lord. I waited and watched each day for the postman – seven months, September to March. It got to me; sometimes I was very run down. *Who was saying what to whom? –' do him.'* Uncertainty - the killer.

Months earlier the Jobcentre had discovered I was often too ill to work, and refused to allow me to sign on. Doctors ruled that I was so ill long-term (from exposure to dalmane) that I must be placed on permanent Disability Benefit. The Bingham Order that I live out my days condemned a thief effectively left me unemployable in any meaningful position. But as I hadn't worked for so long, I didn't qualify for the extra benefit - just bottom base; I am a statistic.

Eight months and on 30 March the order arrived:
Kaberry v Freethcartright and Oliver Thorold:

> *Leave to appeal should be refused because the Petition 'does not raise an arguable point of law of general public importance' which ought to be considered by the House at this time, bearing in mind that the cause '**has already been subject of judicial review**'."*

This is the advice of the committee of:
Lord Nicholls,
Lord Scott,
Lord Brown
29 March 2004

In Lords Nicholls, Scott and Brown, I had struck the 'code of silence' (Omerta) of the powerfully unaccountable. The unwritten rule is that no judge may find another guilty of dishonesty - hence I had no chance. If any judge ever has to give evidence, he doesn't take the oath - for he wouldn't lie, would he? How corrupt is that? Within months, in another case, Nicholls ruled that the courts must do all possible to enable a litigant to present his evidence at a trial – 'to preserve public confidence in the system'. A highly duplicitous man.

A week or so later, my old friend John Patchett invited me to lunch at the Pizza in Street Lane. I related the history of events:
"I'm sorry Simon, but I've known you many many years, what is it - since 1972... and this isn't you... you love a fight, if there's one thing you've hated since I first met you, its pompous lawyers.... and arrogant conceited men, preferably Jewish - for god's sake man.... don't give in now."

"Thank you JBP - I hope you aren't suggesting that a man called Aldous could possibly be Jewish, or I have prejudices - just a little problem with one or two Welshmen."

Yet he was right. I wrote to the Lord Bingham, asking him to review the Petition - as he had started the cover-up. I suggested the clerks *'can't have put the evidence before the three judges.'*.

Brendan Keith, senior clerk wrote - *"You cannot question the law lords like this"* - Oh but I can, and we must! Appease wrongdoing and it will only get worse. I wrote to Bingham many times asking that he intervene in accordance with his oath to do justice, as he had led the cover-up. Once Brendan Keith replied on his behalf:

> *"Lord Bingham the senior law lord instructs me*
> *to tell you he has your letter"*

That's all. Lord Bingham then travelled to Windsor to accept the 'Order of the Knight of the Garter' from Her Majesty in acknowledgement of his chivalry - defined as 'honour of gallantry and a courageous defender of the weak.' As the saying goes – "it takes all to make a world."

Once again it was off to the library to read the European Convention of Human Rights. It took me May, June and July to research and complete an Application to Declare 'Breach of my Human Rights' and a 'Direction to House Lords' to hear me.

I waited nine months; then this letter from Strasbourg…:

30 May 2005

Dear Sir,
> *I write to inform you that on 18 May2005... a Committee of three judges (Caflisch, Tsatsa-Nikolovska and Thor Bjorgvinsson) ... decided under Article 28 of the Convention to declare that the above Application be inadmissible because it did not comply with the requirements set out in Articles 34 and 35 of the Convention.*

> *This decision is final and not subject to any appeal to either the Court, including its Grand Chamber, or any body. You*

278

will therefore appreciate that this registry will not provide any further details about this decision and deliberations, or conduct any further correspondence relating to this decision. You will receive no further documents from the Court concerning this case, and in accordance with instructions, the file will be destroyed.
Yours faithfully,
Mark Villager,
Deputy Section Registrar.

Baffled, I read up Articles 34 and 35 which I had apparently breached – they read – verbatim:
Article 34: Subject to the provisions of Articles 28 and 29, the Convention shall make its decisions by a majority of the members present and voting.
Article 35. The Commission shall meet as the circumstances require. The meetings shall be convened by the Secretary General of the Council of Europe.

I wrote to Mr. Villager - *'how could I possibly have failed to comply– they are nothing to do with this Application?'* A Registrar's assistant replied that I have no right to query anything; any attempt to re-issue addressing the same issues will be struck out and not answered. That's the end.

It really could be you next time…..or your wife or husband, mistress or lover, son or daughter, friend or brother. Did you find any honour and integrity in this account? Human frailties, sadly, are that absolute power, over time, has always corrupted; it always will.

Simon Kaberry

CHAPTER NINETEEN

- your right to judge these lawyers and judges
- and what's happened to these characters

With gusto and pride, we belch out - "*Land of Hope and Glory...*
Mother of the Free." Fine values... but pretty useless if you have
a justice system operating as a closed shop. Parliament and
executive account to us, but not our judges who are unelected,
often do things in secret and are in jobs for life, chosen from a
closed shop. No one would invent such a system today.

When Charles 1 lost his head, the 'Divine Right' to do no wrong
and never to account was meant to end. Unwittingly, it slipped
straight into the laps of the Lord Chancellor and King's Judges,
where it has remained for nearly 400 years. Save the Lord
Chancellor, now 'Minister of Justice' - all are in jobs for life,
selected from a closed shop, protected by a special omerta - a
silent code that they protect the very system that gives them that
special protection – the Legal Establishment. It's a simple accident
of history that we have such a system. But any system whereby
those entrusted with such enormous power, without any
accountability, is, by the rules of human nature, open to deceit,
corruption, abuse and cover-up. They arrogantly tell us to have
blind faith in them. This story surely shows why we cannot hold
that faith. So what's to do? I know where Chadwick and Aldous
should be... and would be, if in any other job.

There is no equivalent, as there should be, of the government's
Committee on Standards in Public Life (into government
ministers, MPs and civil servants) of any allegations of
incompetence or dishonesty in office. It wouldn't be difficult to
put such a committee together, properly accountable to the public
– chaired by anyone but a judge. Alternatively, something similar
to the Independent Police Commission. It's a mockery of our
democracy that one doesn't exist. We are meant to have 'blind
faith' in a closed system, but blind faith died long ago, shortly
after deference in public life post war.

For centuries, judges were accountable to the Lord Chancellor's
office, which had appointed them In April 2006, Chas Falconer

and Harriet Harman implemented yet another of it's ill-thought good ideas, which actually makes that pretty poor closed-door system *worse*. Under the sound-bite of 'transparency,' it created another quango - an 'Office for Judicial Complaints,' to take control of all such complaints. OJC is another unelected quango, accountable to the Lord Chief Justice (now Nicholas Phillips), and investigation is in private. And you have seen in this story how Phillips covered up what SDT had done. OJC can investigate only 'misconduct' - essentially limited to non-PC conduct. It cannot, or rather will not, examine allegations of dishonesty in office of the man it reports to. So the new system is worse from beginning to end. Lord Woolf commented "there is room for double standards to protect public confidence" (in judges as a whole). Well, you will say – '*he would say that wouldn't he!*' The same argument, with similar veracity, could be made of government ministers, policemen, teachers, doctors, and bus and train drivers, in each of whom we must have confidence. Another part of those 'Reforms' is that prospective judges appear before a commitee of MP's. What good can that ever do! Its what they get up to once there that counts, and that mustn't be left to Parliament

The head of OJC Mrs. Dale Simon (did she get her job on ability and zeal, or sex and ethnicity - you don't know nowadays) ruled on this case, she would consider no complaint. In its first year, Phillips ruled that _not_ _one_ single complaint or Finding on complaint to OJC may be made public; the reverse of transparency. Well - what did you expect of Phillips? OJC is a waste of taxpayers money; not even a good idea. It was part of the Falconer/Harman attempts to appease Judges for the other ill-thought reforms – make them more unaccountable.

Each Judge knows any complaint about them just 'fritters away,' with the complainant painted a dick-head, or, in my case, a crook as well. As our Trustees, they never account in their jobs for life.

Am I deluded or has there not been, and is ongoing, a complete cover-up at the top of our judiciary, which has also blocked an important civil claim to set precedent? – all originally to protect Williams and Isaacs, then extended to Balen and Thorold? The recent Clementi Report into the Law Society and Bar advised removing all self-regulatory and disciplinary powers. Nicholas

Phillips and behind-the-scenes pressures decimated parts of the 2007 Act but in 2010 a new Solicitors Regulatory Board will take over - said to be "Independent and Transparent." – to protect the public. Now I read a first appointed Board member is Mike Napier who, in 2000 as President held chapter and verse, from me, of the Sting, the consequences for me and the public, and the cover-up thereafter. He refused to make or allow any inquiry. And we are told to accept things have changed. Not on this evidence.

It proved impossible to bring Isaacs, Thorold, Balen or any of the characters to account. Disgraceful, sad or both.

So, I offer you the chance to judge them - they won't like that.

But first, what became of all these people and organizations in this tale?

Law Society's Solicitors Disciplinary Tribunal continues as before. Its secretary remains **Mrs. Susan Elston**. **Anthony Isaacs** sat on the fiasco of a Kangaroo Court, later covered-up for the wrong Geoffrey Williams did all of us, was promoted by Phillips to **'President' of the Tribunal.'** SDT is comprised of people like **Lady Bonham Carter and Boyd Holmes.** Clementi says they must go, and one can see why. The omerta has blocked that.

'**Murgatroyds**' remains a very successful large Fish and Chip 'Emporium' on the outskirts of Leeds, which flourishes today, making very substantial profits, with a staff of about ninety – all built originally on fraud. The truth is suppressed by Law Society and Lords Bingham, Phillips, Nicholls, Aldous etc.

Peter Harper sold out his interest in Murgatroyds; he is very comfortably placed in life. He will forever be deeply obliged to Geoffrey Williams, Isaacs etc. I saw him ahead of me recently in a queue at M&S; he bought champagne, flowers, chocolates and all things good, and walked to his new 740i BMW. I hope he sends annual Xmas cards to their lordships Bingham and Phillips, and Thurston, Balen and Thorold.

Graham Carter returned to life as a broker earning a crust. He received mis-direction in life, but made no long-term gains. I wish him well. He also sends Xmas cards to Geoffrey Williams QC, the

Penson team and the lords of cover-up - and Pam Hudson at CPS. Later he identified the man caught on CCTV at my bank, and I accept he knew nothing of the forgeries, and received none of that money.

After the Sting of July 1995, **Tony Heatherington** was effectively left in charge of a very great deal of money. It seems he owed old favours to strange men with guns, who, as a branch of serious crime enjoy judicial protection. Just how much he and his mates forged on my client account, we can never know. Our judges preferred cover-up. Every now and again, I read flat is sold at Howgate to raise a little more cash. Tony was left with 100's of £1,000s of funds and assets from their frauds and forgeries. He died suddenly of mesotheleoma. The cash and assets are with the crooks. **'Frank'** was last seen attending the Leeds cancer hospital, but there is a team with the assets and cash.

Aidan Marron QC continued as a barrister with an enhanced reputation - his skills secured my acquittals. In July 2006 he was appointed a Crown Court Judge based in the South East circuit at Blackfriars. **David Hatton QC** and **Robin Frieze** continue as criminal trial lawyers, although I am told the former is a specialist in defending rather than putting Crown prosecutions.

Geoffrey Williams continues as a solicitor-advocate in Cardiff, with an enhanced reputation as a QC; he is too well protected 'to protect public confidence in the system.' The clerk **Penson** and his 'team' of **Head, Wade, Qasim, Rogerson** continue, but with the name changed again. What would practicing solicitors do if they knew the truth? **Geoffrey Negus** continues as Press Spokesman for Law Society. The SCB changed its name to OSS, then/now Solicitors Regulatory Authority - but it's the same people doing the same jobs, with the same attitude problems. Would you trust any of them?

Paul Balen continues as an expert in clinical negligence at Freethcartright - an 'acknowledged leader in the field'. Ask him about his advice to me, and he will say 'the courts ruled we could have done nothing – Kaberry was the cause of lost chance.' It's not true is it? His partner **Michael Thurston** left to form a specialist criminal practice Cartwright King. He did nothing for me -

probably incompetent, but his name was added to the List of 'Leading Five Hundred' solicitors in criminal work.

OliverThorold continues as a valued member of leading chambers at Doughty Street, London. He inherited his great-great-great grandfather's baronetcy - 'Sir' Oliver Thorold. His personal website advises of his 'expertise' in benzodiazepine claims - surely a fraudulent representation. Was his advice to the LAB in my case not 'misleading, incompetent, flawed and deceptive?' (how they vilified Roy Meadows). But he was fully protected by the Judiciary, and chambers. And the question remains - why did he get everything so wrong? How compelling is the evidence? He appears as a trustee of Social Audit - a check on drugs companies. I think he's dangerous. Well... *help or hindrance?*

Counsel for the two lawyers **Susan Carr QC** and **Martin Spencer QC** continue as senior advocates. Spencer sits as a Recorder as well. A barrister was recently been sent to prison for deceiving a court as to facts...? Both **Guy Mansfield QC** and **Tim Dutton QC** later became chairmen of the Bar Council – so little point in reporting Thorold there either - a busy private members club. Many chairmen subsequently become High Court Judges, so the closed shop's in safe hands - 'the greater good.'

Det. Sgt. Jock Clark was quickly moved from the fraud squad. Best to blame the person least able to defend himself. When tested in court - he told the truth - there was no evidence I ever received any of this 'missing' money; I owe him for that. **Pamela Hudson** continues as a decision-maker in CPS; to conceal this story, she failed to prosecute anyone, despite holding vast evidence of fraud - well protected by Kennedy LJ. Or am I wrong?

Janet Paraskeva was appointed Chief Commissioner to the Civil Service by our PM. Anyone discriminating against homosexuals will be brought to account by her, but whether she will expose wrongdoing in public office? – history doesn't fit.

Lord Bingham became Senior Law Lord; due to retire in September 2008. He fervently believes in the Divine Right - that judges be unaccountable to the public they serve as trustees. Deluded - he thinks we have blind faith. We can never know how many times he has protected public wrongdoing and judicial failings. He was asked ten times to allow the hearing of evidence in any of my cases, and refused each time. He had the first print of this book - and refused to comment, or allow my Petition. He could - it's his oath to all of us to do justice. But – no sanction.

Lord Phillips was promoted in 2005 to Lord Chief Justice. He has enormous power over our daily lives, but he covered-up what Law Society did, when he should have punished them. Or am I wrong? Tell me this - if Establishment was an issue, could you, on this evidence, trust him to act without fear or favour? I put details of the impossible ruling of Chadwick and Aldous to him, receiving the reply from him as LCJ no one may complain about a Judge. He will shortly be your senior law lord on Bingham's retirement.

Lord Justice Aldous (**Sir William Aldous**) retired after my case. He leaves a legacy of no evidence being allowed in any benzodiazepine claim; how sinister is that? He became a big-wig in the British Eventing Association. Lord Justice Chadwick (**Sir John Chadwick**) continues as a Court of Appeal Judge - his dishonesty fully exposed. He and Aldous knew the Omerta would protect them 'to maintain public confidence.' Lord Justice Tuckey (**Sir Simon Tuckey**) continues in the belief that exposing the lies published by Establishment is akin to 're-writing history'! **Mr. Justice Douglas Brown** retired - still incompetent. Judges **Behrens, MacGill and Ibbotson** continue as Judges in Leeds. **Sir Mark Potter** was promoted to President of the Family Division (but we need fearless men like him to head civil courts).

Lords Nicholls, Scott and Brown covered it all up. These are top men who operate an Omerta to protect their system. They were also sent this book and asked to review the refusal to hear me.

Graham Sykes, as manager at Courage, with the truth known, tried to have the bankruptcy annulled – I never should have been. In 2004 he was sentenced to four years in prison. He's not a lawyer you see.

Louise finally charged off one day, unable to take my situation any longer. Words cannot do justice to the debts I owe her. **Petrina** finally was able to rebuild her life in 2002, and is happily married with a family and secure; but life is never that simple or kind, and it dealt her a nasty blow. I speak with her from time to time and her husband, who has been of immense assistance to me.

I last saw my brother **Andrew** in January 1995. In the late 1990s he made millions by sitting on his partner's shirttails; clever man, as he got my inheritance as well. We each know we will never speak again. Like Thorold, **Kit** became 'a circuit', and he helps me from time to time, when I have no money for milk!

Benzodiazepines continue to ruin the lives of many. Willie Aldous blocked all evidence being heard. Whether that is sinister or incompetence (or right), we can never know, as there is no system at all to question any judge in England. Two pressure groups in Parliament seek public money to help those injured by the drugs. Fault lies with the doctors who ignore the truth, lawyers for failing to bring them to account, and Judges like Aldous and Chadwick. Shame on them.

Ritalin continues to be prescribed to some children suffering with ADHD. Truth is their effects are highly questionable. I understand many university students use Ritalin to increase their brain capacity and attention span for exams. Is that not cheating, just as much as the athlete who uses steroids?

Simon Kaberry's story is told. Was his destiny determined by events over which he had no control, or personal choice? He expected more strength of character from Bingham and Phillips. But for every weak man, we need not fear, for there are thousands of good strong men and women – you meet them each day in life. He knows also he is here to be shot at for writing this. But save for the names of four people, it's all true.

The People's Court

In England, we have a simple way in dealing with men who think they have the Divine Right to be above accountability. The arrogance of it – shame them. We put them before a Peoples Court and judge them. Public Opinion and a free press can shame them. The arrogance of Divine Right must never again be allowed.

I drafted the ending with charges of these lawyers. Then I realised that by the same rules of human nature that control them - you won't vote, save in your minds.

If you voted - what would your judgment have been?
Lawyers - **Thorold and Balen**: had they been doctors, lawyers like them would have destroyed them, and had them suspended from practice for either incompetence of dishonesty; wouldn't they?

Judges - **Chadwick and Aldous:** were they blatantly dishonest in the exercise of judicial office – choosing to protect the two lawyers from accounting?

Judges – **Bingham and Phillips**: would you trust either, to investigate and bring to account, wrongdoing in public office?

Law Lords – **Nicholls, Scott and Brown**: they read the evidence and blocked it. What do you make of their honour and integrity?

Law Society and SDT: should self-regulation be allowed to continue entrusted to types like Isaacs ("it is not even prima facie evidence of unbefitting conduct to mislead a court")?

The Judiciary: should it be made accountable to a proper committee of Inspection?

E P I L O G U E

In search of Virtue?

After the European 'ruling,' I wrote each third month to Lords Bingham, Scott and Brown, ending October 2007 requesting that they hear my Petition and that Bingham hear a Petition against the ruling of Phillips. Each request was refused. Their chief clerk Brendan Keith responded they would not review any decision.

A recent publication by novelist Grisham ('The Appeal') exposes the dangers in the American system whereby judges are subject to five-year public election process. Our system gives absolute power for life – and absolute power has always, by the vanities of human nature, corrupted, and always will. We are entitled to better and to bring all bad men to account and punish them, whatever their jobs.

As a final throw of the dice I put these facts and that Miss Harman's 'transparent' OJC actually is the reverse, leaving all judges completely unaccountable to us, to Parliament via the **House of Common Justice Select Committee**. I suggested that they must consider advising that something akin to IPCC or their own Commissioner must have power to look at obvious judicial failings as absolute power always corrupts.

Chairman **Alan Beith** refused to allow the issue to be considered (having heard from Bingham and Phillips 2002-5) and their Clerk (**Roger Phillips**) advised M.P.'s that Parliament has no power to investigate any judicial cover-up or wrongdoing, or the concept that Judiciary should account to the public they serve as trustees. Same day a journalist, also called Phillips, published an article that we are governed by clerks, and politicians are irrelevant wimps. One could not possibly comment. But - one day…., and until then, just hope it isn't you taking on our best closed shop.

Printed in the United Kingdom
by Lightning Source UK Ltd.
132297UK00001B/22-30/P